DE200 Investigating psychology 2

Investigating psychology 2 – From social to cognitive

Edited by Rose Capdevila, John Dixon and Gemma Briggs

This publication forms part of the Open University module DE200 Investigating psychology 2. Details of this and other Open University modules can be obtained from the Student Registration and Enquiry Service, The Open University, PO Box 197, Milton Keynes MK7 6BJ, United Kingdom (tel. +44 (0)845 300 60 90; email general-enquiries@open.ac.uk).

Alternatively, you may visit the Open University website at www.open.ac.uk where you can learn more about the wide range of modules and packs offered at all levels by The Open University. To purchase a selection of Open University materials visit www.ouw.co.uk, or contact Open University Worldwide, Walton Hall, Milton Keynes MK7 6AA, United Kingdom for a brochure (tel. +44 (0)1908 858793; fax +44 (0)1908 858787; email ouw-customer-services@open.ac.uk).

The Open University, Walton Hall, Milton Keynes MK7 6AA

First published 2015

Edited, designed and typeset by The Open University.

Printed and bound in the United Kingdom by Page Bros, Norwich.

ISBN 978 1 7800 7855 7

1.1

Contents

Chapter 1

Investigating psychology: an integrative approach

John Dixon, Rose Capdevila and Gemma Briggs

Contents

1 Introduction

Psychology is often defined as the study of how individuals think, feel and act. This definition is a useful starting point, conveying a general sense of the discipline's core concerns, but it doesn't capture the kinds of concrete, everyday questions that make psychology so fascinating.

- Why do we sometimes help or cooperate with others and why do we sometimes dislike or mistreat them?
- With whom do we form friendships?
- Why do some relationships endure happily while others fail miserably?
- How do we organise what we know of the physical and social world, including what we see, hear, pay attention to and remember?
- How do basic perceptual and cognitive processes feature in everyday activities, such as driving a car, listening to music or revising for the exam that will conclude this module?
- How does the brain work?
- What happens when particular areas of the brain stop working because of disease or physical trauma?
- What is the point of childhood?
- How do children become moral beings, acquiring a sense of right and wrong?
- How do we acquire a sense of ourselves as gendered and sexualised beings?
- How do we develop across our lifetime?

Your module textbooks are designed to provide a critical overview of the current state of psychological knowledge about these and other important questions. Working through these books, you will develop a richer understanding of the kinds of answers psychologists have provided and a better sense of the diversity of psychological research. You should also be able to evaluate the strengths and limits of current knowledge.

The textbooks do not simply offer a series of independent discussions of key topics however. They are also designed to explore some of the deeper themes, perspectives and debates that enrich the discipline of psychology, several of which are addressed across a number of chapters. For example, what is the role of genetic and environmental factors in shaping our thoughts, feelings and behaviours? Should psychologists adopt research methods that seek to measure and quantify psychological processes, producing universal laws of human behaviour? Should they adopt methods that embrace the qualitative richness of human experience and acknowledge that behaviour is often specific to particular social contexts? How can psychology help us to not only understand the world, but also to change it, helping to solve social problems and improve people's lives?

Of these deeper and recurring themes, one is particularly central to this module. It concerns the organisation of psychology into sub-disciplines that are characterised by specialist concepts, theories and methods of inquiry. Indeed, these textbooks are designed to take you on a journey through four of these sub-disciplines, exploring their distinctive and overlapping contributions. Book 1 is thus subtitled 'from social to cognitive', Book 2 'from cognitive to biological', and Book 3 'from biological to developmental'. Equally important, the module is designed to highlight work that crosses the boundaries between sub-disciplines, for example, by employing concepts or methods developed in one field of research to elucidate psychological problems that have been studied mainly in another.

Later on, this chapter will describe in more detail the topics you will cover across the three textbooks. However, it begins by considering two more general issues.

First, we outline the nature of the four sub-disciplines explicitly covered in the module textbooks, namely social psychology, cognitive psychology, biological psychology and developmental psychology. Second, and related, we present a worked example that explores an everyday psychological question ('Why do we feel empathy for others?') and illustrates how psychologists working in these different sub-disciplines have tried to address this question. In practice, psychologists often draw on more than one sub-discipline in their work. As you will see, however, the development of an *integrative approach* to psychological inquiry poses many challenges and problems, as well as offering many opportunities and possibilities.

Learning outcomes

On completing this chapter you should:

- be familiar with the core characteristics of the four psychological sub-disciplines covered across the three volumes, i.e. social, cognitive, biological and developmental psychology
- be able to describe some of the main differences, links and points of overlap between these sub-disciplines
- have an understanding of the organisation, content and central themes of the module textbooks.

2 The historical emergence and institutionalisation of psychological sub-disciplines

It is sometimes said that psychology has a long past but a short history. Many basic psychological questions on how we experience and think about the world were debated with considerable sophistication in early Greece and Egypt, and many psychological concepts, including the concepts of memory, identity and emotion, have ancient precursors (Billig, 1987). The emergence of psychology as a modern institution is relatively recent, however, dating back to the later years of the nineteenth century. In many ways, psychology remains a young science whose core concerns, defining concepts and methodological frameworks are still emerging. Indeed, the very definition of psychology as a science – at least in the sense that disciplines such as physics, chemistry and biology are sciences – is far from settled (Brown and Stenner, 2009).

Psychology has, of course, matured over the course of the past century. As this module richly illustrates, it has contributed to our understanding of an array of topics. One sign of this maturation is the emergence of a range of psychological sub-disciplines, designed to address particular kinds of practical or theoretical problems and shaped by both factors internal to the field and the broader contexts in which the discipline has evolved.

The sub-discipline of *social psychology*, for example, originally emerged as a framework for understanding the relationship between the individual and the social – that is, where 'you' meets up with 'the world'. In 1908, two books considered to be the first bearing the words 'social psychology' in their title were published. One was written by sociologist E.A. Ross (1908), the other by psychologist William McDougall (1908), and both focused on the rich possibilities of working at the intersection of the social and psychological. This focus was captured by the early assertion of George Mead (1934, p. 1) that: '… in the study of the experience of and behaviour of the individual organism or self in its dependence upon the social group to which it belongs we find a definition of the field of social psychology.' Social psychology subsequently provided an orienting framework within which psychologists explored topics such as crowd behaviour, social conformity, social cohesion, group identity, attitude formation and intergroup conflict. While it is tempting to view the field's emergence purely as a reflection of the preoccupations of psychologists themselves, it was also powerfully shaped by wider factors. For instance, social psychology, as an experimental and applied science, was able to establish itself just after the First World War with the rise of the factory assembly line and an interest in maximising industrial productivity. The Second World War and the subsequent Cold War between the United States of America (USA) and the Soviet Union made urgent certain kinds of social and political problems – for example, problems of racial and ethnic prejudice, of group morale during combat, and of the effects of political propaganda on the masses. Similarly, social psychology's development was shaped by the value systems of the societies in which it took root. Most early social psychological research was conducted in Western liberal democracies, particularly in Europe and the USA, and this informed the kinds of values that came to permeate the field. Because they prioritised individualistic values, such as autonomy and personal freedom, social psychologists came to see the influence of the social group on the individual as dangerous and potentially corrupting (e.g. see Chapters 2 and 5 of this book), and they neglected the positive role of groups as agents of social change (e.g. see Chapter 3).

There is not space here to elaborate the historical emergence of the other specialist areas of psychology on which this module focuses. Our aims are simpler. First, we want to note that all of these sub-disciplines emerged as the result of a complex combination of factors internal and external to the discipline; they are thus as much a product of wider social, political, historical and technological processes as they are a product of the free-floating ideas of psychologists themselves. For example, it is not irrelevant that cognitive psychology developed just as information processing was revolutionising understandings of computing, while the invention of **fMRI** technology has provided an important tool for the more recent developments in biological understandings. Second, we want to note how, once established, these sub-disciplines provided a powerful lens through which generations of psychologists came to view the project of formulating research questions, conducting research and generating theories. In this sense, they served both as traditions on which psychologists could build and as straitjackets that sometimes constrained innovation. Third, we want to note how sub-disciplines also became part of psychology as a professional and educational institution, shaping how the field is now taught, marketed, funded, accredited and practised across the world. Thus, this module covers a 'syllabus' of topics that is informed by guidelines laid down by the British Psychological Society (BPS) – the

Functional magnetic resonance imaging (fMRI)
A neuroimaging technique that measures brain activity by detecting changes in blood oxygen levels.

body that accredits psychology degree programmes in the United Kingdom but that is very similar to equivalent bodies in other geographical locations. This syllabus is designed to offer students balanced exposure to work across a set of core areas including social, cognitive, biological and developmental psychology.

The next section will introduce the core characteristics – distinctive and overlapping – of these four areas of psychology. It does so by means of a concrete example, exploring some recent studies on the topic of empathy. To begin with, by way of orientation, you might want to consider Figure 1.1.

	Sub-discipline			
	Social	Cognitive	Biological	Developmental
Core focus	The relationship between individual psychological processes and the social and cultural contexts in which they unfold	The mental processes through which we perceive, think and reason about the world	The role of biology and neurology in human psychological functioning and behaviour	The psychological changes that occur across the lifespan, from early infancy to later life
Illustrative topics	Social cognition Attribution Attitudes Group processes and intergroup relations Close relationships Social constructionism	Attention Study of perception Learning Memory Thinking Language Consciousness Cognitive neuropsychology	Biological bases of behaviour Hormones and behaviour Behavioural genetics Neuroimaging Neuropsychology Evolutionary psychology	Childhood, adolescence and lifespan development Development of attachment Social relations Cognitive and language development Social and cultural contexts of development
Most commonly used methods of data collection	Experiments Questionnaires Observation Interviews Diary method Visual methods	Experiments Interviews Observation Questionnaires Tests and scales	Experiments Interviews Observation Questionnaires Tests and scales	Experiments Interviews Observation Tests and scales Diary method Visual methods
Most commonly used methods of data analysis	Statistical Thematic Discursive	Statistical	Statistical	Statistical Thematic Discursive
Examples of practical applications	Health promotion, prejudice and conflict reduction, advertising and marketing, team building	Improving decision making, advising on safe practice (e.g. driving behaviour), accessing memory (e.g. cognitive interviewing)	Improving outcomes for patients who have suffered brain damage, developing treatments for neuropsychological disorders (e.g. Parkinson's disease)	Advising parents and carers, designing educational programmes and strategies, providing support for those facing developmental challenges (e.g. autism)

Figure 1.1 Four psychological sub-disciplines and their core characteristics

3 Why do we feel empathy for others?

3.1 The concept of empathy

Empathy
The ability to take another person's point of view and to imagine how they are thinking, feeling or perceiving.

Empathy is the psychological process through which we are able to 'put ourselves in others' shoes', for example, by imagining how they might be thinking or feeling in a particular situation (Hodges and Myers, 2007). It encompasses both cognitive and emotional dimensions. Cognitively, it involves the ability to use existing information to make intellectual judgements about what others might be experiencing in a particular situation (a process that is sometimes called 'perspective taking'). Emotionally, it involves the ability to feel what others might be feeling in a situation (e.g. shame) and, as a result, to experience vicariously their distress. Activity 1.1 below illustrates one technique that psychologists have used to measure individual differences in the ability to experience cognitive and emotional forms of empathy.

Activity 1.1: Measuring empathy

The empathy questionnaire: measuring cognitive and emotional empathy

For each of the following questions indicate the extent to which you agree or disagree. The first five questions are designed to measure cognitive empathy; the second five to measure emotional empathy. Write down your own scores for each of these ten questions where: Strongly disagree = 1; Disagree = 2; Neither agree nor disagree = 3; Agree = 4; and Strongly agree = 5.

Cognitive empathy	Strongly disagree	Disagree	Neither agree nor disagree	Agree	Strongly agree
1. When I am angry or upset at someone, I usually try to imagine what he or she is thinking or feeling.	☐	☐	☐	☐	☐
2. I can tell by looking at a person whether they are happy.	☐	☐	☐	☐	☐
3. When I am arguing with my friends about what we are going to do, I think carefully about what they are saying before I decide whose idea is best.	☐	☐	☐	☐	☐
4. I can tell what mood members of my family are in by the look on their faces.	☐	☐	☐	☐	☐
5. I notice straightaway when something makes a close friend unhappy.	☐	☐	☐	☐	☐
Emotional empathy					
6. When I see someone suffering I feel bad too.	☐	☐	☐	☐	☐
7. When I walk by a needy person I feel like giving them something.	☐	☐	☐	☐	☐
8. It upsets me when a child is being shouted at.	☐	☐	☐	☐	☐
9. When members of my family get upset I feel bad.	☐	☐	☐	☐	☐
10. I get upset when I see an animal being hurt.	☐	☐	☐	☐	☐

Figure 1.2 Empathy questionnaire

(Source: adapted from a scale developed by Zoll and Enz, 2010)

Pause for thought

The questionnaire in Activity 1.1 yields an overall score ranging from ten (low empathy) to 50 (high empathy). Remember that these are just a few items from a more complex scale and are used for illustrative purposes here. You should not therefore read too much into how you have personally scored.

Bearing that in mind, what might someone who scored towards the bottom end of this kind of scale be like as a person? What might someone who scored towards the top end of this scale be like?

Why do you think the ability to experience cognitive and emotional empathy might be important?

Might it sometimes be important not to empathise?

The capacity to empathise can be important for a number of reasons. For one thing, it underpins a number of other basic psychological abilities and behaviours. Empathy allows us to engage in moral reasoning about what is right and wrong, and to know when and why to perform prosocial behaviours such as helping. More broadly, it also allows us to anticipate the behaviours of other people in everyday situations and to react appropriately. A person breaking bad news to someone else, for example, must typically draw on both cognitive and emotional forms of empathy in order to behave in a socially effective and accepted manner. As this example suggests, empathy is arguably fundamental to what it means to be a fully developed human being, an idea illustrated starkly by how we view those deficient in the ability. Sociopaths and sadists fall into this group, as do young children.

Let us now consider some examples of how psychologists have investigated empathy, drawing on studies conducted across the four main sub-disciplines of psychology.

Box 1.1 Is empathy always a good thing?

In October 1987, eighteen-month-old Jessica McClure – Baby Jessica – fell into a narrow well in Texas, leading to a 58-hour rescue operation (see Figure 1.3). The resulting public interest and media attention was so intense that then President Ronald Reagan observed: 'Everybody in America became Godmothers and Godfathers of Jessica'. However, every day thousands of children die, far less dramatically, as the result of malnutrition, political instability or lack of access to potable water and life-saving drugs, with little media or public attention...

Most of what psychologists have written on the topic of empathy presupposes that it is a positive psychological response that makes the world a better place. However, in a provocative article written in *The New Yorker*, the psychologist Paul Bloom advances the case against empathy. Bloom (2013) argues that the explosion of interest in empathy and enthusiasm for its promotion disregards the fact that it is also, often, a 'parochial, narrow-minded and innumerate' emotion.

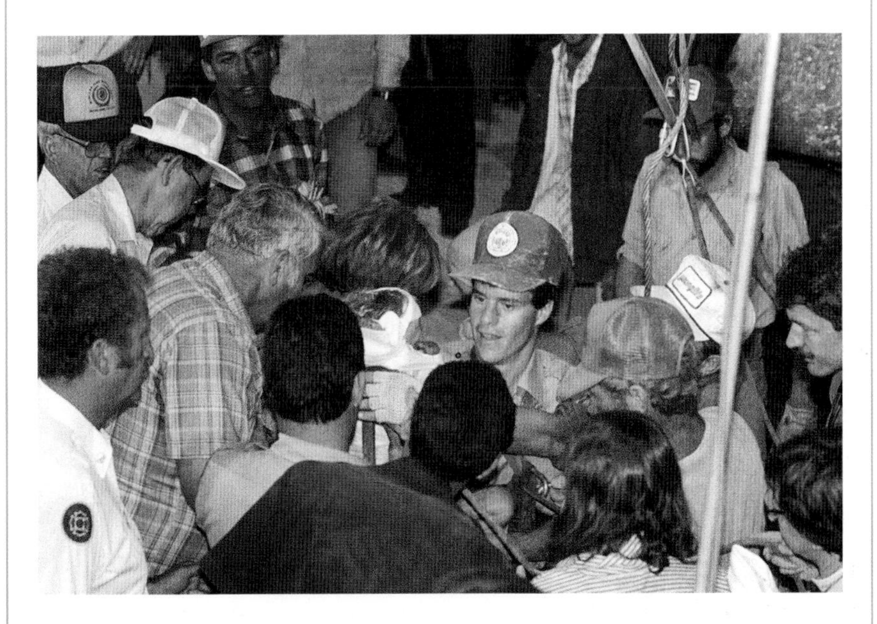

Figure 1.3 The baby in the well

He does not dispute the power of empathy to move people to do good deeds, for exmaple to donate their money, time and passion to worthy causes. However, he points out that the causes that tend to trigger our empathy may lead us to irrational and disproportionate responses that blind us to more rational and measured responses to human suffering. As the economist Thomas Schelling once observed:

> Let a six-year-old girl with brown hair need thousands of dollars for an operation that will prolong her life until Christmas, and the post office will be swamped with nickels and dimes to save her. But let it be reported that without a sales tax the hospital facilities of Massachusetts will deteriorate and cause a barely perceptible increase in preventable deaths – not many will drop a tear or reach for their check books.
>
> (cited in Bloom, 2013)

Bloom's point is not that empathy per se is a bad thing, but that it is often better to rely on rational deliberation and calculation to solve human problems. As he notes: 'Our hearts will always go to the baby in the well; it's a measure of our humanity. But empathy will

> have to yield to reason if humanity is to have a future,' (Bloom, 2013).

3.2 Four perspectives on empathy

3.2.1 A social psychology perspective

Riva and Andrighetto (2012) explored the social conditions that influence how we judge the severity of the pain suffered by others, focusing on both physical pain (e.g. watching someone being beaten) and social pain (e.g. hearing that someone's partner has died). They hypothesised that such judgements may vary depending on whether or not we share group membership with the victims, and they explored this hypothesis in two experiments. In one of their experiments, they asked 89 Italian students to rate the severity of physical and social pain suffered by men belonging to one of three social groups: Marco Rossi (a fellow Italian), Bai Guo Ye (a Chinese out-group member), and Edison Mendez (an Ecuadorian out-group member). Responses were recorded on a scale from 0 (no pain) to 10 (most intense pain). Physical pain items included being punched in the face or deprived of water; social pain items included being humiliated in front of colleagues or being dumped by a girlfriend.

Some of their results are presented in Figure 1.4. They indicate that social but not physical pain estimates varied as a function of the group membership of the victim. When the victim was a fellow Italian, participants tended to rate his social suffering as more intense than when the victim was a member of the two out-groups (Chinese or Ecuadorian).

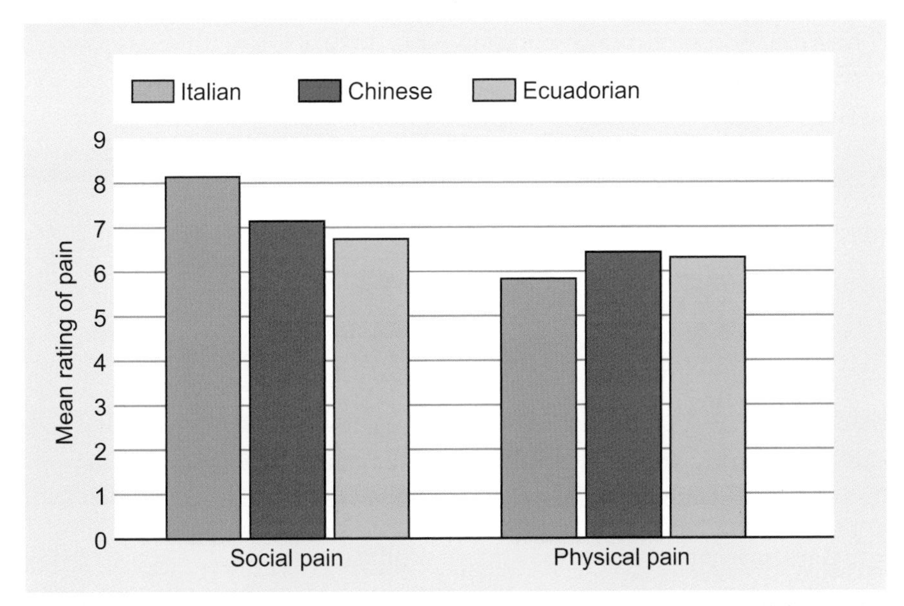

Figure 1.4 Mean ratings of social and physical pain for the three target groups used in Riva and Andrighetto's (2012) study

> ### Pause for thought
>
> Why do you think that this difference emerged for social but not physical forms of suffering?

According to Riva and Andrighetto, their findings reflect a tendency to 'dehumanise' members of other groups. While we can empathise with others' pain on a physical level – just as we might empathise with the physical suffering of animals – we tend to feel that more 'uniquely human' forms of social suffering (e.g. heartbreak at the end of a relationship) are felt more acutely by people who are 'like us'; that is, people with whom we share group membership. In Chapter 4, you will explore more fully why this may be the case.

Riva and Andrighetto's study also captures some key features of a *social psychological* perspective (see also Figure 1.1). Perhaps most fundamental, it is designed to explore how broader contextual processes influence our everyday thoughts, emotions and behaviours – in this case how our membership in wider networks of intergroup relations can shape our capacity to empathise with others. Riva and Andrighetto argue that this process has important implications for tackling a number of social and political problems. It may help us to understand better, for example, why both ordinary people and military personnel are able to tolerate the humiliation of those who are perceived as belonging to an out-group. Moreover, if a lack of intergroup empathy is the problem, then perhaps interventions to change intergroup relations and promote intergroup empathy are the solution? This goal of intervening to change social life and address social problems lies at the heart of the best work in social psychology.

3.2.2 A cognitive psychology perspective

Autobiographic memory
The system of memories that individuals hold about their personal experiences, including memories of places, events, episodes and people that have featured in their lives.

Bluck et al. (2012) reported two studies on how sharing '**autobiographic memories**' may create empathy for others. Autobiographic memories are memories relevant to self, including personal events, episodes and life periods. If someone told you, for example, that when they were six years old they fell off their bike and hurt their knee, they would be recalling an autobiographic memory. Bluck et al. hypothesised that such memories may be particularly important in providing the basis for empathic responses to others. When a speaker shares a memory of a traumatic event, for instance, this may cue memories of a similar event experienced by a listener, thus forming a common ground between them and promoting greater understanding of both their mental states. Empathy is, at least in part, built around this kind of mutual understanding.

Bluck et al. focused on how this process of sharing autobiographic memory might increase empathy towards both a young (25-year-old) target and an elderly (85-year-old) target suffering from chronic physical pain. In one of their studies, for example, autobiographical pain narratives such as the following were read by participants (80 undergraduate students):

> About a month ago I think it was. Yes, it was actually right after my 85th birthday, I had one of these flares. This time, it was mostly in my hips more than anything else. ... The sun was coming in my window and it looked like it would be a nice day. But I was really stiff. So I lay in bed and took a few minutes to just do some deep breathing and stretching to try to ease the pain a little. After a while, I carefully got out of bed and got my walker from the hall closet right next to my bedroom doorway. I tried to get started with my day. Try is the operative term. I walked out of my bedroom and then was walking toward the fridge to get some

> orange juice. I felt a sharp pain right as I reached for the handle. I froze and leaned over the counter wincing with the pain. Words really can't describe how the pain affects me. The pain ... and then the feeling that I can't do anything about it ... This flare that I had last month, just after my 85th birthday, is one of the worst flares I remember.

Having filled in a 'pre-test' measure of empathy in response to this kind of account, some participants were asked to think of a *personal pain experience to share*, while others were asked simply to think about the *pain narrative* they had just read. They were then asked to again rate their degree of empathy for the target person experiencing chronic pain.

To simplify a more complex set of results, Bluck et al. found that participants who were asked to think about sharing their own autobiographic memories of being in pain displayed higher levels of 'post-test' empathy towards both younger and older targets. Having thought of sharing their own memories of pain, it seems, they were better able to empathise with the pain of others. In this sense, Bluck et al.'s work paints a positive '…picture of how humans can use their past to serve social functions such as understanding the plight of older and younger persons in distress,' (Bluck et al., 2012, p. 89).

Pause for thought

Try to remember an occasion when you experienced something physically or emotionally painful. Write down three words that describe that memory.

Do you think your own autobiographic memories might help you to better empathise with others' experiences of pain?

On a broader level, Bluck et al.'s work illustrates some key features of the cognitive approach to psychology (see also Figure 1.1). First, as its name suggests, the cognitive approach focuses on the mental processes through which we perceive, interpret, store, recall and judge information about the social and physical world. Second, mainly through the use of laboratory experiments, it aims to show how such basic cognitive processes (e.g. remembering) may shape our behaviours in day-to-day life. Finally, as demonstrated in the second textbook for this module, cognitive research has informed many interventions to improve individual mental responses or decision making. Dramatic examples include the improvement of judgements in aviation (e.g. how to make pilots fly better), driving (e.g. how to make us safer on the roads), and the justice system (e.g. how to create more effective line-ups for eyewitness identification). The extension of cognitive research on autobiographic memory into the arena of empathy promotion provides another intriguing illustration.

3.2.3 A biological psychology perspective

Jackson et al.'s (2005) study attempts to provide a 'window' into the neurological processes through which we feel empathy, with a particular focus on our capacity to share the emotional reactions that others are experiencing. Their work exemplifies the *biological perspective* in psychology, which features mainly in Blocks 2 and 3 of this module.

Jackson et al. implemented the following method. Fifteen participants – described as healthy and right-handed – were shown a series of 128 digital colour photographs that displayed *right* hands and *right* feet in *painful* and *non-painful* situations, as illustrated by Figure 1.5. These pictures were presented as a random series of blocks of trials, along with a baseline condition in which participants were shown neutral stimuli (images of crosses). In each trial, an image appeared on a screen and afterwards participants were asked to rate the degree of pain involved on a scale ranging from 'No pain' to the 'Worst possible pain'.

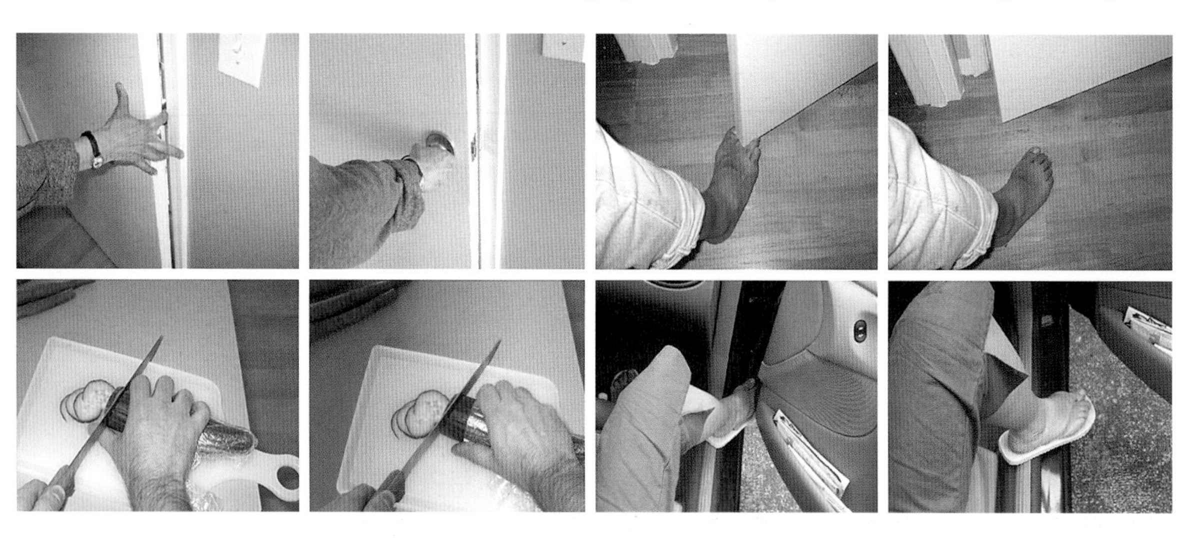

Figure 1.5 Examples of the hand and feet pictures used in painful and non-painful conditions of Jackson et al.'s (2005) study

Crucially, participants completed the study while placed within an fMRI scanner. As Figure 1.6 illustrates, this is a cylindrical chamber that houses a powerful electromagnet and is designed to measure the neural activation of various parts of the brain. Jackson et al. wanted to study their participants' patterns of brain activation across the different conditions of their experiment and also to explore the relationship between such patterns and subjective pain ratings of painful and non-painful situations. They hypothesised that the resulting data would help us to understand the neurological bases of emotional empathy.

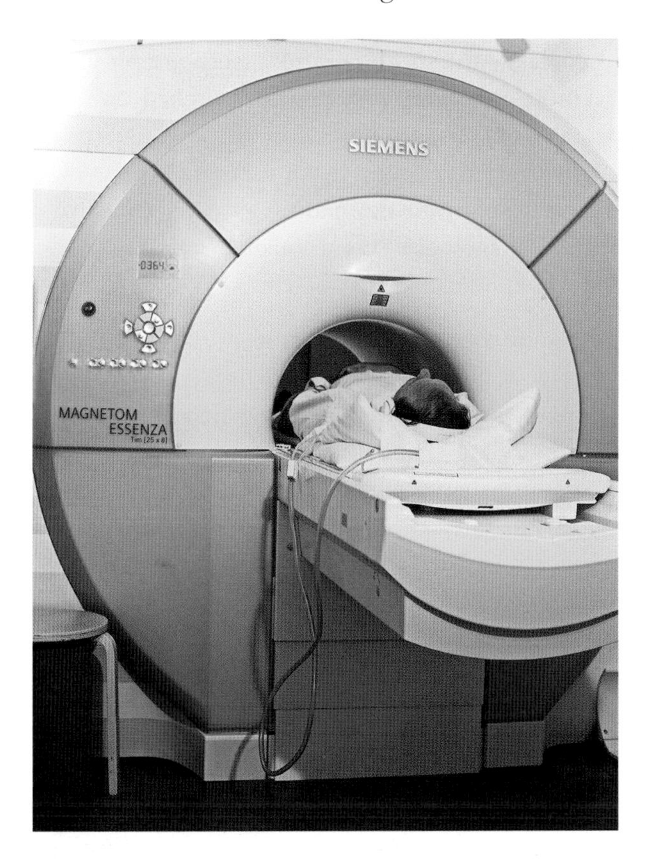

Figure 1.6 An fMRI scanner

Pause for thought

In reporting their research, Jackson et al. (2005) were careful to highlight that they used *right-handed* participants only in their research and that they focused only on photographic stimuli of *right* feet and hands. Why do you think they did so?

Their results showed that watching others in pain-inducing situations (e.g. slicing their finger with a knife) triggers specific neurological responses. Rather intriguingly, it tends to activate neural networks that are known to be involved in processing personal distress. For instance, Jackson et al. found that looking at painful scenarios activated the posterior part of the anterior cingulate (ACC) – an area of the brain associated with the processing of unpleasant experiences of being in personal physical or emotional pain. Moreover, they found a strong association between participants' own ratings of the degree of pain depicted in the particular photographs of hands and feet and the degree of activation of their ACC areas – the more painful a photograph was rated by a participant, the more this brain region was 'switched on'. There are, of course, many possible explanations for why this pattern of neural activation occurs. However, at a broad level, Jackson et al.'s findings provide a fascinating insight into the neurological relevance of empathy. They suggest there is a biological commonality between perceiving pain in others and experiencing it yourself.

This study also conveys some of the main features of a *biological perspective* on psychology (see also Figure 1.1). The focus here is mainly on the neurological and physiological processes through which our thoughts, feelings and behaviours are shaped and, in turn, how those thoughts, feelings and behaviours shape how we respond at a biological level. Increasingly, research in this area of psychology is capitalising on technological advances, as illustrated by Jackson et al.'s use of fMRI equipment, which is providing ever more sophisticated ways of measuring, analysing and visualising neural processes in the brain. As well as fMRI techniques, researchers in this field draw on a number of brain scanning technologies, along with a host of other physiological measures (such as hormonal and other chemical changes in the body). Moreover, although biological psychology is a diverse field, it tends to emphasise theoretical explanations that can account for the development of basic features of the brain, body and nervous system. It thus makes greater use of evolutionary explanations and cross-species comparisons than other areas of psychology.

3.2.4 A developmental psychology perspective

The final of the four studies of empathy has been selected to illustrate the key features of a *developmental perspective* on psychology. Although they take very different approaches, the three studies discussed so far share two features. First, they used adult participants, and second, they investigated participants' responses at a single point in time. Zahn-

Waxler et al.'s study (1992), by contrast, sought to investigate changes over time in the empathic responses of young children, focusing on the period between 13 and 25 months old.

As many parents know only too well, young children sometimes display limited cognitive and emotional empathy for others. Though by no means oblivious to the others' feelings, they are more likely than older children to misinterpret such feelings or act inappropriately in their responses. The child who chucks Grandma's lovingly selected present on the floor, snatches away another child's favourite toy, or stares unblinkingly at the homeless man lying in the street is a figure we can all recognise. Zahn-Waxler et al. wanted to explore the validity of this stereotypic image, however, by investigating the developmental trajectory of empathy and prosocial behaviour in young children.

To do so, they designed a **longitudinal study** to investigate the socio-emotional development of 30 one-year-old children across three key time periods: 13–15 months old, 18–20 months old, and 23–25 months old. They collected various kinds of data at each of these time periods, but their most crucial data took the form of observations of children's responses to others' distress. These data included observations of how children behaved in various naturalistic circumstances along with observations of their responses to simulated distress (e.g. an experimenter pretending to be in pain). Infants' responses were videotaped and then coded for a variety of prosocial (e.g. empathic concern, attempts to intervene and help) and non-prosocial behaviours (e.g. showing amusement or laughing during the distress).

Longitudinal study
Studies that monitor and chart the development of psychological variables over long periods of time.

Pause for thought

Confronted with others in apparent emotional and physical pain, what do you think the children would do and how might their reactions change over time?

Figure 1.7 presents just a few of Zahn-Waxler et al.'s results. The pattern represented here captures the central theme of their study. It shows how children's expressions of concern and willingness to help others steadily increased over the course of their second year of life. Conversely, their readiness to respond 'positively' (e.g. by laughing) steadily declined. Other results in their study suggested that, probably unsurprisingly, children were most responsive when their own mothers simulated distress. However, the fact that empathy was often also extended to relative strangers (e.g. the experimenters) complicates the cultural stereotype of the insensitive child. Children may sometimes treat others in ways that make us cringe, but as early as their second year of life they are already developing the ability to feel empathy.

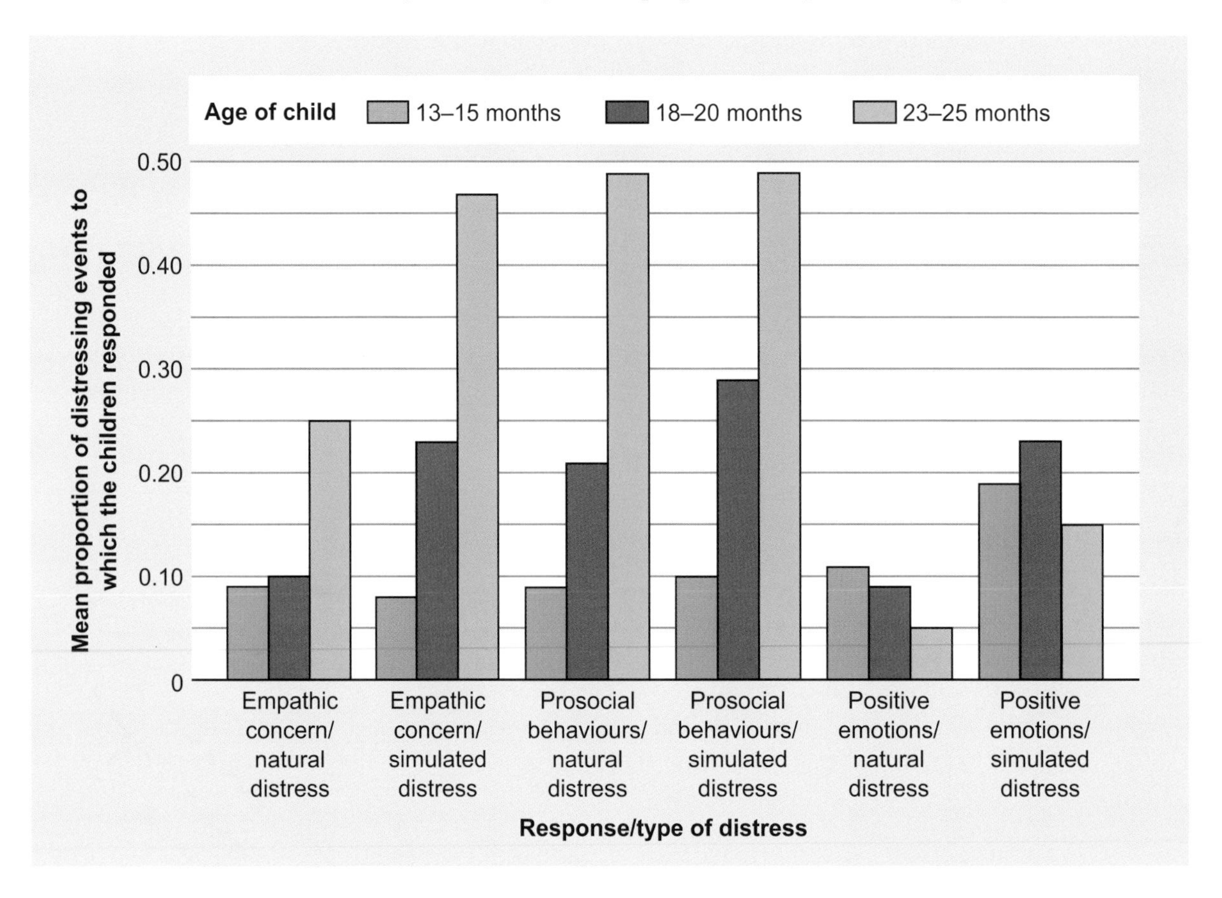

Figure 1.7 Children's shifting responses to others' distress across their second year of life

(Source: adapted from Zahn-Waxler et al., 1992, p.131, Table 1)

In its focus on cognitive and emotional changes that occur during infancy, Zahn-Waxler et al.'s study exemplifies some features of a *developmental psychology* perspective (see also Figure 1.1). As you may have noticed already, this perspective focuses on how our thoughts, feelings and behaviours change over time. In the early years of the sub-discipline, developmental researchers tended to focus on the psychological changes in babies, infants and children. However, as the third textbook for this module demonstrates, this focus has now broadened considerably to encompass developmental trajectories across the entire lifespan, from cradle to grave. Zahn-Waxler et al.'s work also illustrates some of the methodological and conceptual challenges that work in this area involves. Methodologically, it requires techniques for gathering and analysing psychological change and stability over time. Whereas in many other areas of psychology researchers rely heavily on snapshot experiments conducted with undergraduate students, developmental research typically involves investigating complex, longitudinal dynamics amongst a more diverse range of participants. Conceptually, this requires theories that can explain how, when and why we change over time. Explanations in this area must account, for example, for the emergence of prenatal patterns of responses (e.g. early signs of emotion such as proto-smiles and movements in the womb), the development of sexual and gender identity in adolescence, and the cognitive changes that can accompany old age (e.g. the progression of dementia).

4 An integrative approach to psychology: opportunities, complexities and challenges

You should now have a better idea of some core characteristics of the four main psychological sub-disciplines covered in the module textbooks. As the example of research on empathy illustrates, social, cognitive, biological and developmental psychology answer different kinds of questions about the object of study and take different kinds of approaches to psychological research. This section returns to the overarching theme of the module, which is to explore the relationship between these sub-disciplines and, more specifically, to ask questions of psychology that may be answered more fully by bringing together work across conventional academic boundaries.

To begin with, we want to acknowledge that specialisation is often inevitable and in many ways beneficial to the development of any field of inquiry. By focusing on neurological processes and devising specialist equipment for doing so, for example, biological psychologists have clarified basic issues of brain structure and function that might be of less direct relevance, say, to the research interests of social psychologists (e.g. the biology of visual, olfactory and auditory perception). Likewise, by focusing on the role of cultural and group dynamics, social psychologists have explored in depth topics that might be less interesting to biological psychologists (e.g. conformity to group norms, national identification and political attitudes). This division of labour has been beneficial in many ways. It has both extended the range of psychological knowledge and allowed psychologists to build the kinds of domain-specific concepts and methods required to address particular research questions effectively. However, this module is based on the assumption that many psychological topics have simultaneously a social, cognitive, biological and developmental dimension. The topic of empathy is a case in point. How do we understand what others are feeling? Social psychology tells us that who we feel concern for and why is shaped by wider contextual processes such as intergroup relations and group norms (Riva and Andrighetto, 2012). Cognitive psychology explains that it involves particular ways of processing and organising information, including the capacity to store and recall memories (Bluck et al., 2012). Biological psychology indicates that our capacity to feel what others are feeling is made possible by certain brain structures and patterns of neurological processing. Finally, developmental psychology has taught us that whilst empathy is present only in vestigial form in children, it evolves over time (Zahn-Waxler et al., 1992). Given that empathy encompasses all of these dimensions, it seems reasonable to assume that a psychological understanding of the process might require us to consider how its social, cognitive, biological and developmental dynamics might be interrelated and, by implication, how we might build explanations that integrate the insights of different forms of psychological knowledge. This module is designed to encourage you to think about how this project might be accomplished and what challenges and complexities it might entail.

In doing so, of course, the module reflects a wider movement that is gathering momentum in psychology. Attempts to work across academic boundaries and produce integrative accounts of psychological phenomena are increasingly common, and this is reflected in the emergence of hybrid fields such as cognitive neuropsychology, social cognition and developmental neuroscience. Researchers working in these areas are exercising an 'integrative' imagination. In order to answer their research questions, they are combining concepts developed in different sub-areas to construct hybrid theories; they are using methodological frameworks devised to explore one kind of psychological problem (e.g. implicit cognitive processing) to address others (e.g. racial prejudice), and they are exploring the complex interrelation between processes located at different levels of analysis (e.g. how emotions such as disgust operate at neurological, interpersonal, intergroup and cross-cultural levels).

There are two main reasons why this kind of work is the focus of this module. First, it is often located at the cutting edge of the discipline: the frontier between what is known and what is not known. Box 1.2 provides one example. As such, integrative work has the potential to yield the most novel, innovative and imaginative insights into human psychology. Second, such work illustrates the challenges as well as the opportunities involved when attempts are made to unify psychological knowledge. It thus raises provocative questions about the nature and direction of the discipline as a whole. For example:

- How do different areas of psychology conceive the basic nature of the psychological subject, that is, the thinking, feeling and acting individual?
- Do they offer radically distinct (or even irreconcilable) perspectives or is it possible to build a single, holistic perspective?

- How can we integrate research focusing on phenomena located at one level of analysis (e.g. the neurological) with research focusing on processes located at another (e.g. the cultural and historical)?
- For any given psychological process, how do we weigh up the relative influence of social, cognitive, biological and developmental factors?
- How do we decide which kinds of research methods are best able to elucidate particular research topics?
- How should funding for research be allocated across different sub-disciplines?

These are precisely the kinds of questions you should think about as you work through the module textbooks. The next section turns to their basic structure and content, and gives you some tips on how to use them most effectively.

Box 1.2 Crossing boundaries: the cognitive neuroscience of empathy

In recent years, there has been an explosion of work on empathy in the hybrid field of cognitive neuroscience. As its name suggests, this area of research brings together work in the field of cognitive psychology with work in the field of neuroscience (and beyond). A paper by Lamm et al. (2007), published in the *Journal of Cognitive Neuroscience*, provides an excellent example. It is worth noting that this journal, founded in 1989, deliberately aims to foster a cross-discipline approach, inviting contributions that integrate research in neuroscience, neurobiology, cognitive psychology, linguistics, philosophy, and computer science.

On the one hand, their study aimed to explore the effects of two cognitive processes on our concern for others' suffering, namely perspective-taking and cognitive appraisal. In order to do so, they showed participants video clips of patients allegedly suffering from a painful hearing disease (see Figure 1.8). To manipulate perspective-taking, some participants were asked to imagine how they would feel if they were one of the patients (self-perspective), whereas others were asked to imagine how the patients themselves might be feeling (other-perspective). To manipulate cognitive appraisal, some participants were told that the videotaped patients got better after treatment, others that their condition did not improve. Amongst other findings, Lamm et al. reported that participants evaluated patients' pain as more intense and unpleasant when they believed their treatment was not ultimately successful. Moreover, empathic concern for the patient was stronger when participants were asked to focus on the feelings of others rather than how they might feel themselves in a similar situation.

Figure 1.8 Sample frames from a video clip used in Lamm et al.'s study, showing how a painful sound provoked a shift from a neutral to a painful facial expression

On the other hand, Lamm et al.'s study aimed to investigate neural activity in participants' brains across the different conditions of their experiment. To do so, they analysed data gathered using fMRI techniques similar to those employed by Jackson et al. (2005) in the study discussed in Section 3.2.3. They found that watching video clips of others in pain increased brain activity in areas linked to the first-hand experience of being in pain, for example the insular cortex, the cingulate cortex and thalamus (see Figure 1.9). In addition, they found that this pattern of activation was broadly similar across the two perspective-taking conditions (self versus other focus), but that the self-perspective resulted in somewhat greater activation of the left parietal cortex, whereas the other-perspective was associated with greater activation of the right parietal cortex. Based on such findings and other evidence, Lamm et al. argued that this pattern is consistent with the argument that the right parietal cortex is particularly important in processing distinctions between self-produced and other-produced actions.

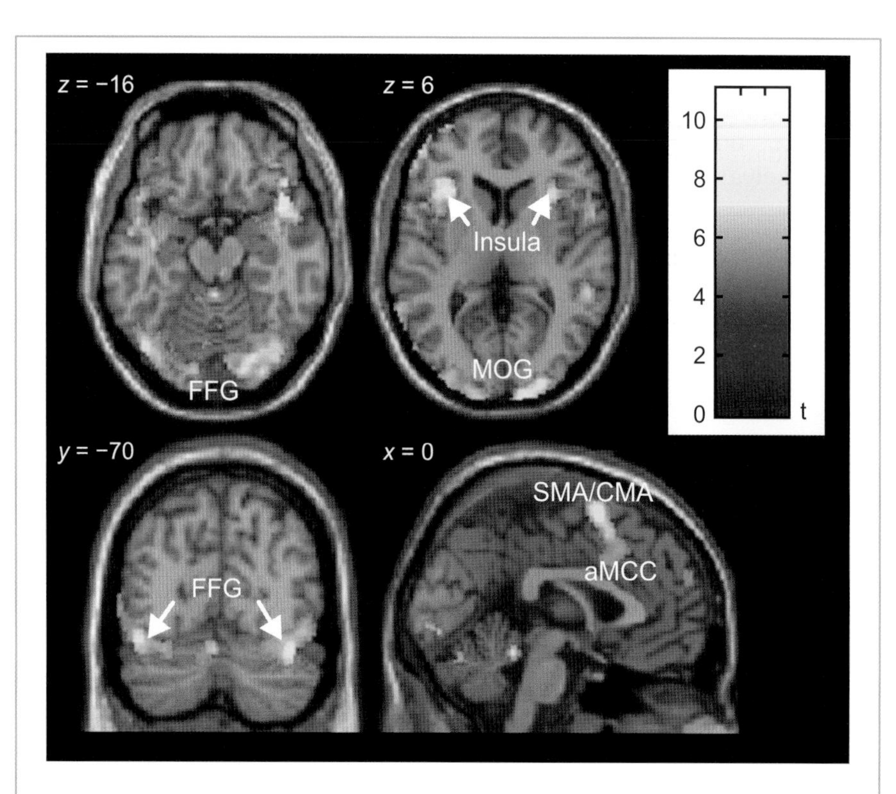

Figure 1.9 Brain areas activated when participants watched patients expressing pain (in contrast to a baseline condition): areas activated in the neural network pictured here include the FFG (Fusiform gyrus), the MOG (middle occipital gyrus), the insula and the aMCC (anterior midcingulate cortex)

(Source: Lamm et al., 2007, p. 49)

It is not possible to discuss here the richer details of Lamm et al.'s findings. Rather, the aim is to use their work to illustrate how recent research on empathy is clarifying the relationship between its cognitive and biological dimensions. This research is combining different conceptual frameworks (e.g. cognitive concepts such as perspective taking with biological concepts such as neural networks). It is also combining a variety of methodological techniques, including experimentation, the manipulation and measurement of cognitive processes, and the tracking and analysis of neural activation.

Interestingly, such research is not simply providing convergent lines of evidence about how we empathise with others. It is also extending our knowledge in new directions. For example, the work of Lamm et al. shows how cognitive perspective and situational appraisal may play a 'top down' role in shaping the nature of our neurological responses to others' pain. How individuals process information about those in pain at a neurological level, it appears, may be dependent on how they define the meaning of a situation.

5 Organisation of the textbooks and chapter outlines

The three module textbooks have been designed to provide you with a critical, up-to-date introduction to psychological research across a broad syllabus of topics and to help you think about the core theme of integration across disciplinary boundaries. Each chapter is organised around an everyday question that can be addressed by drawing on different areas of psychology. As mentioned already, Book 1 is subtitled 'from social to cognitive'. It focuses mainly on classic social psychological topics such as social influence, group and prosocial behaviour and personal relationships, but ends by exploring work on social cognition, i.e. work that has effectively crossed the boundaries between social and cognitive psychology. Book 2 is subtitled 'from cognitive to biological'. It focuses on classic topics in cognitive psychology such as attention and perception, but also explores work on the frontier between cognition (e.g. how we think and learn) and biology (e.g. how the brain works). Finally, Book 3 is subtitled 'from biological to developmental'. As well as continuing to explore the biological bases of our behaviour, it also shows how that behaviour evolves over the course of the individual's life, covering topics such as moral and gender development as well as fixity and change.

As you can see, the books are structured to help you think about how asking questions regarding psychological phenomenona requires engagement with different forms of psychological knowledge that may differ, overlap and interrelate. This reflective process is also facilitated by another design feature. Each chapter includes a 'crossing boundaries' box, the first example of which is provided in Box 1.2, which briefly discusses a piece of research operating at the intersection of different areas of psychology and considers its implications.

5.1 Book 1: From social to cognitive

Book 1 covers eight topics that take you on a pathway from social to cognitive psychology.

In Chapter 2, Stephen Gibson explores the topic of social influence, addressing the question: 'Why do good people do bad things?' He covers classic research on processes such as conformity and obedience as well as emerging work on the role of language in social influence.

In Chapter 3, Rose Capdevila asks: 'Are you with us or against us?' She covers a variety of research in the area of group processes, exploring topics such as social facilitation, social loafing and social comparison, as well as discussing the role of groups in promoting social change.

In Chapter 4, John Dixon addresses the question: 'Why don't we like one another?' He covers a range of research in the social psychology of prejudice and intergroup conflict and also discusses work on conflict reduction.

In Chapter 5, Rachel Manning and Mark Levine ask: 'Why do we help one another?' They cover topics in the field of prosocial behaviour including bystander intervention, altruism and other forms of helping behaviour.

In Chapter 6, Simon Watts and Vicki McDermott address the question: 'Why would I hang around with you?' They cover topics in the field of personal relationships, including work on attraction, self-disclosure, friendship and romantic love.

In Chapter 7, Karen Hagan discusses the psychology of attitudes, addressing the question: 'How do you feel about that?' She covers the history of attitude research and the nature, formation and measurement of attitudes, as well as theories that account for the relationship between attitudes and behaviours.

Finally, in Chapter 8, Lisa Lazard explores how work in the hybrid field of social cognition has provided a valuable foundation for understanding a number of basic social psychological processes discussed in earlier chapters, addressing the question: 'How do we make sense of the world?' Here, she covers topics such as social categorisation, attribution and schematic processing.

5.2 Book 2: From cognitive to biological

Book 2 covers six topics that take you on a pathway from cognitive to biological psychology. Again, each chapter is organised around an everyday question.

In Chapter 1, Simon Davies asks the question: 'Do you see what I see?' to explore the psychology of visual perception. The chapter discusses the sensory and biological bases of sight, along with topics such as the perception–action model, and multisensory and cross-modal perception.

Chapter 2 addresses the question: 'Can I do two things at once?' to introduce cognitive research on attention. Among other topics, Gemma Briggs and Graham Hole consider the role of attention in everyday environments, filter models of attention, and automatic and controlled processing. They also take the role of attention in driving as an applied example.

Chapter 3 asks: 'Is seeing believing?' Gemma Briggs and Simon Davies explore the interplay between attention and perception by investigating change and inattentional blindness.

In Chapter 4, Jane Barrett and Helen Kaye ask: 'Can you do what I do?' Their chapter focuses on the process of learning, exploring topics such as perceptual learning, associative learning, conditioning, social learning and cultural transmission.

Chapter 5 concerns the biology of emotion, addressing the question: 'Why do I feel this way?' In this chapter, Frederick Toates explores some biological (e.g. hormones) and neurological (e.g. synaptic processes) foundations of our emotions and discusses a biopsychosocial model of mood and behaviour. As a practical example, he considers the effects of drugs such as Prozac and heroin.

Chapter 6 asks: 'How does my brain work?' Jeremy Tree introduces the diverse field of cognitive neuroscience, focusing particularly on language perception and production. He discusses neurological impairments such as anomia and aphasia, and, more broadly, addresses the question of how language is related to brain organisation and function. This chapter concludes Book 2.

5.3 Book 3: From biological to developmental

Book 3 covers five topics that take us from biological to developmental psychology.

In Chapter 1, 'Do you hear what I hear?', Jason Rentfrow introduces Book 3 by integrating several core themes from Book 2. He begins by questioning how humans learn to understand music and how we come to process it cognitively, emotionally and neurologically. He goes on to discuss how the music we choose to listen to can help to shape our behaviour, personality and even the everyday choices we make.

In Chapter 2, Andrew Holliman and Sarah Critten ask: 'What's the point of childhood?', taking us on a journey through several core areas of child development, including early attachment relationships, memory, theory of mind and language development. They also consider the role of later influences such as friendship, bullying and social media in shaping children's ability to function well in their environments.

Chapter 3 addresses the question: 'How do we know what is right and wrong?', focusing on the development of moral reasoning in children. In this chapter, Paul Ibbotson discusses the work of key theorists in the field, including Kohlberg, Piaget, Turiel and Gilligan. He also examines the role of moral emotions such as compassion and disgust, and moral behaviours such as sharing and helping.

In Chapter 4, 'Are boys and girls born or made?', Jane Callaghan considers the topic of gender development, comparing the biological, social cognitive and social constructionist perspectives. She also considers the process of sexualisation and the development of sexual identity. Among other examples, she uses the process of 'coming out' as gay or lesbian as a way of exploring the 'heteronormative' nature of much developmental work on gender.

Chapter 5, 'Can people really change?', considers development in a broader sense. Here, Sarah Crafter discusses changes in self-identity and self-relationships over the course of our lifespans. This approach allows her to explore deeper themes such as fixity and change over time, the concept of developmental 'transitions' and the value of a longitudinal perspective.

In the final chapter of the book, John Dixon, Gemma Briggs and Rose Capdevila revisit the central themes of the module – asking questions and working across boundaries – to explore the opportunities, challenges and complexities of taking an integrative approach to psychology. They argue that this is not simply a matter of combining knowledge within and across different areas of psychology. It also requires us to look beyond the discipline's frontiers to developments in companion disciplines including biology, sociology, linguistics, philosophy and history. As well as reflecting on chapters presented in Book 3, this final chapter looks back at material covered across the three books, and invites you to think critically about what you have learned on this module.

References

Billig, M. (1987) *Arguing and Thinking: A Rhetorical Approach to Social Psychology*, 1st edn, Cambridge, Cambridge University Press.

Bloom, P. (2013) 'The baby in the well: the case against empathy', *The New Yorker*, 20 May [Online]. Available at www.newyorker.com/arts/critics/atlarge/2013/05/20/130520crat_atlarge_bloom?currentPage=all (Accessed 26 August 2014).

Bluck, S., Baron, J.M., Ainsworth, S.A., Gesselman, A.N. and Gold, K.L. (2012) 'Eliciting empathy for adults in chronic pain through autobiographical memory sharing', *Applied Cognitive Psychology*, vol. 27, pp. 81–91.

Brown, S.D. and Stenner, P. (2009) *Psychology Without Foundations: History, Philosophy and Psychosocial Theory*, London, Sage.

Hodges, S.D. and Myers, M.W. (2007) 'Empathy', in Baumeister, R.F. and Vohs, K.D. (eds) *Encyclopedia of Social Psychology*, Thousand Oaks, CA, Sage, pp.296–8.

Jackson P.L., Meltzoff A.N. and Decety J. (2005) 'How do we perceive the pain of others: a window into the neural processes involved in empathy', *NeuroImage*, vol. 24, pp. 771–9.

Lamm, C., Batson, D.D. and Decety, J. (2007) 'The neural substrate of human empathy: effects of perspective-taking and cognitive appraisal', *Journal of Cognitive Neuroscience*, vol. 19, pp. 42–58.

McDougall, W. (1908) *An Introduction to Social Psychology*, London, Methuen & Co.

Mead, G.H. (1934) *The Social Self*, Chicago, University of Chicago Press.

Riva, P. and Andrighetto, L. (2012) '"Everyone feels a broken bone, but only we can feel a broken heart": group membership influences perceptions of targets' suffering', *European Journal of Social Psychology*, vol. 42, pp. 801–6.

Ross, E.A. (1908) *Social Psychology: An Outline and Source Book*, New York, The Macmillan Company.

Zahn-Waxler, C., Radke-Yarrow, M., Wagner, E. and Chapman, M. (1992) 'Development of concern for others', *Developmental Psychology*, vol. 28, pp. 126–36.

Zoll, C. and Enz, S. (2010) *A Questionnaire to Assess Affective and Cognitive Empathy in Children* [Online]. Available at www.opus-bayern.de/uni-bamberg/volltexte/2010/235/ (Accessed 21 September 2014).

Chapter 2

Why do good people do bad things? The psychology of social influence

Stephen Gibson

Contents

1 Introduction

> It is arguable that the shadow of the Holocaust lies over the last half century of social psychology.
>
> (Reicher and Haslam, 2006, p. 1)

Much of social psychology since the Second World War has been concerned with understanding why seemingly ordinary, decent people would assent to – and actively participate in – genocide and mass murder on an unimaginable scale. In seeking to understand the Holocaust and a range of other abuses and atrocities, social psychologists have undertaken some of the most creative and enduring work in the social sciences. However, it is also arguable that some of that work has led to blind alleys and misleading conclusions. Perhaps most disturbingly, it has led to suggestions that some social psychologists have become so intent on explaining these evils that they have themselves treated their research participants inhumanely and unethically. This chapter will delve into these issues, and in doing so will introduce the broad topic of social influence.

Hogg and Vaughan (2011, p. 236) define social influence as the 'process whereby attitudes and behaviour are influenced by the real or imagined presence of other people.' They note that this is remarkably similar to one of the classic definitions of social psychology as a whole, which described social psychology as 'the scientific investigation of how the thoughts, feelings and behaviours of individuals are influenced by the actual, imagined or implied presence of others' (Allport, 1954, p. 5). It might therefore be suggested that the study of social influence can be seen as social psychology's key subject matter, and that by conceiving of social influence as a distinct 'topic' in its own right, connections with other areas of enquiry in the discipline have sometimes been lost. This chapter begins with an outline of some of the core areas of inquiry that have typically been understood as 'social influence' research. It then considers connections between social influence and other key concerns of social psychology, most notably the nature of groups and intergroup relations. Finally, it introduces some more recent attempts to explore social influence that have focused on language use.

Learning outcomes

On completing this chapter you should:

- be able to describe the difference between compliance, conformity and obedience
- be able to compare and contrast classic studies of social influence (e.g. Milgram's obedience experiments; Zimbardo's Stanford Prison Experiment) with more recent work in this area
- be able to discuss recent attempts to explore the role of language in social influence.

Not everyone complies, agrees, some people do their own thing.

2 What are the classic approaches to social influence?

Social influence is often divided into three different topics:

- **compliance**
- **conformity**
- **obedience.**

Compliance
Social influence arising as a response to a request.

Conformity
Social influence arising from adherence to group norms.

Obedience
Social influence arising in response to a direct order.

This section explores these three types of influence through some of the classic studies that have been used to demonstrate them. However, let's begin by thinking critically about this distinction. Look at the definitions in the margin and see if you can think of situations that perhaps don't fit neatly into one or other of the categories.

2.1 Compliance: 'Please could you do this?'

How often have you been stopped in the street by someone wanting you to complete a survey? Or received a phone call from someone trying to sell you something? Situations such as these rely on techniques designed to encourage compliance. Psychologists interested in compliance have studied a range of factors that influence how likely someone is to agree to a request. Some of the most influential studies of compliance have made use of very simple but ingenious experimental designs to assess people's willingness to comply. One example is Freedman and Fraser's (1966) study of the 'foot-in-the-door' technique, which suggests it is easier to get people to agree to something that they may be reluctant to do if you first ask them to do something much more straightforward. Freedman and Fraser asked participants whether they would be willing to allow a group of consumer researchers to come into their home for a period of around two hours to record and classify the types of household products they used. When asked in isolation, only just over 20 per cent of respondents agreed to this request. However, when respondents had taken part in a short telephone survey on a similar topic a few days previously, agreement to the more onerous request went up to just over 50 per cent.

Why does the foot-in-the-door technique work? Many researchers have argued that the key factor is a desire to see ourselves as consistent (e.g. Cialdini and Goldstein, 2004; Dolinski, 2000). In general terms, we have a preference for consistency, and having agreed to one request we are thus inclined to see ourselves as being the sort of person who helps out with consumer surveys (or whatever the specific focus of the request may be). When faced with the subsequent, much more demanding and time-consuming, request, the desire for consistency frequently wins out. This interpretation is supported by research that suggests people who score highly on measures of the desire for consistency tend to be more likely to agree to the second request (Cialdini et al., 1995).

If preceding a large request with a small request can increase the likelihood of people agreeing to the large request, then it also seems that changing the order of the requests can lead to increased compliance with the small request. This is known as the 'door-in-the-face' technique (the idea being that the initial large request leads to the slamming of a metaphorical door in the requestor's face!) Cialdini et al. (1975) demonstrated this technique by asking participants if they would give up two hours of their time to take a group of young offenders on a trip to the zoo. When asked on its own, less than 20 per cent of participants complied with this request. However, when it followed an initial request to give up two hours per week over a period of two years for a mentoring scheme for young offenders, 50 per cent of participants agreed to the subsequent smaller request. This can be understood as a result of a norm of reciprocity – the requestor is seen as making a concession in shifting from the large request to the small one, and so the decent thing for the participant to do is to reciprocate and make a concession of their own by agreeing to the small request (Cialdini and Goldstein, 2004).

Subsequent research on compliance has tended to follow the lead of these classic studies by focusing on different techniques for achieving compliance, as well as exploring the variables that affect levels of compliance (see Cialdini, 2008). However, the extent to which such research can help us to address why good people do bad things is limited. Much of the literature on compliance concerns scenarios that involve trying to get people to do things that may be inconvenient or time-consuming, but which are not ultimately activities that are frowned on. More critically, compliance research can be seen as an area characterised by a series of clever and innovative studies that don't really cohere in any meaningful sense. Indeed, as far back as the 1960s, some social psychologists were bemoaning the state of the discipline with its 'fun and games' approach to research leading to a neglect of important theoretical and social issues (Ring, 1967). Compliance research has perhaps gained its most favourable reception in advertising and marketing circles, where the benefits of knowing a range of simple but effective techniques for securing agreement has obvious advantages. It is less clear how it helps us address some of the bigger questions that some critics of 'fun and games' experimentation wanted social psychology to engage with.

2.2 Conformity: 'Everyone else is doing this'

Research on conformity has tended to explore the effects of social pressures on individual judgements. This has often been used to explore why people might be led into doing things they would not ordinarily do if they were acting alone. As such, it appears more promising in addressing the issue of why good people may do bad things. However, as we'll see, there are reasons to be cautious here too.

2.2.1 Sherif and the autokinetic effect

In his classic experimental demonstration of the formation of group norms, Sherif (1966) took advantage of a visual illusion known as the autokinetic effect. This illusion involves participants being placed in a darkened room with a single point of light projected onto a screen in front of them. In the pitch-black conditions, the point of light appears to move, although in reality it remains stationary.

Sherif asked participants to estimate the distance over which the point of light moved. He did this in two conditions: individually and in groups of two or three participants. Some participants were tested first individually, and then in groups; others were tested in groups and then individually. For those who were first tested individually, there was considerable variation between their judgements. When these same participants were subsequently tested in groups of two or three and required to call out their estimates so that other group members could hear, the judgements converged over a series of trials. For participants who were initially tested in groups, the estimates again converged, but then when they were subsequently tested individually, their judgements remained anchored around the norm established in the group condition (see Figure 2.1).

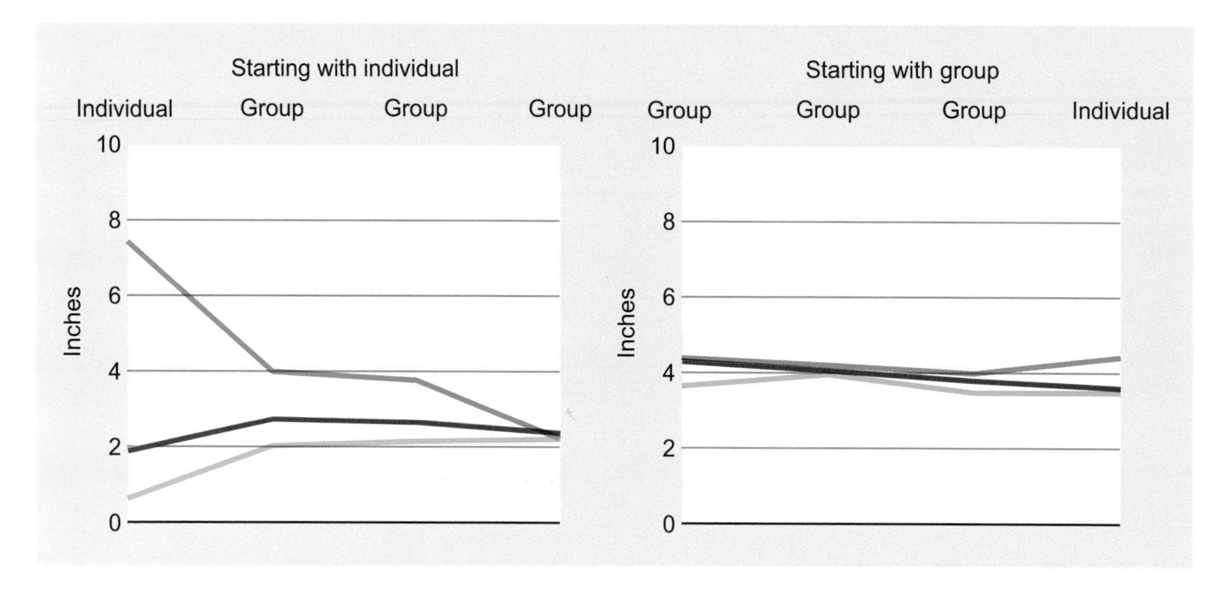

Figure 2.1 Results from two of the groups in Sherif's study of the emergence of social norms using the autokinetic effect
(Source: adapted from Sherif, 1966)

Each line represents the responses of an individual participant. When individual judgements are delivered first, the initial wide variation in participants' estimates narrows over a succession of trials when participants are brought together in a group. When the individual trial comes last, the convergence of judgements is apparent from the outset, and remains in place even when participants are asked to make the final judgement alone.

Sherif's findings can be seen as providing an example of

Informational influence
Social influence based on the belief that others are better informed than we are

informational influence – when the correct answer isn't clear or obvious, we will look to others who we may presume to be better informed than we are. Sherif argued that the experiments provided evidence of the emergence of social norms, and the persistence of these norms even when the group was no longer directly present. He speculated that this helped to shed light on the basic social psychological processes underlying a range of phenomena, including the development of socially shared customs, stereotypes and fashions.

Activity 2.1: Going along with the crowd

Have you ever found yourself in a situation where you have 'gone along with the crowd' and done something because everyone else in your

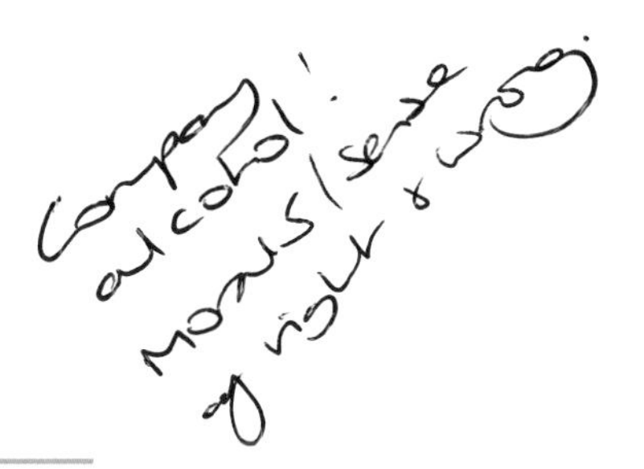

group was doing it? Equally, have you ever rebelled and remained independent despite pressures to conform?

What do you think led you to behave in these ways?

2.2.2 Asch's line-length judgement experiments

Sherif's study involved the creation of a deliberately uncertain situation. In contrast, Solomon Asch (1952, 1956) conducted a series of landmark experiments exploring people's reactions to situations in which they were asked to perform a clear and straightforward perceptual task that other people appeared to be getting consistently wrong. In the best-known of the experiments, each participant took part as a member of a group of between seven and nine people. However, the other members of the group were confederates – people who were employed by Asch to provide the wrong answer. The task itself required participants to look at three lines of unequal lengths and decide which of the lines was the same length as a target line (see Figure 2.2). The correct answer was always clear and unambiguous, but to be on the safe side Asch included a control group who judged the stimuli alone, and found that there were virtually no mistakes.

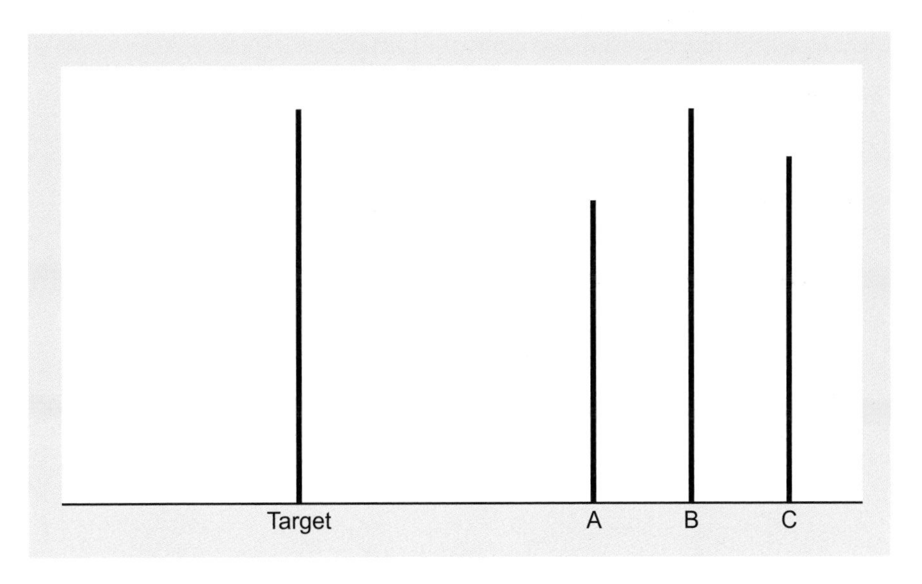

Figure 2.2 Stimuli used by Asch (1956): which line is the same length as the target line?

In comparison with the control group, participants who took part in the experimental condition (i.e. with confederates) made many more errors over a series of trials, with over 75 per cent of them being swayed by the majority on at least one occasion out of the 12 trials (Asch, 1956). However, Asch was keen to point out that, while most participants in the group condition made at least one error, over all the trials the number of incorrect judgements was far outweighed by the number of independent (correct) judgements.

Asch conducted post-experiment interviews with his participants to try to find out what they made of the situation he had created, and why they had behaved as they did. Before being told that the experiment had been a set-up, Asch's participants often said they had been confused by what happened, and tried to rationalise both their own conduct and the conduct of the other group members. Participants frequently referred to the pressure they felt to 'go along with the crowd' (Asch, 1956, p. 31), but also to provide the correct answer. In short, the experiment had led to a dilemma between conforming to the group and providing the objectively correct answer. Even participants whose judgements were highly independent could acknowledge the norm of going along with the group. Asch (1956, p. 31) reports that one such participant began the post-experiment interview by saying, 'I hope you didn't think I was different – I was just calling them as I saw them.' And yet, despite these pressures to conform, as noted above, the majority of responses displayed independence. To the extent that participants were influenced by the group to provide an incorrect answer, Asch's study can be seen as demonstrating **normative influence**. In contrast to informational influence (see above), this refers to occasions when we go along with the group out of a fear of social disapproval. However, it is important to note that in most situations, both informational and normative influence will be at work. Even Asch's experimental situation – despite the easiness of the task – can be shown to have informational pressures (Deutsch and Gerard, 1955). For example, some participants suggested the sheer weight of numbers getting a seemingly straightforward task wrong led them to doubt the evidence of their own eyes.

Normative influence
Social influence that occurs because of pressures to 'fit in' with a group, or more broadly with what we perceive to be expectations about what we should do.

Sherif's and Asch's experiments are often seen as classic examples of the ways in which individual judgement can be skewed by social pressures, typically in group situations. However, it seems that neither Sherif nor Asch was entirely happy that their work should simply be seen as evidence of the irrationality of the individual in the face of group pressures. Sherif (1966) came to reflect somewhat ruefully on the way in which his experiments were understood by many social psychologists. He saw his studies as offering a glimpse of how people arrive at consensus in the face of unclear and confusing information, and believed that his experiments therefore revealed something fundamental about the social nature of the ways in which people arrive at definitions of reality. Similarly, Asch (1956) actually framed his experiments on the judgement of line lengths as examples of the way in which, more often than not, group pressure is *insufficient* to overcome individual rationality.

Some authors have thus attempted to develop alternative accounts of 'conformity' phenomena that take seriously the dynamics of the situation in which participants find themselves. For example, Hodges and Geyer (2006) suggest that Asch's participants who sometimes gave the wrong answer to fit in with the group should not be seen as simply making an obvious error in the face of pressures to conform. Rather, they suggest that the competing values of accuracy and solidarity should both be seen as meaningful responses in this situation. Specifically, Hodges and Geyer argue that errors might represent strategic attempts to keep oneself 'in the conversation' (2006, p. 6) so that subsequent dissent might be more effective. If you are in the difficult situation of disagreeing with a group that is unanimously in opposition to you, then sometimes it might be wise to go along with that group so that when you do subsequently disagree, you have built up a base layer of solidarity with your fellow group members.

This points to the possibility that behaviour that apparently is the result of 'mindless' conformity might in fact be the product of a rather more complex attempt at resistance. Indeed, Asch points to a more general danger in emphasising conformity at the expense of resistance:

> One need not doubt the great power of social forces to realise that conformity is not the sole effect they produce. The striving for independence and resistance to encroachment are as much facts about people as is conformity. It is consequently unduly narrowing to emphasise submission, to the neglect of the not inconsiderable powers persons demonstrate on occasion for acting according to conviction and rising above group passion.
>
> (Asch, 1956, p. 2)

It is notable that, in some versions of his study, Asch (1951) found that if only one additional person dissents from the majority view, conformity is drastically reduced. This suggests that the group processes that sometimes produce erroneous responses can also work in the other direction and encourage people to stick together when they have the right answer. But can such minorities go further and actually influence a majority?

2.2.3 Minority influence and bias in social psychology

This question was addressed by Moscovici (1976), who argued that social influence research exhibited a bias towards conformity. By this he meant that a lot of research on social influence looked at how individuals can be made to fit in with social norms. In contrast, Moscovici suggested that research should explore how social change occurred, and that this required the exploration of minority influence. Moscovici argued that it is minorities – groups who are excluded from, or are on the fringes of, mainstream society – that are the main engines of social change.

Moscovici and his colleagues (e.g. Moscovici et al., 1969; Moscovici and Lage, 1976) conducted a series of experiments designed to explore minority influence. Like Asch's studies, the basic version of Moscovici's procedure involved a simple perceptual task – naming the colour of a series of slides projected onto a screen. When a minority (played by confederates) asserted that blue slides were in fact green, there was a small but nevertheless statistically significant effect on the responses of the majority group composed of naïve participants. Over a series of studies, consistency emerged as the most important factor in the ability of minorities to influence majorities. When the minority was inconsistent, the effect was eroded. Moscovici has argued that a desire to avoid conflict is at the heart of the minority influence effect. Majority group members are motivated to avoid disagreement and achieve consensus, and so when faced with a determined and consistent minority that disagrees with the majority position, there is a preference for moving towards the minority position in order to reduce conflict and minimise tension. Applied to social issues, this sort of influence from a consistent minority can lead to genuine and long-lasting changes in attitudes (Wood et al., 1994). This helps to explain how small groups of determined and vocal campaigners have been able to gradually change the majority view on issues such as gay marriage.

Moscovici's work also highlights another issue – the idea of a bias towards conformity raises fundamental questions about the assumptions underpinning social psychology. Some researchers have also noted that social psychology exhibits biases of this sort, although it is interesting to note that some take a quite different view from Moscovici on the nature of these biases. For example, Reicher and Haslam (2006) have argued that much social psychological theory and research has often assumed that group influence necessarily leads towards dangerous and irrational behaviour. In this sense, then, it can be said that there is a form of **individualistic bias** in which theorists uncritically accept cultural values emphasising the importance of resisting the temptation to 'go along with the crowd' and to instead retain a sense of yourself as an individual.

Individualistic bias
The tendency to either explain social phenomena in terms of individual psychological processes (explanatory individualism), or to see the individual as the locus of rationality and morality (normative individualism).

Nowhere is this bias more apparent than in the concept of deindividuation, defined by Festinger et al. (1952) as arising when:

> individuals are not seen or paid attention to as individuals. The [group] members do not feel that they stand out as individuals. Others are not singling a person out for attention nor is the person singling out others.
>
> (Festinger et al., 1952, p. 382)

As is apparent from this definition, deindividuation is particularly likely to occur in group situations where we can 'lose' ourselves among others. However, it is fairly clear that the apparent common-sense plausibility of the dangers of groups can be countered. Consider the following statement from the start of Festinger et al.'s (1952) paper:

> People obtain release in groups, that is, are sometimes more free from restraints, less inhibited, and able to indulge in forms of behavior in which, when alone, they would not indulge.
>
> (Festinger et al., 1952, p. 382)

On the face of it, this sounds plausible enough, but you might want to ask yourself if the opposite is equally plausible:

> *People obtain release* ***when alone****, that is, are sometimes more free from restraints, less inhibited, and able to indulge in forms of behaviour in which,* ***when in groups****, they would not indulge.*

Isn't it the case that we sometimes do things when we're alone that we wouldn't dream of doing when we're with others? (See Box 2.1.)

Box 2.1 Crossing boundaries: a criminological internet 'sting'!

Given the concern with 'bad' behaviour, it is perhaps unsurprising that social psychology has often crossed boundaries with criminology and other related fields (e.g. forensic psychology). Later you will explore the Stanford Prison Experiment, which was partly a response to deteriorating relations between guards and prisoners in US gaols in the 1960s. More recently, however, the rise of mass communication technologies – especially the internet – has led criminologists to use social psychological concepts to explore how people might be tempted to commit criminal and other forms of socially undesirable behaviour online.

Demetriou and Silke (2003) conducted an ingenious study in which they set up a website that was registered with search engines as offering free games. However, the site itself appeared to contain clearly illegal pirated games, and 'softcore' and 'hardcore' pornography, as well as free games. Demetriou and Silke tracked the numbers of users accessing the site, and the number of people who tried to access the different types of material. Out of 803 visitors to the site, 483 (60 per cent) attempted to access hardcore pornography, and 331 (41 per cent) attempted to access the pirated software. In all, Demetriou and Silke (2003, p. 219) found that 'no more than 331 visitors restricted themselves to just legal and non-pornographic material.' By recording information on the search terms that people had used to locate the website, Demetriou and Silke were able to confirm that the vast majority of participants had accessed the site after searching for legitimately available games.

Demetriou and Silke suggest their findings highlight the potentially deindividuating effects of the internet. However, think of the typical way in which one accesses the internet (and bear in mind that the study was conducted in the early 2000s, before the availability of devices that enable us to access the net in social situations 'on the go'). An individual sitting alone at a computer screen is surely not an example of deindividuation, but instead might be said to be supremely *individuated*. In the attempt to prioritise the morality and rationality of the individual, it thus appears that even a situation in which it seems that people are clearly acting as individuals is explained in terms that maintain the superiority of individual action.

2.3 Obedience: 'You must do this'

Stanley Milgram's (1963, 1974) studies of obedience are perhaps the most well-known and controversial experiments in social psychology. Milgram had worked with Asch and was a great admirer of his studies of conformity (Blass, 2004). However, Milgram was concerned that the judgement required of participants in Asch's experiments was essentially a trivial and inconsequential one. Milgram wanted to understand the processes that had led to the Holocaust, and so he designed an experimental situation where social pressures pushed people to do something that was clearly wrong.

Milgram conducted many variations of the basic obedience procedure (see Chapter 2 of Brace and Byford (2012) for a fuller account of the obedience experiments), but perhaps the best-known version of the procedure involved a participant arriving at the laboratory apparently to take part in a study of memory and learning. The experimental procedure required the participant, in the role of 'teacher', to use an electric shock generator (see Figure 2.3) to punish another participant – 'the learner' – for mistakes on a memory test. The shocks began at 15 volts, and went up in 15 volt increments all the way to 450 volts. As the experiment unfolded, it became clear that the learner was making numerous mistakes, and the teacher was required to progress rapidly through the shock levels. From around 75 volts, the learner began to cry out in pain. Initially these cries were fairly innocuous (e.g. 'Ouch!'), but by 150 volts the learner was apparently sufficiently agitated to demand to be withdrawn from the experiment. In reality, of course, the other 'participant' was in fact a confederate, and the shocks were not genuine.

Figure 2.3 Milgram's shock generator

Unsurprisingly, most participants were unsure whether they should continue, and looked to the experimenter for guidance. At this point, the experimenter had a set of pre-prepared prods that he could use to attempt to get participants to continue with the experimental procedure (see Activity 2.2). If a participant continued to defy the experimenter after receiving the fourth sequential prod, the experimental session was discontinued. Participants who were fully obedient and went all the way to the end of the shock generator were asked to administer the final 450 volt shock a total of three times. By this point in the procedure, the learner had long since fallen silent, apparently unconscious (or worse) after a series of agonised screams. With this version of the procedure, Milgram (1974) found that between 47.5 per cent and 65 per cent of participants were fully obedient (i.e. they continued all the way to the 450 volt level).

Activity 2.2: Obedience or compliance?

The standardised procedure for Milgram's experiment included six 'prods' that the experimenter could use to try to get participants to continue giving electric shocks to the learner. Four of these prods were to be used in sequence, and begun anew for each separate attempt at disobedience:

> Prod 1: Please continue, *or*, Please go on.
>
> Prod 2: The experiment requires that you continue.
>
> Prod 3: It is absolutely essential that you continue.

Prod 4: You have no other choice, you *must* go on.

(Milgram, 1974, p. 21, italics in original)

In addition, the experimenter could use two extra prods to answer specific queries from participants as appropriate. These were: 'Although the shocks may be painful, there is no permanent tissue damage, so please go on' (Milgram, 1974, p. 21) and 'Whether the learner likes it or not, you must go on until he has learned all the word pairs correctly. So please go on' (Milgram 1974, p. 22).

Recently, some authors have begun to question whether these prods are best understood as *orders* designed to elicit *obedience*, or whether they might be better understood as requests designed to elicit *compliance* (e.g. Burger et al., 2011; Gibson, 2013a; Reicher and Haslam, 2011).

What do you think? Are these prods *orders* or *requests*, or a mixture of the two? How should we define an 'order'? What are the implications for our understanding of the experiments if it turns out that the experimenter wasn't really issuing orders as such? Can we have obedience without orders, or is this a different type of phenomenon?

Milgram's findings provoked a range of reactions when they were published in the 1960s and 1970s. While some fêted Milgram as a daring and creative scientist revealing unpalatable but compelling truths about human nature (e.g. Zimbardo, 1974), others challenged the studies on both ethical (e.g. Baumrind, 1964) and methodological (e.g. Orne and Holland, 1968) grounds. This debate has continued to the present day, and has recently taken new twists as researchers have begun to delve into the wealth of material held in Milgram's personal archive at Yale University (e.g. Nicholson, 2011; Perry, 2012; Russell, 2011). For example, my own research has explored the extent to which participants actually obeyed the fourth prod ('you have no other choice, you must continue') (Gibson, 2013a). This prod has been identified as being of crucial importance to whether or not Milgram's studies are seen as demonstrations of people's tendency to follow orders (Miller, 2009; Reicher and Haslam, 2011). Using audio recordings of 70 participants in two conditions that used the basic procedure described above, I found that out of 23 participants on whom the fourth prod was used, only two administered any more shocks, and only one of these went all the way to 450 volts. Rather than following this direct order, participants thus appeared more than capable of resisting it. It therefore appears that, whatever Milgram's experiments show us, they do not provide evidence that direct orders can elicit obedience to authority (see also Burger et al., 2011).

Other researchers have developed Milgram's research in a different direction. For many years, the ethical issues involved in Milgram's experiments meant that it was difficult – if not downright unacceptable – to attempt to replicate the obedience experiments. However, one researcher, Jerry Burger, has recently undertaken a partial replication of Milgram's procedure that retains both the deception and the electric shocks.

Burger's (2009) study of obedience to authority retained almost all of the essential features of Milgram's original procedure described above. However, in order to make his study more ethically acceptable, Burger made several important modifications. Most importantly, he chose to terminate his experiments at the 150 volt point. You will recall from the description of Milgram's procedure outlined above that this was the point at which the learner first demanded to be released. Burger noticed that in Milgram's version of the experiment, 79 per cent of participants who continued past this point ultimately went all the way to the end of the shock generator. He therefore suggested that by stopping the procedure at this point, a fairly good guess can be made at how many people would have continued to 450 volts. Seventy per cent of Burger's participants did indeed begin to continue after 150 volts, at which point the experimenter brought the session to an end. This means that – using the proportion who continued in Milgram's study as a guide – around 55 per cent of his participants would have gone all the way to 450 volts. This was not significantly different from Milgram's obedience levels.

However, as Twenge (2009) has pointed out, this relies on a fairly big assumption. One of the key questions that Burger set out to address was whether obedience levels – as measured using the Milgram paradigm – would be the same in the early twenty-first century as they had been back in the 1960s. There doesn't seem to be a huge change up to the 150 volt point on Milgram's procedure, but what if any cultural change that has occurred has made people less willing to accede to the demands of the authority figure in the face of *repeated* attempts at withdrawal by the learner? In other words, perhaps the cultural change operates on the sustained exposure to the conflicting demands of authority and victim that occurs between the learner's first withdrawal of consent at 150 volts and the end of the procedure at 450 volts.

2.4 Summary

This section has introduced some of the classic studies in the areas of compliance, conformity and obedience. Seminal research by the likes of Cialdini, Sherif, Asch and Milgram has been discussed with a view to exploring what it tells us about social influence processes, and more specifically the extent to which it helps us to answer the question of how good people can be led into doing bad things. You have seen that a great deal of this classic research demonstrates that we are apparently rather susceptible to being influenced into giving a wrong answer on a simple perceptual task (Asch), or administering what we think is a dangerous electric shock to another human being (Milgram). However, you have also seen that there is reason to be cautious about buying into this rather oversimplified version of human nature. If people really were so malleable, how would dissent, resistance and social change come about? This is what authors such as Moscovici have been concerned with, and why the recent re-evaluation of Milgram's obedience experiments points to further layers of complexity that have been hidden from view for perhaps too long. Underscoring this is a concern for the values and assumptions that have shaped social psychology, and the next section will confront this issue directly by looking at one of the most (in)famous studies of group influence, together with a more recent attempt to challenge it.

3 Group influence and social identity

You have already seen that groups have been central to some studies of social influence, particularly in the area of conformity. More recently, there has been a shift in some quarters towards seeing group action as rational and meaningful in its own right, and this has led to the development of new perspectives on social influence (e.g. Turner, 1991). However, the tendency to see groups as a negative influence on the otherwise rational and moral individual goes deeper than simply a few studies. Reicher and Haslam (2006) have argued that social psychology has a much broader tendency to associate the group, the crowd, the collective, with the dangerous and the irrational. This can be traced to long-standing cultural assumptions in the Western world about the primacy of individual reason, allied with more recent twentieth-century suspicions about the supposed dangers of collectivism embodied in Communism (Billig, 1976; Samelson, 1986). One infamous study that has long been used to point to the dangers of group influence – and which continues to exert a fair amount of influence itself to this day – is the Stanford Prison Experiment (SPE).

3.1 The Stanford Prison Experiment

In August 1971, Philip Zimbardo conducted a study that has since become one of the most well-known and notorious pieces of research in social psychology (Haney et al., 1973; Zimbardo, 2007). Zimbardo created a mock prison in the basement of Stanford University's psychology department and randomly assigned his participants, who were all men, to play the role of either prisoners or guards. After an initial period of attempted rebellion by the prisoners, the guards began to clamp down and behaved increasingly oppressively towards the prisoners.

Zimbardo and his colleagues argued that, while at first the guards responded with aggression to the prisoners' attempted rebellion, over time the abusive and dehumanising behaviour exhibited by the guards 'was emitted simply as a "natural" consequence of being in the uniform of a "guard" and asserting the power inherent in that role' (Haney et al., 1973, p. 92). Zimbardo concluded that both guards and prisoners had become subsumed by their roles, losing their sense of themselves as individuals (deindividuation), and instead simply going along with what they felt followed from the role they had been assigned. As such, the prisoners became withdrawn, despondent and resigned to their fate, and the guards became oppressive, abusive and authoritarian. As a result of the extreme behaviour displayed, the study, which had been planned to run for two weeks, was abandoned after only six days. As with Milgram's experiments, this led to a heated ethical debate.

Pause for thought

Zimbardo (2007) describes how he drew on his experiences in the Stanford Prison Experiment when testifying in defence of Sergeant Ivan 'Chip' Frederick, one of the US soldiers tried for the abuse of prisoners at the Abu Ghraib prison in Iraq in 2003. Zimbardo argued that, while Frederick's actions should not be excused, the lessons of the SPE suggest that he should not be judged as harshly as some might think. The conditions under which Frederick and his fellow accused were working promoted the abuses, in much the same way as the social conditions created in the SPE promoted the extreme behaviours exhibited by Zimbardo's guards. In a nutshell, Zimbardo suggests that the Abu Ghraib abuses should not be seen as resulting from the actions of a few 'bad apples', but rather they should be seen as the outcome of 'bad barrels' – corrupt and dehumanising institutions and social practices that create an environment that promotes abusive behaviours. Figures 2.4 and 2.5 attest to some of the surface similarities between the SPE and Abu Ghraib, with anonymising tactics used to humiliate and abuse prisoners.

What do you think? Do the findings of the SPE help to explain abuses such as those committed at Abu Ghraib? Do they suggest we should be more lenient towards the perpetrators of such crimes? What are the implications of suggesting that individuals should not be held responsible for their own actions in this way?

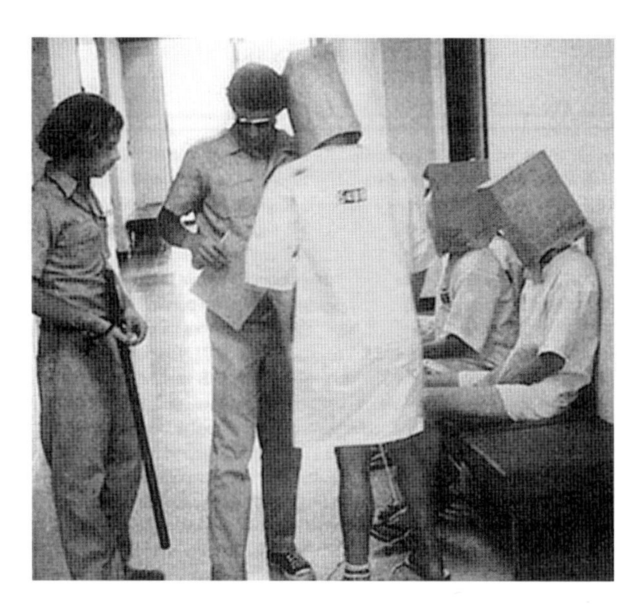

Figure 2.4 Humiliation and torture in the Stanford Prison Experiment

Figure 2.5 Humiliation and torture at Abu Ghraib

3.2 The BBC Prison Study

Reicher and Haslam (2006) argued that the ethical controversy surrounding the SPE had made it difficult for subsequent researchers to attempt similar studies, thus leaving the SPE as 'the last word' on these important issues. Working with funding from the BBC (but with complete control over the design and conduct of the study), Reicher and Haslam set about trying to address what they argued were some serious shortcomings in the theoretical explanation of the SPE provided by Zimbardo and his colleagues.

Specifically, Reicher and Haslam argued that the events of the SPE simply do not support the interpretation that participants' behaviour was a 'natural' result of being assigned to particular roles. Reicher and Haslam point out that in Zimbardo's video of the SPE (entitled 'Quiet Rage'), the footage of Zimbardo briefing the guards on how to treat the prisoners challenges the idea that 'we did not have to teach the actors how to play their roles' (Zimbardo et al., 2000, p. 206). In his briefing, Zimbardo tells the guards that:

> You can create in the prisoners feelings of boredom, a sense of fear to some degree, you can create a notion of arbitrariness that their life is totally controlled by us, by the system, you, me – and they'll have no privacy. They'll have no freedom of action, they can do nothing, say nothing that we don't permit. We're going to take away their individuality in various ways. In general what all this leads to is a sense of powerlessness.
>
> (Zimbardo, cited in Reicher and Haslam, 2006, p. 4)

This suggests that, far from being helplessly subsumed by their role, the guards in the SPE were in fact following Zimbardo's orders! Zimbardo also continued in his role as 'prison superintendent' for the duration of the study, something which arguably served as a constant reminder of his authority. Similarly, Reicher and Haslam note that prisoner and guard behaviour during the study itself appears to contradict Zimbardo's account. It is clear from Zimbardo's accounts of his study that, at various points, several prisoners did, in fact, challenge the authority of the guards. Equally, the guards were not all involved to the same extent in the dehumanising and aggressive treatment of the prisoners. Zimbardo (2007) himself has noted that guards could be placed into one of three categories: those who were frequently brutal and sadistic; those who were 'tough but fair'; and those who were more sympathetic towards the prisoners.

There was a further, more far-reaching concern that led Reicher and Haslam to challenge the SPE. They argued that the theoretical and methodological problems of the SPE were compounded by the politically troubling nature of Zimbardo's interpretation. By presenting an account of how easily people can be led into tyrannical and oppressive actions, they suggest that Zimbardo is in danger of making it appear that such behaviour is normal. Indeed, they draw attention to the use of the SPE in making sense of the abuses at Abu Ghraib, noting that:

> The fact that Zimbardo's analysis of those events was invoked in order to *deny responsibility* for acts of appalling brutality should also serve as a warning to social psychology. For … it points to the way that our theories are used to justify and normalise oppression, rather than to problematise it and identify ways in which it can be overcome. In short, representing abuse as 'natural' makes us apologists for the inexcusable.
>
> (Haslam and Reicher, 2006, p. 62)

For these reasons, Reicher and Haslam (2006) argued that a study along similar lines to the SPE was long overdue. In the BBC Prison Study, they set out to address some of the shortcomings in the SPE, and in particular made sure that they took more of a 'back seat' role in the running of the prison.

The guards in the BBC Prison Study were simply told to run the institution in the best way they saw fit for maintaining order. They had the power to impose punishments – such as solitary confinement and a bread-and-water diet – but were not given the sort of directive instructions that Zimbardo gave to the SPE guards. It quickly became apparent, however, that the guards in Reicher and Haslam's study were not comfortable with their position, and they expressed concerns at being seen to be too authoritarian. Initially, although the prisoners were unhappy with the inequalities in the prison (e.g. their food and living quarters were much more basic than those of the guards), they did not work cohesively as a group to try to bring about a change in their situation. This was because the prisoners had been provided with the opportunity to work for a 'promotion' to be a guard. This promotion was one of a series of interventions planned by Reicher and Haslam, based on predictions derived from social identity theory (SIT; Tajfel and Turner, 1979). SIT is a theory of intergroup relations, with a specific focus on exploring how members of disadvantaged groups can work collectively to overcome illegitimate inequality. In this respect, SIT is principally a theory of *social change*. One of the key principles of SIT is that individuals will move from a lower-status group to a higher-status group when such an opportunity is available. This is known as individual mobility, and whether or not this strategy is adopted by individuals depends on whether the boundaries between the groups are *permeable*, i.e. whether it is possible to move between groups.

In the BBC Prison Study, Reicher and Haslam manipulated permeability by beginning the study with an announcement that there was an opportunity for a prisoner to move to the higher-status group by becoming a guard. This led to several prisoners working hard at being 'good' prisoners in order to try to achieve the promotion. However, after the promotion, the group boundaries were fixed – they were *impermeable* – and the prisoners began working together to effect social change. The key idea here is that when we have the option of improving our own position as individuals, we take it. However, when that option is not available, and group members see the situation as unfair and can figure out alternative ways of organising the relationship between groups, we work collectively with our fellow group members to try to achieve genuine social change on behalf of all group members.

Once the prisoners began to organise themselves and work together collectively, they were able to 'turn the tables' on the guards, who were weak and disorganised as a group. They overthrew the guard–prisoner system, leading to all the participants establishing a communal system where everyone was equal. For a short while this system functioned effectively, with many participants working hard to make it a success. However, Reicher and Haslam argued that the commune had one crucial weakness – no one was willing to put in place and enforce a system of rules. In short, there was no way of punishing those who abused the system. Very quickly, a small group of participants began to make trouble and planned to abolish the commune and replace it with a new guard–prisoner regime in which they would be the guards and would ensure that the prison was run 'properly'. Worried that this would lead to breaches of ethically acceptable behaviour, Reicher and

Haslam called off the study just as it appeared to be on the verge of tyranny!

Reicher and Haslam have argued that, in showing how tyranny can emerge, the BBC Prison Study demonstrates that strong groups are a necessary part of a defence against tyranny, rather than being the cause of tyranny. It is when groups break down that a vacuum of power may emerge, which can then be filled by those who would advocate a more oppressive regime. For Reicher and Haslam, then, good people can be led into doing bad things when groups are ineffective and unwilling to wield power to enforce democratic principles.

Zimbardo (2006) criticised many elements of the BBC Prison Study. For example, he argued that the extensive surveillance used would have led participants to modify their behaviour. In response, Haslam and Reicher (2006) pointed out that participants indicated that they quickly got used to the cameras and forgot they were there. They also note that it would be difficult to 'fake' behaviour over such an extended period of time, and it would certainly be impossible to 'fake' the physiological data collected during the study, such as cortisol levels that provide an indication of stress. Moreover, they question exactly what it means to consider that behaviour might be 'faked', or more generally affected by the very fact of surveillance. Notably, they suggest that their study shows how people's behaviour can be oriented towards the future – people can anticipate how their actions in one context might be responded to by others, and have implications for them in other contexts. But this is part and parcel of everyday human experience. We are constantly thinking about how our behaviour might be responded to, and we are – in one form or another – under surveillance for much of our daily lives, whether it be formal surveillance in the form of CCTV cameras, or more mundane surveillance such as being in a busy workplace where we take it for granted that other people are observing our behaviour.

Activity 2.3: Surveillance and the BBC Prison Study

The nature and effects of surveillance in the BBC Prison Study was a key focus of the debate between Zimbardo (2006) and Haslam and Reicher (2006). However, Zimbardo (2006) was largely concerned with the effects of the cameras on the behaviour of participants in a general sense. More specific attention to the way in which surveillance operated in the study points to the possibility of some interesting consequences of the guards' surveillance of the prisoners. Notably, in the layout of the prison in Reicher and Haslam's (2006) study (see Figure 2.6), the guards' observation post – which featured video screens showing pictures from cameras inside the prisoners' cells – was located in a position where prisoners could see whether or not it was occupied. In other words, the prisoners knew when the guards were monitoring their behaviour.

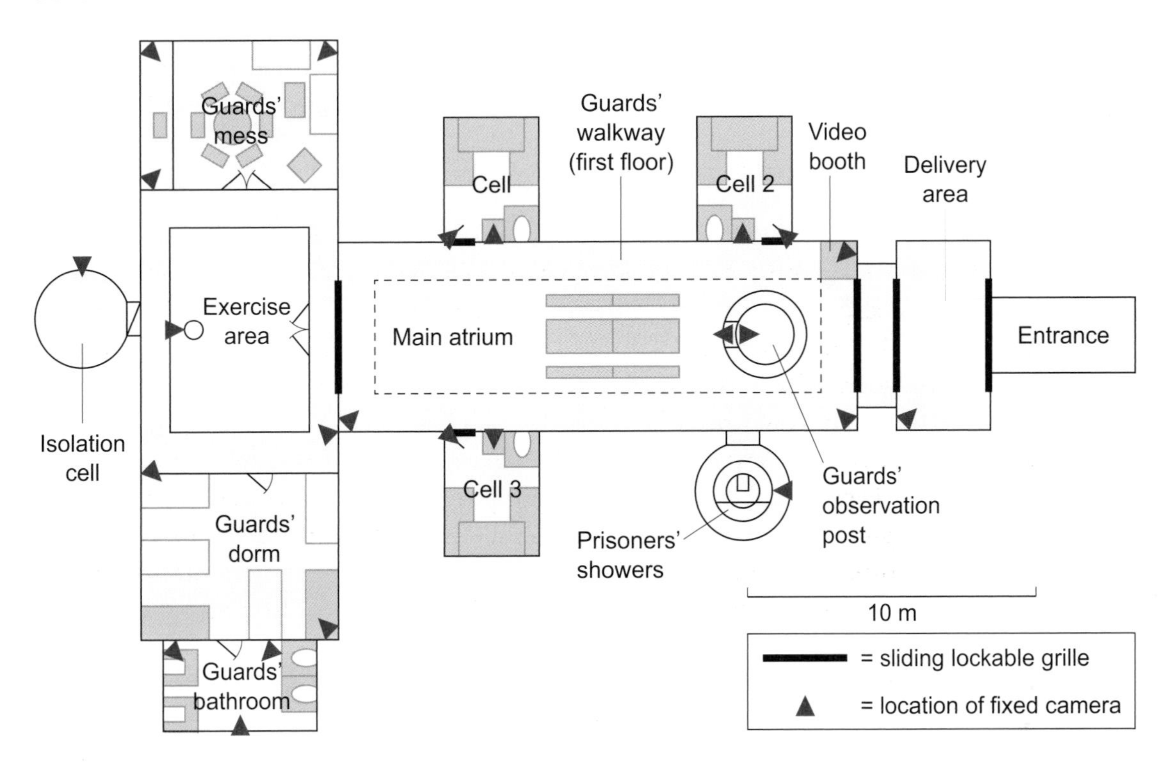

Figure 2.6 Prison layout in the BBC Prison Study
(Source: Reicher and Haslam, 2006, p. 8)

By contrast, imagine if the guards' observation post had been located in a different part of the prison, out of view of the prisoners, thus allowing the guards to keep the prisoners under covert surveillance (see Figure 2.7).

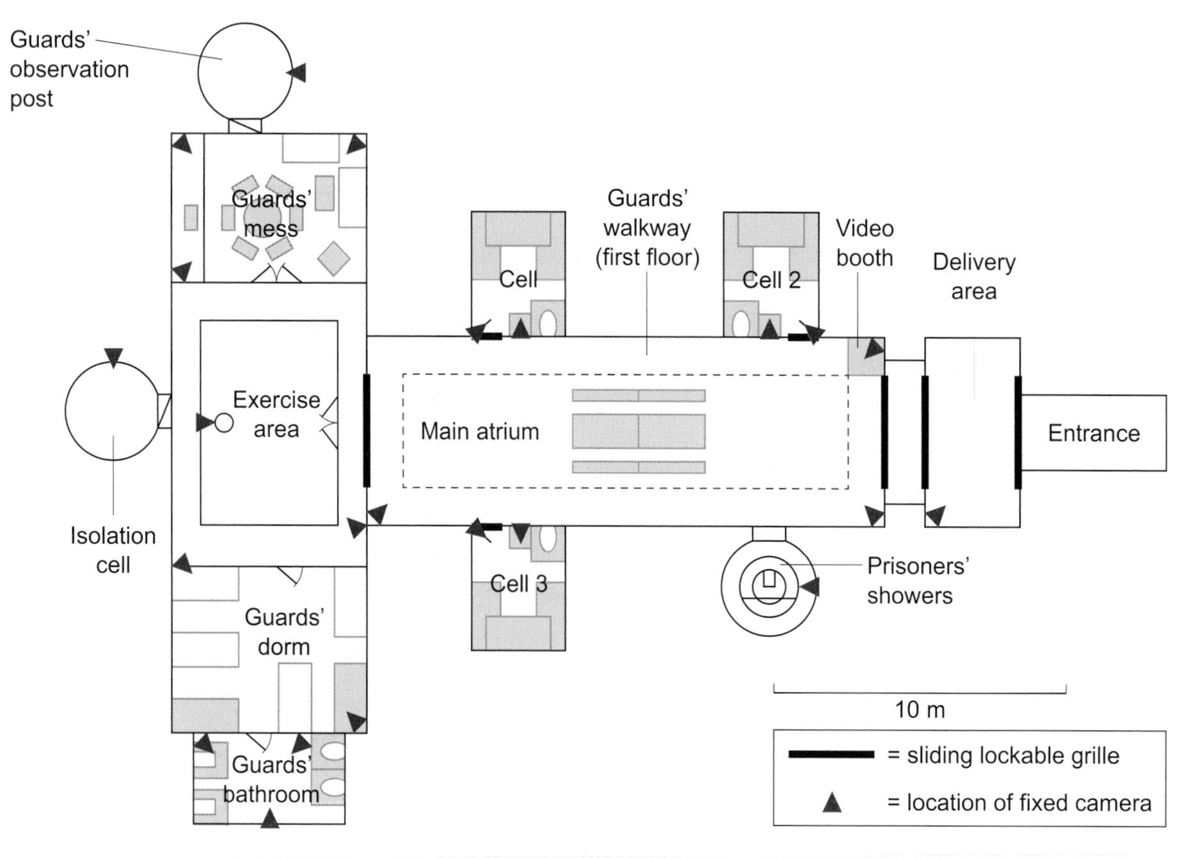

Figure 2.7 Hypothetical prison layout
(Source: Gibson, 2009, p. 18; adapted from Reicher and Haslam, 2006, p. 8)

Consider what, if any, effect this might have had on the prisoners' behaviour. Do you think that prisoners would have found it harder to rebel if they did not know when they might be being watched by the guards? And might the guards have found it easier to exercise their authority if they had access to covert surveillance?

It is possible that if the guards had had access to the sort of covert surveillance shown in Figure 2.7, things might have panned out a little differently. For example, at one point in the study, a group of prisoners planned to break out of their cell. In order to do this, they taunted the guard who was on duty until he left the observation post to return to the guards' quarters. Safe in the knowledge they were now unobserved by the guards, the prisoners put their plan into action, and eventually managed to take control of the guards' quarters. If the guards' observation post had been out of sight of the prisoners, then the escapees would not have been able to tell whether they were being observed or not, and at the very least this would have made it far harder for them to escape.

The way in which the location of the surveillance cameras made the prisoners' escape possible can be understood in terms of the idea of the panopticon, introduced by the philosopher Jeremey Bentham in the eighteenth century. Foucault (1979) developed this idea into an analysis of the way in which governments and other authorities maintain discipline in modern societies. A panoptic system ensures that an individual (who may be an inmate of a prison, or simply someone going about their day-to-day business) is potentially under surveillance at any given time. However, the individual cannot see the person keeping them under surveillance, and so never actually knows whether they are indeed under surveillance or not. But, because surveillance remains an ever-present possibility in such a system, the individual ultimately has to act as if they are under surveillance at all times. If they do something they shouldn't be doing, then they may be lucky and get away with it, or they may be seen and punished. The safest thing to do, therefore, is to avoid any actions that may be seen as undesirable by those maintaining the surveillance. Perhaps the most famous example of a panoptic system can be found in literature. In George Orwell's dystopian classic *Nineteen Eighty-Four*, the surveillance operated by the sinister 'Thought Police' on behalf of the mysterious 'Big Brother' leads to chilling effects on individual behaviour:

> There was of course no way of knowing whether you were being watched at any given moment. How often, or on what system, the Thought Police plugged in on any individual wire was guesswork. It was even conceivable that they watched everybody all the time. But at any rate they could plug in your wire whenever they wanted to. You had to live – did live, from habit that became instinct – in the assumption that every sound you made was overheard, and, except in darkness, every movement scrutinised.
>
> (Orwell, 1983, p. 744)

It is not possible to say exactly how things might have unfolded in the BBC Prison Study had the prison layout resembled that presented in Figure 2.7, but it nevertheless raises some intriguing possibilities. Moreover, these ideas also point to some broader processes of social influence that have not yet been touched on. Specifically, they raise questions concerning the influence of mass surveillance technologies on our own lives.

Activity 2.4: Surveillance society

Some authors (e.g. Lyon, 2001) have noted that we live in a 'surveillance society', with seemingly ever-increasing numbers of CCTV cameras, electronic devices that allow our movements to be tracked, and sophisticated means of collecting a huge amount of data via the internet.

What do you make of the idea that we live in a 'surveillance society'? How does it influence people's behaviour? Does it have any specific effects on your own behaviour? Are there positive aspects to the wealth of surveillance technologies used in the modern world? If so, do these outweigh the drawbacks?

3.3 Summary

The contrast between the two prison studies discussed in this section is striking, and arguably represents a direct clash between different views of what social psychology should be, and how it should be practised. It is worth emphasising that Zimbardo and Reicher and Haslam agree that any answer to the question of why good people do bad things has to be answered with reference to the role of group processes. The key point of contrast, however, is that whereas for Zimbardo it is groups themselves that are the source of danger, for Reicher and Haslam groups are important in overcoming that danger.

4 Discourse, rhetoric and influence

In response to the sorts of criticisms of experimental social psychology discussed above – that it has all too often adopted a 'fun and games' approach, and that its supposedly objective scientific theories in fact mask hidden biases and assumptions – some authors have developed radically different approaches to social psychology. These take many diverse forms, but a feature common to many is a concern with discourse – spoken and written language. Until recently, authors in these newer traditions had not directly addressed questions of social influence, but in the past few years this has begun to change. In this section you will briefly explore two ways in which these discursive perspectives have begun to take a rather different approach to matters of social influence.

4.1 Discourse and social influence

Hepburn and Potter (2011) have developed an approach to social influence based on **discursive psychology**. They point out that although a huge amount of research has been conducted on social influence, the overwhelming majority of this work has been conducted in artificial laboratory settings. In contrast, they aim to explore actual examples of people trying to 'influence' one another. To do this, they explore data from video recordings of family mealtimes in which parents try to get their young children to behave themselves and eat their food, often resorting to threats of one sort or another. These mundane, everyday occurrences are quite different to the sorts of creative and dramatic experimental procedures developed by the likes of Sherif, Asch, Milgram and Zimbardo, but Hepburn and Potter argue that these ordinary activities will tell us more about how people actually live their lives. For example, in the following extract you can see how one mum tries to get her young daughter, Kath, to sit quietly and eat her breakfast:

Discursive psychology
The detailed study of how language is used to construct the world and perform social actions.

Kath: I don't want to watch you.

Mum: Katherine, Katherine, Katherine, if you carry on whinging and whining. Had enough of it. This is your warning now. If you carry on whinging and whining during breakfast time I'll send you to the bottom step. We don't wanna listen to it.

(Source: adapted from Hepburn and Potter, 2011, p. 105)

Hepburn and Potter (2011) note that, like many 'threats' in their data set, mum's threat to send Kath to 'the bottom step' takes the format of an *if–then conditional statement*. This can therefore be rephrased and simplified as follows: *If* you keep 'whinging and whining', *then* I will send you to 'the bottom step'. More generally, then, the structure of threats can be summarised as: *if* you continue doing the undesirable action, *then* I will bring about certain negative consequences. This sets up two possible types of response for the recipient (in these data, the child): compliance or defiance. Hepburn and Potter argue that this gives us an insight into how phenomena typically understood in terms of social influence are built into ordinary practices and activities, and they suggest that it provides an insight into the dynamics of power relations in everyday life.

But how can this approach help us to get at our key question of how good people do bad things? Surely parents and toddlers over the breakfast table is some way removed from the questions of genocide, tyranny and abusive behaviour that the likes of Milgram and Zimbardo sought to address? To finish off, let's apply some of these ideas to one of the classics of social influence.

4.2 Discourse and rhetoric in the obedience experiments

Rhetorical psychology
The study of how social life consists of rhetoric (argumentation), with people constantly engaged in rhetorical struggles to define the world in one way or another.

In some of my recent work, I have used a related approach – **rhetorical psychology** – to further explore some of the archived recordings from Milgram's obedience experiments (Gibson, 2013a). This approach can be used to reframe the experiments as rhetorical encounters, and to focus on the tussle between the experimenter trying to keep participants in the experiment, and participants trying to extricate themselves from it. Exploring the data in this way shows not only how many people 'obeyed' the experimenter and how many resisted, but also how they attempted to defy the experimenter. Moreover, when the experiments are viewed in this way, attention must also be paid to the rhetorical character of the experimenter's prods (see Activity 2.5).

Activity 2.5: Obedience and rhetoric

Read the dialogue in Figure 2.8 below and consider the questions that follow it.

1	T:	I'm going to administer a hundred and twenty
2		volts.
3		((SHOCK))
4	L:	Urgh! Hey these really hurt.
5		(3)
6	T:	I don't think I wanna be a part of this anymore.
7		(2)
8	E:	Please continue.
9	T:	No.
10		(11)
11	E:	It's absolutely essential that you go on.
12		(2)
13	T:	Well if he says it's all right, it's all right with me.
14		Will you ask him if he wants to go on?
15		(3)
16	E:	Whether he likes it or not, er, we must
17		continue.
18	T:	I wouldn't contin–
19	E:	((inaudible))
20	T:	I wouldn't continue without asking him.
21		(2)
22	E:	As I explained to both, er, er, to him when you were
23		there, er, although the shocks may be extremely
24		painful there is no permanent tissue damage.
25	T:	Well I still th– I still don't want to go on unless he
26		says all right.
27		52) ((During this time period movement can be
28		heard, and what sounds like a door shutting.
29		From what follows it seems reasonable to
30		presume that E went out of the room, ostensibly
31		to ask L if he wished to continue.))
32	E:	He seems willing enough to go on so please
33		continue.
34		(8)
35	T	Wet, night, grass, duck, cloth.

59	L:	Experimenter! Get me out of here! I won't be in
60		the experiment anymore. I refuse to go on. Let
61		me out!
62	E:	Please continue.
63	T:	Not under those conditions. Not with him
64		hollering.
65	E:	I just checked on him, and he, er, seemed pretty
66		willing to continue so please continue.
67	T:	No, not unless I think– You see he's hollering in
68		there. It's just, er
69		(16)
70	E:	It's absolutely essential that you continue.
71	T:	Well, I'm not gonna continue with the man
72		hollering that he wants to get out of there. I mean
73		er (2) it might be essential to you but it's not that
74		essential for me.
75		(3)
76	E:	I was just in there and he seemed willing enough
77		to continue.
78	T:	Well, that's what he says but you know it's not
79		er
80		(14)
81	E:	((inaudible))
82	T:	I mean i– I'd be glad to walk in there. If he says to
83		me go on I'll go on but I'm not going to go on
84		with the man hollering in there to stop.
85	E:	You have no other choice. You must go on.
86	T:	Well, I don't say that. I mean I'm just not gonna go on
87		unless he says to go on.
88	E:	Well, we'll have to discontinue the experiment then.

Figure 2.8 Extract from participant 8 in condition 2 of Milgram's obedience experiments

(Source: Gibson, 2013a, pp. 297–9)

How does the participant (teacher, T) get the experimenter to leave the room and check on the learner? What does the experimenter (E) do in response? How are the 'prods' used? How is the visit to the learner (L) used as a rhetorical resource once the participant begins to resist again? What does this tell us about standardisation in the obedience experiments? (If you need a reminder of the standardised prods, see Activity 2.2.)

This extract shows us how participants could get the experimenter to depart – sometimes quite radically – from his standardised script. Note how the participant asks the experimenter to go and check on the learner in lines 13–14, line 20 and then once again in lines 25–26. This clever strategy effectively puts a condition on his continued participation, and as with the examples of family mealtime interaction studied by Hepburn and Potter (2011), can be summarised as an *if–then* conditional statement: *If* the learner says he wants to carry on, then I will continue. Rather than sticking to the standardised prods, however, the experimenter responds to the participant's repeated requests by apparently leaving the room to speak to the learner, before returning to assure the participant that the learner is indeed 'willing enough to go on'! This part of the procedure was not included in any of Milgram's published work on the obedience experiments, and – together with numerous other, smaller, departures from standardisation – casts doubt on the idea that the experiments were in fact standardised in any meaningful sense (Gibson, 2013b). For example, not only does the experimenter leave the room, but this visit to the learner is then drawn upon as a rhetorical resource when the participant subsequently tries to defy the experimenter again (see lines 65–66; 76–77).

4.3 Summary

The approaches considered in this section represent a rather different way of studying social influence. Indeed, once it is seen how actions are discussed and performed in the to-and-fro of conversation and argumentation, it is questionable whether anything is left that can properly be described as 'influence'. What can be said, however, is that it is through language that those phenomena typically seen as examples of social influence occur. This suggests something of potential importance in relation to the key concern for how good people can be led into doing bad things. If we want to find out how people are led down the slippery slope to atrocities and abuses of all kinds, then actually studying the detail of what happens in such situations is crucial. If we do this, we may find that it takes rather more effort on the part of those who would lead us astray to convince us to go along with something that we wouldn't ordinarily think is right.

5 Concluding thoughts

This chapter has explored classic and more recent studies of social influence. It has shown how people can be led to comply with requests that they may otherwise have refused, how the influence of groups can lead to confusion and error, but also to rebellion and collective action, and how straightforward orders from an authority *don't* actually appear to be very good at getting us to commit harmful acts against another person.

Can we, therefore, arrive at an answer to the question to which we have returned at various points throughout this chapter? What is it that leads seemingly ordinary, decent people into committing wicked deeds?

As ever, simple answers to such questions are elusive, but what can perhaps be suggested is that the processes involved are not likely to be those of blunt authority. The re-evaluation of Milgram's experiments, together with the work of scholars such as Foucault on the subtle processes of influence at work in our everyday lives, suggest that simple obedience is, at best, only a small part of the equation. Similarly, the resurgence of interest in positive aspects of group behaviour suggest that when people are led astray, it is not simply a matter of 'losing' one's identity in a group.

Ultimately, it is also important to note that the answer to this question goes some way beyond social psychology. Milgram (1974) claimed that a fascist dictator could find enough people to set the wheels of genocide in motion in any medium-sized US town, but as Goldhagen (1996) points out, this ignores the political and historical context. The Holocaust took place against an ideological backdrop of virulent anti-Semitism. Might it have been this, rather than any general tendency to go along with the crowd, or to obey orders, that made the Holocaust possible?

Further reading

Burger, J.M. (2009) 'Replicating Milgram: Would people still obey today?', *American Psychologist*, vol. 64, pp. 1–11.

Gibson, S. (2013) 'Milgram's obedience experiments: a rhetorical analysis', *British Journal of Social Psychology*, vol. 52, pp. 290–309.

Milgram, S. (1974) *Obedience to Authority*, London, Tavistock.

Perry, G. (2012) *Behind the Shock Machine: The Untold Story of the Notorious Milgram Psychology Experiments*, Brunswick, Scribe.

- Zimbardo's commentary and Haslam and Reicher's reply (in the same issue of the journal) are also well worth a look:

Reicher, S. and Haslam, S.A. (2006) 'Rethinking the psychology of tyranny: the BBC prison study', *British Journal of Social Psychology*, vol. 45, pp. 1–40.

- Chapters 4–8 are particularly relevant for the material covered here:

Smith, J.R. and Haslam, S.A. (2012) *Social Psychology: Revisiting the Classic Studies*, London, Sage.

Zimbardo, P. (2007) *The Lucifer Effect: How Good People Turn Evil*, London, Rider.

References

Allport, G.W. (1954) 'The historical background of modern social psychology', in Lindzey, G. (ed.) *Handbook of Social Psychology*, Reading, MA, Addison-Wesley.

Asch, S.E. (1951) 'Effects of group pressure upon the modification and distortion of judgments', in Guetzkow, H. (ed.) *Groups, Leadership and Men: Research in Human Relations*, Oxford, Carnegie.

Asch, S.E. (1952) *Social Psychology*, Englewood Cliffs, NJ, Prentice-Hall.

Asch, S.E. (1956) 'Studies of independence and conformity: a minority of one against a unanimous majority', *Psychological Monographs: General and Applied*, vol. 70, pp. 1–70.

Baumrind, D. (1964) 'Some thoughts on ethics of research: after reading Milgram's "behavioural study of obedience"', *American Psychologist*, vol. 19, pp. 421–3.

Blass, T. (2004) *The Man Who Shocked the World: The Life and Legacy of Stanley Milgram*, New York, Basic Books.

Brace, N. and Byford, J. (eds) (2012) *Investigating Psychology*, Oxford, Oxford University Press/Milton Keynes, The Open University.

Burger, J.M. (2009) 'Replicating Milgram: would people still obey today?', *American Psychologist*, vol. 64, pp. 1–11.

Burger, J.M., Girgis, Z.M. and Manning, C.M. (2011) 'In their own words: explaining obedience to authority through an examination of participants' comments', *Social Psychological and Personality Science*, vol. 2, pp. 460–6.

Cialdini, R.B. (2008) *Influence: Science and Practice*, 5th edn, Boston, MA, Pearson.

Cialdini, R.B. and Goldstein, N.J. (2004) 'Social influence: compliance and conformity', *Annual Review of Psychology*, vol. 55, pp. 591–621.

Cialdini, R.B., Trost, M.R. and Newsom, J.T. (1995) 'Preference for consistency: the development of a valid measure and the discovery of surprising behavioural implications', *Journal of Personality and Social Psychology*, vol. 69, pp. 318–28.

Cialdini, R.B., Vincent, J.E., Lewis, S.K., Catalan, J., Wheeler, D. and Darby, B. L. (1975) 'Reciprocal concessions procedure for inducing compliance: the door-in-the-face technique', *Journal of Personality and Social Psychology*, vol. 31, pp. 206–15.

Demetriou, C. and Silke, A. (2003) 'A criminological internet 'sting': experimental evidence of illegal and deviant visits to a website trap', *British Journal of Criminology*, vol. 43, pp. 213–22.

Deutsch, M. and Gerard, H.B. (1955) 'A study of normative and informational social influences upon individual judgment', *Journal of Abnormal and Social Psychology*, vol. 51, pp. 629–36.

Dolinski, D. (2000) 'On inferring one's beliefs from one's attempt and consequences for subsequent compliance', *Journal of Personality and Social Psychology*, vol. 78, pp. 260–72.

Festinger, L., Pepitone, A. and Newcomb, T. (1952) 'Some consequences of de-individuation in a group', *Journal of Abnormal and Social Psychology*, vol. 47, pp. 382–9.

Foucault, M. (1979) *Discipline and Punish: The Birth of the Prison*, Harmondsworth, Penguin.

Freedman, J.L. and Fraser, S.C. (1966) 'Compliance without pressure: the foot-in-the-door technique', *Journal of Personality and Social Psychology*, vol. 4, pp. 195–202.

Gibson, S. (2009) 'An imperfect Panopticon? Surveillance and the BBC Prison Study', *Social Psychological Review*, vol. 11, pp. 15–21.

Gibson, S. (2013a) 'Milgram's obedience experiments: a rhetorical analysis', *British Journal of Social Psychology*, vol. 52, pp. 290–309.

Gibson, S. (2013b) '"The last possible resort": a forgotten prod and the in situ standardization of Stanley Milgram's voice-feedback condition', *History of Psychology*, vol. 16, pp. 177–94.

Goldhagen, D. (1996) *Hitler's Willing Executioners: Ordinary Germans and the Holocaust,* New York, Vintage.

Haney, C., Banks, C. and Zimbardo, P. (1973) 'Interpersonal dynamics in a simulated prison', *International Journal of Criminology and Penology*, vol. 1, pp. 69–97.

Haslam, S.A. and Reicher, S. (2006) 'Debating the psychology of tyranny: fundamental issues of theory, perspective and science', *British Journal of Social Psychology*, vol. 45, pp. 55–63.

Hepburn, A. and Potter, J. (2011) 'Threats: power, family mealtimes and social influence', *British Journal of Social Psychology*, vol. 50, pp. 99–120.

Hodges, B.H. and Geyer, A.L. (2006) 'A nonconformist account of the Asch experiments: values, pragmatics, and moral dilemmas', *Personality and Social Psychology Review*, vol. 10, pp. 2–19.

Hogg, M.A. and Vaughan, G.M. (2011) *Social Psychology*, 6th edn, Harlow, Pearson.

Lyon, D. (2001) *Surveillance Society: Monitoring Everyday Life*, Buckingham, Open University Press.

Milgram, S. (1963) 'Behavioral study of obedience', *Journal of Abnormal and Social Psychology*, vol. 67, pp. 371–8.

Milgram, S. (1974) *Obedience to Authority*, London, Tavistock.

Miller, A.G. (2009) 'Reflections on "Replicating Milgram" (Burger, 2009)', *American Psychologist*, vol. 64, pp. 20–7.

Moscovici, S. (1976) *Social Influence and Social Change*, London, Academic Press.

Moscovici, S. and Lage, E. (1976) 'Studies in social influence: III. Majority versus minority influence in a group', *European Journal of Social Psychology*, vol. 6, pp. 149–74.

Moscovici, S., Lage, E. and Naffrechoux, M. (1969) 'Influence of a consistent minority on the responses of a majority in a color perception task', *Sociometry*, vol. 32, pp. 365–80.

Nicholson, I. (2011) '"Torture at Yale": experimental subjects, laboratory torment and the "rehabilitation" of Milgram's "obedience to authority"', *Theory and Psychology*, vol. 21, pp. 737–61.

Orne, M.T. and Holland, C.H. (1968) 'On the ecological validity of laboratory deceptions', *International Journal of Psychiatry*, vol. 6, pp. 282–93.

Orwell, G. (1983 [1949]) 'Nineteen eighty-four', *The Penguin Complete Novels of George Orwell*, Harmondsworth, Penguin.

Perry, G. (2012) *Behind the Shock Machine: The Untold Story of the Notorious Milgram Psychology Experiments*, Brunswick, Scribe.

Reicher, S. and Haslam, S.A. (2006) 'Rethinking the psychology of tyranny: the BBC prison study', *British Journal of Social Psychology*, vol. 45, pp. 1–40.

Reicher, S. and Haslam, S.A. (2011) 'After shock? Towards a social identity explanation of the Milgram "obedience" studies', *British Journal of Social Psychology*, vol. 50, pp. 163–9.

Ring, K. (1967) 'Experimental social psychology: some sober questions about some frivolous values', *Journal of Experimental Social Psychology*, vol. 3, pp. 113–23.

Russell, N.J.C. (2011) 'Milgram's obedience to authority experiments: origins and early evolution', *British Journal of Social Psychology*, vol. 50, pp. 140–62.

Samelson, F. (1986) 'Authoritarianism from Berlin to Berkeley: on social psychology and history', *Journal of Social Issues*, vol. 42, pp. 191–208.

Sherif, M. (1966 [1936]) *The Psychology of Social Norms* (Torchbook edition), New York, Harper & Row.

Tajfel, H. and Turner, J.C. (1979) 'An integrative theory of intergroup conflict', in Austin, W.G. and Worchel, S. (eds) *The Social Psychology of Intergroup Relations*, Monterey, CA, Brooks/Cole.

Turner, J.C. (1991) *Social Influence*, Buckingham, Open University Press.

Twenge, J.M. (2009) 'Change over time in obedience: the jury's still out, but it might be decreasing', *American Psychologist*, vol. 64, pp. 28–31.

Wood, W., Lundgren, S., Ouellette, J.A., Busceme, S. and Blackstone, T. (1994) 'Minority influence: a meta-analytic review of social influence processes', *Psychological Bulletin*, vol. 115, pp. 323–45.

Zimbardo, P.G. (1974) 'On "obedience to authority"', *American Psychologist*, vol. 29, pp. 566–567.

Zimbardo, P.G. (2006) 'On rethinking the psychology of tyranny: the BBC prison study', *British Journal of Social Psychology*, vol. 45, pp. 47–53.

Zimbardo, P. (2007) *The Lucifer Effect: How Good People Turn Evil*, London, Rider.

Zimbardo, P.G., Maslach, C. and Haney, C. (2000) 'Reflections on the Stanford Prison Experiment: genesis, transformations, consequences', in Blass, T. (ed.) *Obedience to Authority: Current Perspectives on the Milgram Paradigm,* pp. 193–237, Mahwah, NJ, Lawrence Erlbaum.

Chapter 3

Are you with us or against us? Group processes and decision making

Rose Capdevila

Contents

1 Introduction

> Every time a social phenomenon is directly explained by a psychological phenomenon, we may rest assured that the explanation is false.
>
> (Durkheim, 1895)

> There is no psychology of groups which is not essentially and entirely a psychology of individuals.
>
> (Allport, 1924)

This chapter asks the question: *Are you with us or against us?* as a means of considering the psychological study of group processes and decision making. Schachter (1959, p. 1) argued that 'the study of the processes and products of human association' is at the heart of social psychology if not the social sciences as a whole. Not only is it a significant topic academically; trying to understand these processes in practice is something we all grapple with every day. Whether we are trying to get along with a difficult neighbour, negotiating with a co-worker, picking a fantasy football team or making our way down a crowded street, getting along in life is, to a large extent, about getting along with others (Figure 3.1). But why should we bother? Why should we want to get along with others? To answer these questions, we will look at what psychology has to say about groups, what they are and how they work. Throughout this chapter we will be interrogating the relationship between the individual and the group. We will look at relationships both within and between groups and what this can tell us about our everyday lives.

Figure 3.1 Getting along with others is a part of life

Learning outcomes

On completing this chapter you should:

- have an understanding of groups and how they work
- have an understanding of key psychological theories and research about the concept of groups and group processes
- have considered the role of groups in both psychological theories and everyday life.

2 Asking questions about groups

2.1 What's wrong with being alone?

Activity 3.1: Is anybody out there?

Read the scenarios below and consider your response to the question that follows each one.

You are walking down a dark street late one evening. You look around and realise you are completely on your own. Suddenly the street lights go out and you become keenly aware of the darkness around you. Then, around the corner comes a smartly dressed young couple cheerfully chatting as they walk up the street hand in hand. You feel your body relax.

> Why does the presence of this unknown couple make you more comfortable?

You are waiting at a bus stop on an unfamiliar route. You've been waiting for what feels like a long time. You start to wonder if you've made a mistake and for some reason the bus isn't coming. A family that includes three small children walks up to the bus stop and forms a queue behind you. Then a woman with a shopping basket walks up, followed by a young man talking on his phone. They all join the queue for the bus. You stop worrying and assume the bus must be due soon.

> How does the appearance of the other travellers dispel your doubt?

You walk into a crowded room; people are milling around chatting in pairs or small groups. A few people are on the move from one place to another. You glance around the room, spot an old friend and immediately walk towards them.

> Why are you drawn immediately to a familiar face?

These are examples of occasions when the presence of others matters to us. From early on psychologists argued that we have a need for affiliation (McDougall, 1908; Murray, 1938; Maslow, 1954) and that this affiliation, or contact with others, is both rewarding and useful. Festinger (1954) proposed a **social comparison theory** that suggests that in order to make sense of how to behave in the world, we compare our abilities and opinions to those of other people. Buss

Social comparison theory
A theory that suggests we compare our abilities and opinions to those of other people in order to make sense of how to behave in the world.

(1995) argues, from an evolutionary perspective, that groups that cooperate with each other have a greater chance of surviving so evolution will have favoured these groups. In evolutionary terms, those who possessed adaptations such as cooperativeness, loyalty and fear of being socially excluded would have been more likely to procreate and pass these qualities on to future generations. From your previous study of psychology (e.g. Brace and Byford, 2012), you might recall the work of Harlow (1958) and Bowlby (1969), both of whom argued that in order to thrive babies needed nurturing as well as nourishment. Furthermore, research seems to indicate that the outcome of isolation, that is, long-term separation from other people, even when it is one's own choice, can be detrimental (Baumeister and Leary, 1995). Overall, psychological research has consistently shown that, while we enjoy and also require time spent alone, we need the company of others (e.g. O'Connor and Rosenblood, 1996).

Anonymity
According to LeBon (1960), anonymity refers to the loss of the sense of responsibility in the context of a crowd.

2.2 Are groups real?

At the beginning of this chapter there are quotes from Emile Durkheim and Floyd Allport, two seminal figures in the history of psychological thought, each epitomising one of two extreme positions on the existence of the group. One proposes that individual behaviour can only be understood with reference to the social. The other proposes that groups are never anything more than a collection of individuals. What evidence is there for either of these positions?

Contagion
According to LeBon (1960), this refers to the idea that, in a crowd, every sentiment and act is contagious to the extent that an individual will readily sacrifice their personal interest to the collective interest.

In 1896, Gustav LeBon put forward the notion of a 'group mind' to explain the behaviour of crowds. LeBon's theory of crowd behaviour was more appropriately a theory of what was considered to be 'mob behaviour'. Writing during a time of civil unrest in France, LeBon attempted to explain the belief that crowds behave in ways that would be unthinkable to the individuals that make them up. He saw this as evidence of a loss of individual rationality and the formation of a 'group mind'. According to LeBon (1960, p. 36), 'by the mere fact that he forms part of an organised crowd, a man [*sic*] descends several rungs in the ladder of civilisation. Isolated, he may be a cultivated individual; in a crowd, he is a barbarian – that is, a creature acting by instinct.' LeBon proposed that three mechanisms were involved in this process: **anonymity**, **contagion** and **suggestibility**. This was a very useful way of conceptualising crowds, particularly from the perspective of those in power who have to deal with mass protests. If you identify

Suggestibility
According to LeBon (1960), an individual in a crowd enters a special state not unlike hypnosis, in which they lose consciousness of their acts and are directed by the behaviour of the crowd as by a hypnotiser.

the problem of crowd behaviour as pathological and inherent in the crowd itself, you no longer need to consider the possibility that the behaviour might be caused by government policy. A fundamental issue with LeBon's theory, however, rests in the notion of a 'group mind'. It is a rather vague and metaphysical concept that doesn't easily lend itself to scientific scrutiny (Allport, 1924).

However, while many psychologists were not convinced by the theoretical underpinnings of LeBon's approach, they still pursued an explanation for group behaviour that was distinct from that of individual behaviour. For instance, Solomon Asch (1952, cited in Brown, 2000) proposed a chemical analogy to describe how groups might come together. He suggested that such a process could be seen as analogous to the relationship between hydrogen and oxygen. Separately they have their own identity. However, when they are combined, they can become something new and different – water. That is to say, they can become a completely different substance with different properties from the components that make up the whole. Yet the components of water are not irrelevant. Asch argued that we cannot reduce group behaviour to individual behaviour, but neither can we reduce the individual to being merely a victim of group forces. For Asch it was important to acknowledge the reality of both individual and group.

2.3 What is a group?

Activity 3.2: The groups in your life

Pause for a few minutes and try to list some of the groups you belong to. Make a note of these on a piece of paper. Think about what they have in common and what makes them different from each other. Did you choose to belong to these groups? Why did these groups form? Do they serve a purpose? What do you share or have in common with the other group members?

It appears simple, but when you get right down to it agreeing on a definition of a group can be very complex. How do we differentiate a group from a mere collection of individuals such as those that might be sitting in the waiting room of the dentist's office?

As with many concepts in psychology, one of the complications of defining terms is that the word 'group' is one we commonly use in everyday life, so we presume we already know what it means. In research and theory, however, it is important to be clear about what a word refers to. In everyday talk, the word 'group' refers to many different types of collectives of many different sizes – from a few individuals to millions. Examples of different kinds of groups include: families, juries, sports teams, student unions, political parties, armies, countries and religions, to name but a few. These groups vary across multiple criteria such as size, duration, organisation and function, so they are all very different in terms of how members relate to each other.

One way of dealing with the problem of definition is to ask what crucial characteristics define a group in a psychological sense. Many of the most renowned psychologists in the history of the discipline have taken on the challenge of trying to define the group. For instance, Lewin (1948) proposed that interdependence was what constituted a group, in particular *interdependence of fate* and *task interdependence*. The former refers to the dependence of one's fate on that of the group as a whole, the latter to situations in which a collection of individuals are dependent on each other in order to achieve a group task. Bales (1950a) suggested that reliable group membership relied on face-to-face contact. Sherif et al. (1961) defined a group as individuals with interdependent status and role relationships who adhere to a set of group norms and values. For Sherif and his colleagues these qualities provided the social structure that characterises the group. (You will learn more about Sherif's work with groups in Chapter 4.)

Self-categorisation
An awareness of one's membership in a social group.

Turner (1982) proposed a definition of a group that relied on the concept of **self-categorisation**. He suggested that a group exists when individuals perceive themselves to be members of that group. This approach is interesting because it provides a more fluid reading of what might constitute a group than one based on interdependence, structure or face-to-face contact. However, it is at the same time a very subjective understanding of the group. Brown (2000) added a further and significant concept to this definition by incorporating the 'other'. He proposed that a group could be defined as 'two or more people possessing a common social identification and whose existence as a group is recognised by a third party' (Brown, 2000, p. 19).

It really is quite difficult to capture the variety of groups in a single definition. Part of the reason is that the boundaries around groups, what we consider to be or not to be a group, are both conceptual and consensual – that is, they depend on how we conceptualise or think of groups and what we agree with others constitutes a group.

What do you think of the definitions we have looked at so far? Do you find them convincing? Do they resonate with your ideas when you started reading this chapter? Do they reflect the 'reality' of groups, in your opinion? Definitions, of course, don't only tell us what something is, they also tell us what it is not. So how we define a group has implications for what questions we ask and what areas we choose to study.

Activity 3.3: Face(book) to face(time) interaction

In 2010, a 14-year-old girl in a small town in England posted an invitation on her Facebook page. The invitation was to her 15th birthday party and intended for 15 of her friends. Within days she received 21,000 responses. Although it would have been clear to most of those who responded that they hadn't actually been invited, they were playing with the construction of boundaries around friendship groups. Consider for a minute the impact social media has had on how you think about 'groups' in an everyday sense.

Early on, some psychologists based their understanding and analysis of groups on the premise that they involved face-to-face interaction such as families or committees (e.g. Bales, 1950a). Consider how important face-to-face interactions are in your day-to-day life. What proportion of your interactions with others occurs face to face? Do you spend a lot of time using electronic communication or social media?

Things have changed since the 1950s and there has been what many would consider a revolution in communication that has been accompanied by a rethinking of social interaction. According to Wilson et al. (2012), who conducted a review of Facebook research in the social sciences, 27 per cent of this research focused on social interaction. One of the issues consistently identified was the tension created by the overlapping of social groups – that is, the crossing of boundaries between different groups.

What impact do you think social media will have on psychological understandings of what constitutes a group? Can face-to-face interaction be replicated electronically?

— No.

2.4 Why study groups?

Why study groups? Indeed, why care about them at all? Whether we recognise it or not, we all belong to some kind of group, often not by choice. We grow up in them, we work in them, we learn in them, play in them, make decisions in them, fight in them and they can even influence how we behave when we are alone. The groups we belong to can affect what language we speak, what accent we have, what attitudes we hold, what cultural practices we adopt, what education we receive, what level of prosperity we enjoy and, to a point, who we are. At the same time, the groups we don't belong to, either by choice or by exclusion, can also have an important impact on our lives. So understanding what groups are and how they might affect our lives can be very useful.

But this is not the only consideration. Apart from our direct experience with them, groups can affect us indirectly by acting on the society in which we live. For this reason, social psychology (along with other disciplines such as anthropology, politics and sociology) studies groups as a way of trying to understand the world around us.

2.5 Summary

This section has focused on asking some questions about groups: *What's wrong with being alone? Are groups real? What is a group?* and *Why study groups?* Other people are an important part of our life and psychological research has established that we need the company of others. However, while some psychologists have endeavoured to define and understand groups, others have argued that they have no reality outside of the individuals that make them up. This debate has provided a starting point for considering the distinction between individuals and groups and what this might mean for psychological theory and research. Groups can be understood in many different ways, and even what we consider to be a group has changed over time, for instance with the advent of social media. Groups are crucial to how we engage with our environment and, because they are ever-present and ever-changing, studying and understanding them helps us to understand our world.

3 How do we 'come together'?

Pause for thought

Why do we join groups? Earlier in this chapter you were asked to think about what groups you belonged to and what made them similar or different. Some of these groups are chosen for you, but others you choose yourself. What factors do you take into account when deciding whether or not to join a group? Groucho Marx famously claimed he would never join a club that would have him as a member. Why would you join one group and not another? Once you've joined a group, what affects whether you choose to stay with the group or to go?

Maybe you like the group activity, such as playing basketball or singing in a choir. You may also join and stay with a group because you like the people in the group, even if the activity is not your first choice. Many psychologists would argue that the group is a means of satisfying many of our needs.

Research about groups has traditionally followed two separate but closely related paths. One is the study of large groups and relationships between these groups or **intergroup processes**. The other is the study of small groups and the internal workings of those groups or **intragroup processes**. Earlier we asked a question about the latter: *What's wrong with being alone?* At that point we discussed why individuals might choose to come together and mentioned some of the explanations that psychology has proposed. While psychologists generally agree that humans have a need for affiliation, explanations of how we go about it have been diverse.

Intergroup processes The relationships between groups.

Intragroup processes The internal workings of a group.

3.1 Social comparison theory

One of the dominant theories in this area has been Festinger's social comparison theory (1954), which was mentioned above. As noted, this theory proposes that humans are driven to compare their abilities and opinions with those of other people in order to make sense of the world (Figure 3.2).

Figure 3.2 We learn about who we are by comparing ourselves with others

However, according to Festinger, we tend to compare ourselves with those we perceive as similar to ourselves rather than random individuals. Comparing yourself with someone whose abilities, interests or opinions in a specific area were very different from yours would not give you a very meaningful evaluation. So, if you go skiing for the first time and want to get a sense of how you are doing, you are unlikely to compare your performance with that of an Olympic skier. Similarly, a lover of classical music will not benefit from comparing their opinion on the performance of a specific piece of music with that of someone who has no interest and is unlikely to be attentive to the subtleties. For this reason, Festinger argues, we are more attracted to those who are similar to us.

To demonstrate this, Festinger et al. (1952) carried out a revealing experiment. They asked participants to write their opinion on a given issue on a piece of paper. Before engaging in a discussion on the topic with other participants, they were given a note with the opinions of the other members of their experimental group. Some were told that the members of their group had opinions similar to their own, while others were told that the opinions of the others were different from theirs. The discussion was conducted through note writing. Once the experiment was over, participants were asked how much they liked the other members of their group. According to Festinger et al., participants were consistently less attracted to group members whose views differed from their own. From this perspective, we need others in order to obtain an accurate assessment of ourselves and our place in the world, and we prefer others who are similar to ourselves as they allow the greatest precision in evaluating ourselves.

So what happens when we are faced with those not like ourselves? According to social comparison theory, we respond to difference in one of three ways:

- we attempt to change ourselves to fit in with our reference group
- we attempt to convince the reference group to change to fit with us
- we disassociate ourselves from that group and maybe even disparage it.

The implications here are important because the opinion or ability that group members share will come to define the group and thus, pressure to ensure uniformity of the group will increase. This then leads to the segmentation of a society into different groups according to relevant abilities and opinions. A clear illustration of this can be found among the adolescents at most secondary schools. The broader group of students is often divided up by interest or ability: the 'jocks', who excel at sport, the 'geeks' who are academically inclined, the musicians, the 'fashionistas', etc.

3.2 Bales's phase model and interaction process analysis (IPA)

In psychological research, however, discussion about group formation tends to focus on small groups that come together for a particular purpose or task: for instance sports teams, therapy groups or work groups. Bales (1950a) developed a phase model of group processes, according to which groups exist to achieve tasks, so ultimately all activity is directed to this end. However, in understanding group processes, it is important to make a distinction between task-related (instrumental) behaviour and social-emotional (expressive) behaviour. The reason for the latter is that task activity can be threatened by social instability (see Box 3.1). Simply stated, this means that, if your group is constantly bickering, you won't get much done. Disagreements, conflicting values and time constraints can lead to tensions that will keep the group from achieving its goal. To deal with this the group develops processes that focus on interpersonal relations and that help to manage emotions, 'bleeding off' the tensions inevitably generated by instrumental, goal-directed behaviour. Bales argued that all task-oriented groups need to constantly balance task-oriented concerns with social-emotional concerns as too much attention to one puts a strain on the other. For Bales, all groups tend towards equilibrium.

Box 3.1 Expressive/emotional versus instrumental acts

Research using Bales' approach has consistently found that the patterning of instrumental and expressive acts in small group interactions predicts how satisfied group members are with their overall performance on a particular task. Consider, for example, the interaction profiles presented in Table 3.1.

Table 3.1 Interaction profiles of satisfied and dissatisfied discussion groups

Type of act	Satisfied group	Dissatisfied group
Positive emotional	33.5%	17.2%
Instrumental	61.2%	65.6%
Negative emotional	5.3%	17.3%

How and why might the distribution of acts represented here relate to group satisfaction?

Bales identified three phases that a group engages in to complete the task at hand:

- The *orientation phase* is predominant at the beginning of the task and then declines. During this phase, as the group orients to the problem, clarifies tasks and identifies relevant information, it is highly communicative, expressing opinions and ideas.

- The *evaluation phase*, in which ideas are assessed, starts out low, rises during the middle of the session and then declines again.
- The *control phase*, during which members manage and police each other, exerting efforts on reaching a decision, is low at the beginning but rises progressively, reaching its height at the end.

Social-emotional levels continue to increase across the three phases; if the group is successful in meeting its goals, positive reactions will be dominant. As a result of these processes, Bales argued, different roles become differentiated within the group, with some taking on the more task-oriented roles and others focusing on social-emotional behaviours.

What is most attractive about this theory is how neatly it lends itself to empirical investigation. Based on the phase model, Bales developed interaction process analysis (IPA), a coding scheme to observe and analyse group interaction in terms of task and social-emotional behaviours (see Figure 3.3). While he revisited and adapted his original design over the years, the original IPA approach has left a legacy in areas such as organisational and industrial psychology. According to Brown (2000, p. 44): 'IPA has been strikingly successful' as a result of its detailed and objective observation of group behaviour. It has been able to 'shed new light on the phenomena of interest' (p. 44), which Brown argues is the criterion by which the value of a methodological innovation should be judged. For instance, this approach has allowed researchers to observe that high status members of a group give a higher proportion of answers to questions, address the group as a whole, and give out more information than they receive. Lower status members give out more agreements, disagreements and requests for information, address other individuals rather than the group as a whole, and receive more information and answers than they give out. This has provided an insight into the relationship between the distribution of talk and status hierarchies within a group.

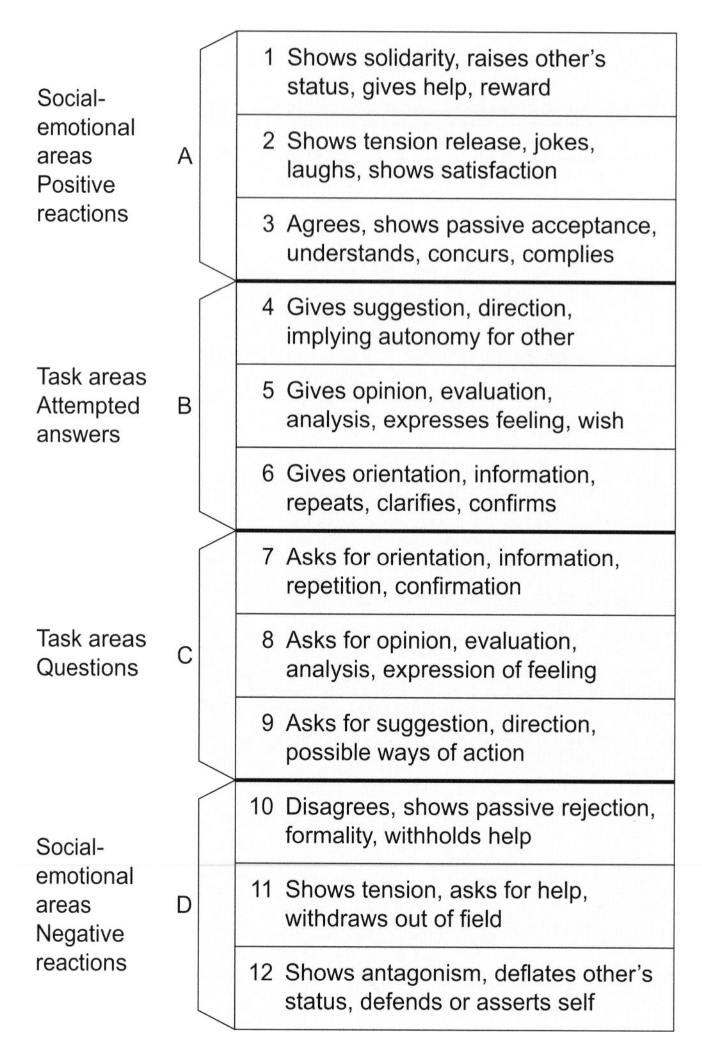

Figure 3.3 Bales's coding scheme
(Source: Bales, 1950b)

3.3 Tuckman and Jensen's stage model of group development

Bales took a particular approach to understanding how groups work that is generally referred to as a phase model because group behaviour develops through different phases as the group addresses a given task. Another dominant approach is the stage model of group development. The best-known example of this approach is Tuckman and Jensen's (1977) five-stage model. Based on a review of the existing literature in the area, each stage involves both interpersonal and task-related processes (as well as catchy rhyming titles, which may have contributed to its success!).

- The first stage, *forming*, is allied with testing and dependence. This stage involves the initial coming together of members, in which they form new relationships and look to each other to establish the appropriate interpersonal and task behaviours in the group.
- This is followed by a period of intragroup conflict, called *storming*. In this stage, because individuals are more comfortable they are more willing to question authority, attempt to express their individuality and resist control.
- This is followed by *norming*, which is aligned to the development of group cohesion. During the norming stage, members accept each other, begin to act harmoniously and accept the implicit and explicit rules of behaviour appropriate to the group.
- In *performing*, the group has developed a supportive environment and energy is focused on completing the task.
- In *adjourning*, the task moves to closure and the members accept the anticipated change in personal relationships.

This has been an incredibly popular approach to understanding task-related group behaviour. Many organisations have adopted Tuckman and Jensen's stages to understand and plan work groups and teams as it is generally perceived to be a highly practical and successful approach.

3.4 Keeping it together

A key element of group development is maintaining unity. Psychology has traditionally aimed to explain this through the concept of **group cohesiveness**, which refers to the processes that hold the group together. Festinger (1950, p. 274) defined it as: 'the resultant of all forces acting on the members to remain in the group.' However, in the intervening years, the concept has accumulated more and more marginally different definitions in response to growing engagement with different types of groups (Friedkin, 2004). The primary motivation for much of the research on cohesiveness has been the belief that cohesiveness promotes productivity and so has very real applications in the world, particularly in the world of work.

Group cohesiveness
All those processes that function to hold the group together.

Until the early 1990s, group cohesiveness was primarily conceptualised as the outcome of interpersonal attraction. Very simplistically put, if all the members of a group like each other the group will be cohesive. This reflects a particularly individualistic perspective that focuses on the group as a collection of individuals, in the spirit of the Allport quote at the beginning of this chapter. However, since then there has been a move to conceptualise it as an outcome of group processes such as the development of social identity and self-categorisation theory (Hogg, 1993). (These ideas are explored further below.)

One of the issues concerning the conceptualisation of group processes as an individual phenomenon is nicely illustrated in a stand-up routine by US comedian Jerry Seinfeld on sport. Seinfeld describes sports fans as supporting clothes rather than individual athletes. After all, it is not uncommon for players to change teams, yet the fans generally remain loyal to the team and whichever players are wearing those particular shirts at the time. What is it that lends continuity to that team? In the 1990s, psychologists rediscovered a concept first introduced by Donald Campbell (1958) that initially garnered little attention (Yzerbyt et al., 2000): the concept of **entitativity**. Entitativity refers to the recognition of a collective as a coherent and distinct entity and is an emergent quality of the group rather than of the individuals who comprise it. Consider how the concept of entitativity brings together many of the definitions discussed earlier in the chapter. It is, for instance, highly resonant with Asch's water analogy described above.

Entitativity
The degree to which a group is a unified and coherent whole.

3.5 Summary

This section has focused on an area traditionally referred to as group formation. Social comparison theory had attempted to explain how groups form around affinities and similarities. Bales and Tuckman and Jensen developed more structured theories of group formation that follow groups from their inception to their demise. Both approaches have developed systems for analysing small group interactions that have been successfully used in organisational contexts. One of the key elements for understanding groups, however, is what keeps them together. Group cohesiveness is an important area of study in group processes as research indicates that cohesive groups are productive groups. More recently, psychologists have rediscovered the notion of entitativity to describe the phenomenon of what makes a group coherent.

4 How do groups (fail to) work?

So far this chapter has looked at what groups are and how they develop. Much if not most of the research on group processes looks at how groups work and the relationship of that to group productivity. This research has traditionally focused on **social facilitation**, **social loafing** and group decision making.

Social facilitation
How individual performance is impacted by the presence of others.

Social loafing
The tendency of individuals to make less of an effort when they are working collectively with others than when they are on their own.

4.1 Behaviour within groups (intragroup processes)

4.1.1 Social facilitation

Here we have to step back again to interrogate the relationship between the individual and the group. Are we different when we are alone compared with when we are with others? Does the mere presence of other people affect how we behave? Certainly, in many cases this is true. There are many behaviours we would normally never consider performing with others around, many of which respond to cultural norms. For instance, most people would be greatly embarrassed if they were discovered picking their nose!

In the early days of psychology, research most often focused on productivity and comparing group and individual performance. Norman Triplett kick-started this research with his work on *social facilitation*. A fan of bicycle racing, Triplett noted that cyclists seemed to race faster when competing with other cyclists than when they were racing against the clock (Triplett, 1898): see Table 3.2.

Table 3.2 Clock versus competitors

	Average time per mile
Paced against time	2 minutes, 29.9 seconds
Paced competition	1 minute, 50.35 seconds

He hypothesised that competition between people energised and improved performance on motor tasks. To test his theory he designed an experiment that involved children winding up fishing reels as fast as they could. The children were asked to do this either alone or with another child also completing the task independently alongside them.

Triplett confirmed that children were faster when completing the task at the same time as another child than when they were on their own.

From around the turn of the twentieth century until the 1930s, a steady stream of research followed in which psychologists showed that individual performance is enhanced when being 'watched' by 'conspecifics' (those of our own species) or when conspecifics are engaging in the same behaviour. Cockroaches run faster; chickens, fish and rats eat more; and pairs of rats copulate more (Baron, 2010). However, some research found that the presence of others could also impair performance. Even in Triplett's original research, while the majority of children performed faster with others, for some it made no difference and some actually performed better when alone. Such conflicting evidence led to the demise of this area of research after the 1940s. Until an acceptable explanation could be advanced for the inconsistencies, studies in this area seemed to have reached a dead end. This situation persisted until 1965 and the work of Robert Zajonc.

Zajonc conducted research with cockroaches. In his experiments, he discovered that the cockroaches would run faster through a simple maze if they were in the presence of other cockroaches. However, in a complex maze they would take longer if others were present (Figure 3.4).

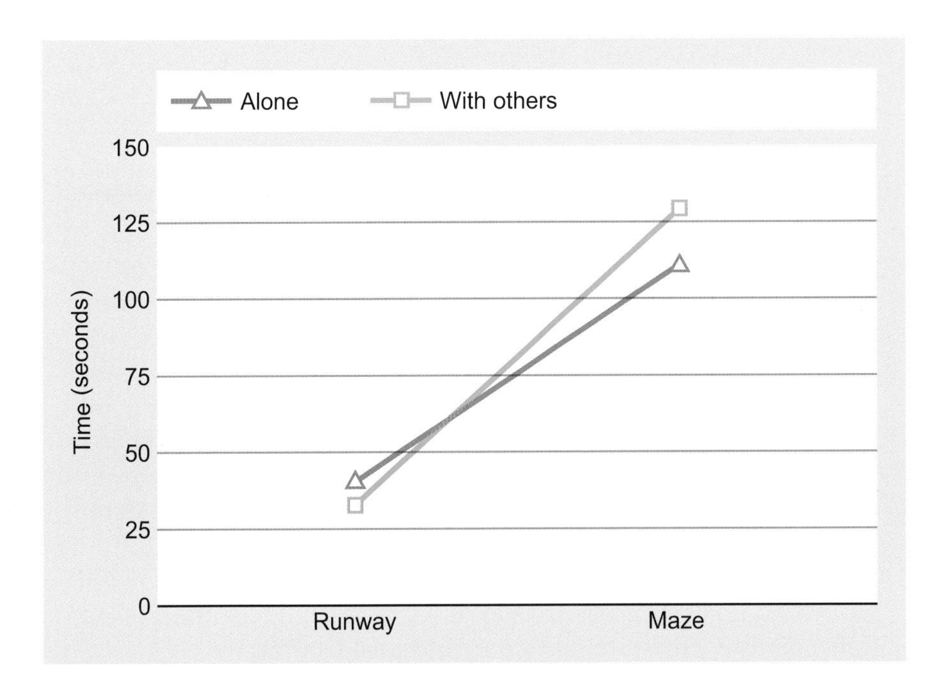

Figure 3.4 Cockroach running times
(Source: Zajonc et al., 1969)

Zajonc argued that the presence of others (in whatever capacity) increases the drive level or level of arousal. Up to a certain level, this arousal enhances performance, but past this point it makes it more likely that incorrect or irrelevant responses will be performed, and more mistakes will be made. So, the level of arousal is heightened by the presence of others and the challenge of a new or complex task similarly produces an increase in the level of arousal. According to Zajonc, together these can be overwhelming and will hinder performance. To illustrate, think of playing a musical instrument, say a piano. If the piece you are playing is simple or you are particularly skilled at playing, then the presence of others may well facilitate your performance. However, if it is a complex piece of classical music, or you are just learning to play, then you are likely to perform better on your own than in front of an audience. That is why it is often recommended that we practise new skills on our own, and then, when we become more proficient at them, perform them in public. These two situations maximise performance.

Zajonc's theory seemed to account quite effectively for the inconsistent results that had been found over the decades and might be seen to have brought research into social facilitation back to life. However, not all psychologists were convinced that an explanation in terms of 'drive' or 'arousal' was necessary.

Pause for thought

Many psychological concepts are not directly observable, but are construed to describe relationships between events or behaviours that show clear patterns and can be reliably predicted. An example of this is the concept of 'drive'. Some psychologists have questioned the usefulness of this term for social facilitation, arguing that the phenomenon can be much more easily explained through the use of straightforward concepts such as the worry of being judged or simply being distracted (Aiello and Douthitt, 2001). More recently, with advances in the field of psychophysiology, experiments conducted by Blascovich et al. (1999), while confirming Zajonc's predictions in terms of task performance, failed to support the drive–arousal theory of social facilitation.

Step back here for a moment and consider the wider question being asked. That is, does the presence of another person impact on our behaviour? This question in itself has implications for how we think about the relationship between the individual and the group. First, this is an interesting question because it assumes that it is the physical presence of others that is the determining factor in how we are influenced by others. However, when are we ever, really alone and beyond the influence of others? How might we actually go about isolating the individual from the context in which we find ourselves?

At the same time, it would surely be unreasonable to expect that a change in the environment, especially a change as profound as the adding of a living, sentient human being, would have no effect on us. Yet, a **meta-analysis** of 241 social facilitation studies argued that the presence of others accounted for only 0.3 to 3 per cent of variation in behaviour (Bond and Titus, 1983). How might this be explained? Might it have something to do with how the question was formulated? Social facilitation research does not represent the full variety of human behaviour. It is limited to those behaviours that are task-oriented only. Is that a fair representation of human behaviour? Is your task performance a reasonable indicator of who you are? It is important to always pay close attention to the specificities of the question that is being asked and answered.

Meta-analysis
A technique for combining data from different studies on the same topic, and analysing them together, to derive an overall conclusion.

4.1.2 Social loafing

Social loafing was first brought to the attention of psychology by Ringelmann (1913, cited in Kravitz and Martin, 1986), a French professor of agricultural engineering. In an experiment involving rope pulling he noted that the pull of a group of individuals appeared to be less than the sum of their individual pulls would indicate (Figure 3.5).

Figure 3.5 Social loafing

Ringelmann attributed this to coordination loss, though he did recognise that motivation might play a part. However, while Ringelmann's observation was tangential to the experiment he was conducting, Latané et al. (1979) conducted one of the first studies specifically into this phenomenon. They asked students to clap or cheer as loudly as possible for a set amount of time. They did this alone or in groups of two, four or six. Social facilitation would have predicted that, on this simple task, performance would improve in the presence of others. However, cheering was reduced by 34 per cent in two-person groups and up to 64 per cent in six-person groups. Across numerous studies, the bigger the group, the less effort each individual puts into it. It appears that the range in which group size has significant impact is between 2 and 8 members. Latané et al. (1979, p. 831) termed this phenomenon *social loafing*, describing it as a social disease because 'it has negative consequences for individuals, social institutions, and societies.'

Box 3.2 Social loafing versus social facilitation

While at first it appeared that social loafing contradicted social facilitation theory by demonstrating reduced ability in the group condition, Jackson and Williams (1985) present a case for integrating the findings from the two streams of research. They argue that social loafing can be seen as the flip side of social facilitation because in social loafing you find low arousal or low evaluation threat, while in social facilitation you find high arousal or high evaluation threat. The effects on performance in social loafing are precisely the opposite of those in social facilitation. When we are an anonymous part of a group, we do not try as hard on simple, well-learned tasks, but this very same relatively relaxed state may improve our performance on the sorts of complex tasks that are impaired by high evaluation apprehension.

We might want to consider, however, that while evaluation may bring together theorisation on facilitation and loafing, these are both extremely individualistic understandings. They do not provide a theory of groups, only theories of individual behaviour within groups.

Does being in a group make you lazier than you 'really' are or do groups allow you to be as lazy as you 'really' are? Latané et al. (1979) suggested that as group size increases, responsibility is diffused, so each member feels less responsible for the outcome (social impact theory). In a meta-analytic review of the social loafing literature, Karau and Williams (1993) suggested that the best explanatory tool for the finding could be found in the **collective effort model**. This model suggests that social loafing results from a reduction in motivation because the participants realise that their individual contributions cannot be evaluated on an individual basis. In other words, when individuals work together with others, the relationship between their own effort and group performance and rewards is more uncertain than when they are alone so they are less likely to make the effort. So you shouldn't be surprised to find that making that relationship more certain improves performance. For instance, relay racers swim faster when individual lap time is announced than when only the overall team score is given (Williams et al., 1989).

Collective effort model
This model suggests that working as a group reduces motivation because participants realise that their individual contributions cannot be evaluated on an individual basis.

Pause for thought

Statisticising groups is a common method for comparing individuals and groups in which researchers add together measures of individual performance and compare these with the performance of real groups. Ringelmann's and Latané et al.'s studies involved a comparison between performance in real groups and statisticised groups. What do you think of this method of comparison? What might be its strengths? How might it be limited?

As you can imagine, maximising the productivity of groups is important in many different settings, from sport to business to health care to education, to mention but a few. This being the case, some research has gone into identifying ways in which social loafing might be minimised. In his overview of group processes, Hogg (1996) proposes that social loafing can be reduced by increasing the importance and relevance of the task, how enjoyable it is, how identifiable each group member is and, importantly, group cohesiveness.

It has been suggested also that social loafing might be a symptom of Western culture, which is highly individualistic. In their meta-analysis, Karau and Williams (1993) found support for the claim that groups made up of women or people from Asian cultures are less prone to loafing. However, subsequent comparative studies on social loafing are contradictory. Much research claims that the phenomenon is universal in that it occurs: in both males and females; among children and adults; differently but consistently across cultures; under a wide variety of work conditions; and on cognitive as well as physical tasks.

Pause for thought

Having taken a look at some of the key work on social loafing, consider what the implications are for conceptualisations of the group. The evidence seems to support the notion that groups perform rather differently from individuals. However, are both valued equally, or does the research appear to conceive of one as hindering the other? Evidence seems to suggests groups are deficient in comparison with individuals and that individuals do better on their own or equally as well as when in groups.

What might be some of the issues with this assumption? Like social facilitation, it is based on theory and research that assumes it is simple to measure individual performance alone – but a participant is never actually performing alone. Usually they are in the presence of the experimenter, or at least aware that their performance is being evaluated. Guerin (1986) conducted a meta-analysis of mere presence studies – that is, studies investigating the effects of the mere presence of others on our behaviour. His research exposed the difficulty in meeting the comparison criteria for 'mere presence'. Were the participants in these studies ever actually alone?

As you have seen in both this chapter and Chapter 2, there is a considerable body of evidence showing that the presence of other people influences individual performance. That would imply that actually both group and individual measures of performance in an experiment are subject to social influence.

4.1.3 Making decisions

So far you have been looking at how individuals behave within groups and how this may impact on group productivity. However, there are situations in which a group will need to engage in the process of group decision making to produce a single unified outcome. Failure to reach a common decision could potentially, depending on the circumstances, spell the end of a group. This could be as consequential as the dissolution of parliament or as trivial as some friends splitting up to attend two different films. However, group decision making is an intricate part of our everyday lives. It is likely that most of the decisions made by and about you are made in groups. Politicians, bankers, medical professionals, juries, committees and student unions, to name but a few, all have to make decisions in groups.

Group decision making can be understood as the process by which the group chooses one out of several possible courses of action. One of the areas of study has been the process by which groups reach a consensus. (This was touched on earlier in the section on how groups form and develop with respect to Bales's IPA and the work of Tuckman and Jensen.) It has been argued that the final decisions reached by groups can often be predicted quite accurately by relatively simple rules known as *social decision schemes* (see Davis, 1973). This model suggests that for tasks that have a single, correct answer, for instance a mathematical puzzle, groups adopt a 'truth wins' approach, which means the group discusses the problem until the correct solution is found. However, for tasks that have no demonstrably correct solution, such as choosing the best film of all time or the best pizzeria in town, the 'majority wins' rule is typically used. According to this social decision scheme model, how decisions are made depends on the procedures used by the group to reach the decision regardless of the information available to the group members. The reason for this is that, although we expect groups to employ all the resources available to them, often only shared knowledge is used. The resources or information held by *just* one member are less likely to be raised or discussed in this situation and the larger the group the more likely this is (Stasser et al., 1989). Does this reflect your experience of working in groups? Do you find yourself being shy about introducing information that you think others might not know or want to hear? Does it become more difficult as group size increases?

If you ask most people, they might well tell you that they would expect groups to behave in quite moderate ways and that this would be reflected in less 'risky' decisions (e.g. in deciding how much money to invest in a new start-up venture). However, early research into group decision making seemed to indicate that, actually, the opposite was the case. James Stoner (1961), as part of his master's thesis, used 12 decision dilemmas to ask participants to give advice as to how much risk to take. Participants worked alone and in groups of five. To Stoner's surprise, the group decisions were found to be clearly and consistently riskier than those made by individuals. Also, according to Stoner, this was not just a case of public conformity but rather one of actual opinion change. This was initially identified as the *risky shift phenomenon*. However, it was then found that sometimes groups tended to become more conservative than the individuals within them, for instance when making decisions about betting on horse races or burgling houses.

This general phenomenon was termed **group polarisation** by Moscovici and Zavalloni (1969). Group polarisation refers to the way in which group members tend to shift towards a more extreme opinion than they originally expressed after engaging in group discussion. Myers and Lamm (1976) established that as well as risk taking, group polarisation extended to many other areas, including jury decisions, ethical decisions, judgments, person perceptions and negotiations. Drawing on the existing research, Isenberg (1986) suggested that the explanation for this phenomenon could be found in a combination of social comparison theory and **persuasive arguments theory**. Currently, there are three competing or possibly complementary theories of group polarisation that dominate the literature.

Group polarisation
The tendency of group members to shift their position to a more extreme one after group discussion than the one they expressed initially.

Persuasive arguments theory
An informational approach to social influences, it describes the process by which arguments are drawn into and used in decision making.

Social comparison theory, a normative approach to social influence (Sanders and Baron, 1977), predicts that participants will shift towards the socially desirable pole. Because the decision issues presented to the participants often involve social values, there is an implied social preference for one of the outcomes. When participants decide individually, they reflect this preference. Then, in group discussions, the individual participants realise that others are nearer to this outcome than they themselves are. In wanting to be seen to be adhering to this social value they shift further towards it. This further explains why those who are already nearer that end show less of a shift.

Burnstein and Vinokur (1977), however, argue that social comparison theory fails to account for the actual content of the discussion. They suggest that it is the exchange of information and arguments in the discussion that leads to polarisation. The reasoning here is that in any discussion there is never a precise balance of arguments and evidence. If you combine them all, you will find that one choice is favoured. This means that during the discussion more evidence and arguments will be raised in favour of the dominant view. Thus, Burnstein and Vinokur contend that *persuasive arguments theory*, an informational approach to social influence, is sufficient to explain a shift to a more extreme position based on the group discussion.

Turner et al. (1989), however, suggest that group polarisation is a form of conformity through *self-categorisation*. The most important finding from their research is that while, as expected, risky groups shift towards risk and cautious groups shift towards caution, individuals who are risky or cautious show either no shift or a shift in the opposite direction from their label. This can be explained in terms of a social identification process whereby group members attribute characteristics to themselves that are typical of the group members as a whole, so they conform to the norms of the group. From this perspective, one crucial function of norms is to differentiate between groups, and differentiation is achieved by accentuating intergroup differences. So participants would be more affected when listening to the in-group (members of their own group) and more motivated to conform to the norms of that group and differentiate themselves from the out-group (members of another group).

More recently Krizan and Baron (2007) have argued that the explanatory power of the self-categorisation approach is limited in this area. They hold that social comparison and persuasive arguments are still required to account for the phenomenon overall. According to Brown (2000) evidence suggests that all three processes are involved in group decision making in the real world, varying from situation to situation, with one never operating exclusively. One way to think about this is that:

- *Social comparison theory* is most applicable in situations where there is little opportunity for argument but information is available on how others behave and on the socially preferred way of behaving. An example of this would be gambling.
- *Persuasive arguments theory* is most applicable when the group has more scope for argument, which can be controlled in an experimental context.
- *Self-categorisation theory* seems to apply when individuals are identified with a specific group. Thus, it would be unlikely to apply in a situation where there was no obvious out-group. A possible example of this might be a jury.

You need to remember, of course, that taking a more polarised position does not imply that the decision is necessarily wrong. However, it is also true that sometimes groups make really bad decisions. You may be familiar with the adages about a camel being a horse designed by a committee and too many cooks spoiling the broth. Irving Janis (1982) attempted to explain bad decision making by groups through a phenomenon he identified as **groupthink**. Groupthink refers to the situation in which group members are so keen to reach a unanimous decision that they fail to follow proper and rational procedures for making the decision.

Groupthink
A mode of thinking in which the desire to reach unanimous agreement overrides the motivation to adopt proper, rational, decision-making procedures.

According to Janis, if you take a cohesive group with no systematic procedures for reaching a decision and a directive leader who already favours one decision over others, isolate it from outside influences and put it in a high-stress situation, groupthink will occur. This is, as you may imagine, because the desire to achieve consensus and avoid dissent becomes paramount. This means that group members will have the illusion that the group is invulnerable, moral and unanimous, so they will police the group to ensure conformity among themselves and others (see also Baron, 2005). The problem with this is that it produces bad decisions because the group doesn't properly and fully address and assess all the possible options and fails to make contingency plans.

At the same time, cohesive groups can make good decisions – even better than those taken by individuals – if groupthink is controlled.

Janis (1982) identified these methods for achieving this:

- be impartial – don't endorse any specific position
- assign a devil's advocate, thus encouraging critical evaluation
- sub-divide the group occasionally then reunite it to air differences
- consult outside experts or colleagues
- call a 'second-chance' meeting before implementing decisions.

Box 3.3 Crossing boundaries: groupthink

Janis's concept of groupthink provides one of the most conspicuous examples of working across boundaries in psychology. To develop the concept of groupthink, Janis drew on his background in the military, his interest in politics and his training in psychology to analyse historical accounts of decision making, in particular bad decision making.

The classic example of groupthink is that of the Bay of Pigs invasion in 1961 when the immensely powerful United States of America failed to defeat the forces of the comparatively tiny island of Cuba. Janis argued that the members of the US government who made the decision were led astray by the need to form a cohesive group, resulting in the failure of members to properly consider, question or challenge decisions. It has been argued that the decision to invade Iraq in search of weapons of mass destruction (WMDs) followed a similar process in which flawed evidence was used to inform unrealistic appraisals of the situation.

Over the years the concept of groupthink has been applied to group decision making in a multitude of contexts, from high-level military, political and technical groups to business and management groups in the private sector. In his review of Janis's 1972 ground-breaking book *Victims of Groupthink: A Psychological Study of Foreign Policy Decisions and Fiascoes*, Hart (1991) argued that Janis's study has had a major influence on students of group processes, decision making and management, as well as influencing international relations analysts in managing the complexities of international crises.

According to Baron (2005, p. 219), Janis 'offered this formulation as a compelling bridge between principles documented by laboratory research and "real life" problems.'

4.2 Behaviour between groups (intergroup processes)

Having looked at what goes on inside groups, the focus will now shift to what happens outside them. Chapter 4 will address the question of intergroup processes in greater depth, but this chapter looks a bit more closely at the distinction between acting as an individual and acting as a group member and how those two relate to each other. Are they the same or are they distinct behaviours?

Tajfel et al. (1971) conducted some experiments that led them to the conclusion that simply allocating someone to a group was sufficient cause for them to prefer their own group over others. Tajfel et al. used paintings by Klee and Kandinsky to divide groups of boys into two groups. The only information the participants had was who belonged to which group. When they were asked to allocate money to recipients, but not to themselves, they showed a preference for members of their own group, an in-group bias – even though this was the only thing they knew about the other participants. This methodology, known as the minimal group studies, allowed the researchers to argue that in-group favouritism is intrinsic to groups. This can be seen as one of the foundational studies of what has become known as social identity theory (SIT) (Tajfel and Turner, 1979), as you read about in the previous chapter.

SIT distinguishes interaction between people from interaction between groups. It further proposes that there is a difference between interpersonal and intergroup behaviour in which the latter means acting as a group member rather than as an individual. According to Brown (2000), behaviour can be plotted along a continuum, the two extremes being identified as interpersonal and intergroup. In terms of SIT, interpersonal behaviour is determined by individual characteristics of the person, whereas intergroup behaviour is determined by membership in the group and the relationship with other groups. The theory draws on this distinction to propose a personal identity and a social identity. Personal identity refers to self-definition in terms of personal and idiosyncratic characteristics, for instance loving jazz or enjoying parties. Social identity refers to self-definition in terms of category membership, such as being a woman or a Barcelona FC supporter. Group behaviour is based on the similarities among members because the key characteristic of groups is that of uniformity. At the same time, group behaviour ignores the variation across individual members of a group. That is to say, people acting as group members show uniform behaviour and treat the behaviour of members of other groups as uniform. Individual differences are not relevant to group behaviour but group norms are crucial to any understanding of intergroup processes.

SIT thus allows us to dispense with the vague, metaphysical notion of a 'group mind', discussed earlier in the chapter, but still acknowledges that the group has *psychological reality* for its members. Tajfel (1982) has argued that being in and behaving as a member of a group has psychological consequences, and these consequences arise whether or not one is in the presence of other members. When group norms and values are salient, we will respond in accordance with these norms, even if we are alone. Moreover, as social identity involves attributes and norms associated with the group, members, in a sense, stereotype themselves as much as they stereotype members of other groups. Rather than the group mind being outside the individuals who comprise it, the group becomes located in the mind of its members, so to speak.

The theory argues that the most persuasive explanation for intergroup behaviour relies on self-categorisation and social comparison and thus explains the emergent properties of group processes in relation to shifts in self-perception from personal to social identity, varying with the social context (Turner et al., 1994). Switching between intergroup and interpersonal behaviour is not necessarily related to finding yourself in an interpersonal and intergroup setting, however, but rather in a social setting in which groups are, or are not, salient. For instance, discrimination of individuals based on a social identity, such as class, can take place in what might otherwise be construed as an interpersonal setting, such as a dinner party.

Abrams and Hogg's (1988) presentation of SIT includes both the original intergroup theory about the need for a positive social identity for one's in-group in comparison with the out-group, and also self-categorisation theory, which relates to intragroup behaviour and is a general theory of group processes. This combination of social identity theory and self-categorisation theory is referred to as the social identity approach. Postmes et al. (2005) have presented a developed model of social identity formation that, they argue, overcomes the dualism of group-level versus individualistic analysis of small group processes, by incorporating both factors at both levels of analysis as well as their interaction. They suggest that intragroup negotiation and debate are, in practice, key to constituting and redefining identity over the course of the group's life. For social identity theorists this combination is crucially important to the study of group processes, be they intragroup or intergroup, as it offers a 'complete approach' to this area.

4.3 Summary

This section began by focusing on how groups work. It looked first at the phenomenon of social facilitation to consider how the presence of others can affect individual performance. It then moved on to social loafing to discuss individual performance within a group. Box 3.2 briefly considered the relationship between the two. The section then moved on to the question of group decision making, which included discussion of group polarisation and groupthink. Finally, the topic of intergroup behaviour was introduced through a discussion of social identity theory.

5 The power of groups – so you want to change the world?

Both this chapter and Chapter 2 have looked at the way individual behaviour is affected by the presence of others and the context of the group. It has been argued that the reason social influence research dominates social psychology is that the role of resistance has been individually theorised. This has led to a tendency in social psychological research to present the group as dangerous and something that must be understood and managed, if not controlled. There is certainly evidence that groups produce apparently negative behaviours: deindividuation, social loafing, group polarisation and groupthink, to name but a few. Are groups bad for us? It is true that we often conform in groups, but is it also true that we resist and rebel in them. Figure 3.6 shows an example of such resistance: the 1930 Salt March in India.

Figure 3.6 Gandhi and fellow activists in the Salt March of 1930

Gamson and his colleagues were interested in studying resistance and rebellion in the face of unjust authority. They were surprised by the results of Milgram's obedience studies. They wanted to understand the mechanisms that produced such high levels of obedience, and what would happen if they varied them. Focusing on the phenomenon of rebellion, they set up an intriguing study using a fake company they created called MHRC Encounter (Gamson et al., 1982). They told participants they were running focus groups to gauge community standards for evidence in an upcoming court case. People were asked their opinion of a Mr C., who had lost his petrol station franchise because he was 'living in sin'. Mr C. was suing the oil company. Participants were told that their discussions would be videotaped. After some discussion, they were asked to argue in favour of the oil company on tape; however, the tape was stopped when they were given these instructions. They were then asked to sign an affidavit giving MHRC the right to edit the tapes as they chose and use them as evidence in court. As was intended, the participants concluded that this was a scam by the oil company to collect evidence and refused to sign the affidavits. Participants were so annoyed that Gamson et al. were only able to run 33 out of the 80 'focus groups' planned. Of these, 16 groups unanimously refused to sign, in nine groups the majority of members refused to sign, and in the remaining eight the majority signed, but still expressed some amount of rebellious sentiment.

Why did this study produce such different results from those of Milgram? Why did the majority of Gamson et al.'s participants rebel? Based on their own research, Postmes et al. (2005, p. 34) have argued that: 'it is precisely because individuals actively engage with each other that a small group of unconnected individuals can be transformed into an entity capable of taking a collective stance and undertaking collective action.'

However, is this only the case for small groups? From the very inception of research into group behaviour, one of the most challenging groups for study has been the crowd. It doesn't lend itself to the experimental cubicle and it is difficult to capture the complexity of it through simple observation. However, it has been of significant interest because the crowd can represent a challenge to the social order. As mentioned above, the crowd was the focus of LeBon's classic text, which advanced the concept of the 'group mind'. Are crowds groups or are they just a collection of individuals?

Research indicates that while crowds can often be a simple collection of individuals, they can also sometimes be a group, or indeed a number of groups. Reicher (1984) has argued that to understand crowds, we need to recognise that they do not exist in a vacuum. There is always a context and this context will include other groups, not least of which might be the police. In his study of the St Paul's (Bristol) riot in 1980,

Reicher found that while reports of the event claimed that the crowd had been out of control, his research did not support that conclusion. Contrary to LeBon's (1960) claims that the crowd was irrational and barbaric, Reicher's research indicated that crowd behaviour was far more sophisticated and creative than previously believed. Behaviour appropriate to group norms was prevalent and behaviour not in line with group norms was not present or, if it occurred, was immediately controlled. Based on his early work using SIT, Reicher (1996) later extended his analysis to the broader social identity approach.

Thirty years later, Reicher and fellow crowd behaviour expert Clifford Stott brought their analytical tools to bear on the riots that took place in the UK, primarily in London, in August 2011 (Figure 3.7).

Figure 3.7 Riots in London, August 2011

In their book *Mad Mobs and Englishmen*, Reicher and Stott (2011) argue that the way the riots were characterised in public discourse at the time did not represent what we know from psychology about how and why riots happen. During and after the riots, those involved in them were once again presented in one of two ways: as irrational barbarians, as per LeBon, or as mindless criminals intent on causing damage and destruction. As in previous situations, Reicher and Stott argued that the behaviour of the rioters was far more complex and nuanced than was being acknowledged and that to understand these behaviours it is critical to acknowledge that much of it was intergroup behaviour, shaped by social norms and identities rather than random individual acts.

Pause for thought

During the riots in London in August of 2011, much was made of the fact that the rioters used instant messaging to communicate, thereby allowing unprecedented coordination in organising. Moreover, in recent years social media is being used by researchers to study this crowd phenomenon. YouTube, Twitter, Instagram, etc. all provide information that comes from different and diverse perspectives, allowing the researcher the opportunity to access data that would have been inconceivable in the past.

When looking at media representations of these events it is difficult to see the patterns. However, in order to get an understanding of crowd behaviour, you need to consider that crowds are very rarely violent or destructive. Even when groups are made highly salient, as in the case of many sporting events, such as the Olympics, crowd behaviour is often friendly, joyous and inclusive (Figure 3.8). What crowds can be, however, is immensely powerful, so how you theorise and respond to them can have an important impact on society.

Figure 3.8 Crowds at the Olympics in London, 2012

5.1 Summary

This final section began by addressing the question of resistance to social influence and the role of the group in this process. The discussion then broadened to consider the question of crowds and crowd behaviour and how these fit into the theorisation of groups. The section raised some questions about the role of groups in society.

6 Concluding thoughts

This chapter considered the question: *Are you with us or against us?* It has looked at some of the psychological research that attempts to address this question, primarily through a focus on group processes. Because we live our lives within and surrounded by groups, understanding these processes is key to understanding 'real life'. Here you have looked at some of the main theories and research in psychology. However, group research is relevant to education, sociology, management and business studies, communications, anthropology, political science, economics and more beyond. Because groups are relevant to so many areas of study and so intertwined with everyday practices, to understand them it is crucially important to always keep attention on what is going on inside the group and outside the group, and the relationship between them.

The world can be a very messy place to do research. In the laboratory things can appear as isolated and clear, in a way that they would never play out otherwise. To attempt to make sense of a situation, it is necessary to focus questions at different levels of analysis, constantly moving back and forth between the individuals in a group, the group itself, the relationship with other groups and the location of the group within a particular society. Isolating situations and trying to look at them in a vacuum can be a first step in this process, but it can never be the last one.

Further reading

- This is a classic text that covers most of the history and dominant theories around group processes:

Brown, R. (2000) *Group Processes: Dynamics Within and Between Groups*, 2nd edn, Oxford, Blackwell.

- Steven Reicher and Clifford Stott use up-to-date social psychological knowledge to provide an explanation of a real-world event:

Reicher, S. and Stott, C. (2011) *Mad Mobs and Englishmen? Myths and Realities of the 2011 Riots*, London, Constable & Robinson Ltd.

- This is a good overview of key concepts in the study of groups. It is available as an ebook at many academic libraries:

Levine, J. and Hogg M. (eds) (2010) *Encyclopedia of Group Processes and Intergroup Relations*, Thousand Oaks, CA, Sage.

References

Aiello, J.R. and Douthitt, E.A. (2001) 'Social facilitation from Triplett to electronic performance monitoring', *Group Dynamics: Theory, Research, and Practice*, vol. 5, no. 3, p. 163.

Abrams, D. and Hogg, M.A. (1988) *Social Identifications: A Social Psychology of Intergroup Relations and Group Processes,* London, Routledge.

Allport, F.H. (1924) 'The group fallacy in relation to social science', *Journal of Abnormal Psychology and Social Psychology*, vol. 191, no. 1, p. 60.

Bales, R.F. (1950a) *Interaction Process Analysis: A Method for the Study of Small Groups*, Cambridge, MA, Addison-Wesley.

Bales, R.F. (1950b) 'A set of categories for the analysis of small group interaction', *American Sociological Review*, vol. 15, no. 2, pp. 257–63.

Baron, R.S. (2005) 'So right it's wrong: groupthink and the ubiquitous nature of polarized group decision making', *Advances in Experimental Social Psychology*, vol. 37, pp. 219–53.

Baron, R.S. (2010) 'Social facilitation', in Levine, J. and Hogg, M. (eds) *Encyclopedia of Group Processes and Intergroup Relations*, Thousand Oaks, CA, Sage Publications, pp. 792–4.

Baumeister, R.F. and Leary, M.R. (1995) 'The need to belong: desire for interpersonal attachments as a fundamental human motivation', *Psychological Bulletin*, vol. 117, no. 3, p. 497.

Blascovich, J., Mendes, W.B., Hunter, S. and Salomon, K. (1999) 'Social facilitation as challenge and threat', *Journal of Personality and Social Psychology*, vol. 77, pp. 68–77.

Bond, C.F. and Titus, L.J. (1983) 'Social facilitation: a meta-analysis of 241 studies', *Psychological Bulletin*, vol. 94, no. 2, p. 265.

Bowlby, J. (1969) *Attachment*, New York, Basic Books.

Brace, N. and Byford, J. (eds) (2012) *Investigating Psychology*, Oxford, Oxford University Press/Milton Keynes, The Open University.

Brown, R. (2000) *Group Processes: Dynamics Within and Between Groups*, 2nd edn, Oxford, Blackwell.

Burnstein, E. and Vinokur, A. (1977) 'Persuasive argumentation and social comparison as determinants of attitude polarization', *Journal of Experimental Social Psychology*, vol. 13, no. 4, pp. 315–32.

Buss, D.M. (1995) 'Evolutionary psychology: a new paradigm for psychological science', *Psychological Inquiry*, vol. 6, no. 1, pp. 1–30.

Campbell, D.T. (1958) 'Common fate, similarity, and other indices of the status of aggregates of persons as social entities', *Behavioural Science*, vol. 3, no. 1, pp. 14–25.

Davis, J.H. (1973) 'Group decision and social interaction: a theory of social decision schemes', *Psychological Review*, vol. 80, no. 2, pp. 97–125.

Durkheim, E. (1982) [1895] *The Rules of Sociological Method and Selected Texts on Sociology and its Method*, London, Macmillan.

Festinger, L. (1950) 'Informal social communication', *Psychological Review*, vol. 57, no. 5, pp. 271–82.

Festinger, L. (1954) 'A theory of social comparison processes', *Human Relations*, vol. 7, no. 2, pp. 117–40.

Festinger, L., Gerard, H.B., Hymovitch, B., Kelley, H.H. and Raven, B. (1952) 'The influence process in the presence of extreme deviates', *Human Relations*, vol. 5, no. 4, pp. 327–46.

Friedkin, N.E. (2004) 'Social cohesion', *Annual Review of Sociology*, vol. 30, pp. 409–25.

Gamson, W.A., Fireman, B. and Rytina, S. (1982) *Encounters with Unjust Authority*, Homewood, IL, Dorsey Press.

Guerin, B. (1986) 'Mere presence effects in humans: a review', *Journal of Experimental Social Psychology*, vol. 22, no. 1, pp. 38–77.

Harlow, H.F. (1958) 'The nature of love', *American Psychologist*, vol. 13, pp. 673–85.

Hart, P.T. (1991) 'Irving L. Janis' victims of groupthink', *Political Psychology*, vol. 12, no. 2, pp. 247–78.

Hogg, M.A. (1993) 'Group cohesiveness: a critical review and some new directions', *European Review of Social Psychology*, vol. 4, no. 1, pp. 85–111.

Hogg, M.A. (1996) 'Group processes', in Manstead, A.S.R. and Hewstone, M. (eds) *The Blackwell Encyclopedia of Social Psychology*, Blackwell Publishing, Blackwell Reference Online, 2 March 2014.

Isenberg, D.J. (1986) 'Group polarization: a critical review and meta-analysis', *Journal of Personality and Social Psychology*, vol. 50, no. 6, pp. 1141–51.

Jackson, J.M. and Williams, K.D. (1985) 'Social loafing on difficult tasks: working collectively can improve performance', *Journal of Personality and Social Psychology*, vol. 49, no. 4, pp. 937–42.

Janis, I.L. (1972) *Victims of Groupthink: A Psychological Study of Foreign Policy Decisions and Fiascoes*, Boston, MA, Houghton Mifflin.

Janis, I.L. (1982) *Groupthink*, 2nd edn, Boston, MA, Houghton Mifflin.

Karau, S.J. and Williams, K.D. (1993) 'Social loafing: A meta-analytic review and theoretical integration', *Journal of Personality and Social Psychology*, vol. 65, no. 4, pp. 681–706.

Kravitz, D.A., and Martin, B. (1986) 'Ringelmann rediscovered: the original article', *Journal of Personality and Social Psychology*, vol. 50, no. 5, pp. 936–41.

Krizan, Z. and Baron, R.S. (2007) 'Group polarization and choice-dilemmas: how important is self-categorization?', *European Journal of Social Psychology*, vol. 37, no. 1, pp. 191–201.

Latané, B., Williams, K. and Harkins, S. (1979) 'Many hands make light the work: the causes and consequences of social loafing', *Journal of Personality and Social Psychology*, vol. 37, no. 6, pp. 822–32.

LeBon, G. (1960) [1896] *The Crowd: A Study of Popular Mind,* New York, Viking Press.

Lewin, K. (1948) *Resolving Social Conflict*, New York, Harper & Row.

Maslow, A.H. (1954) *Motivation and Personality*, New York, Harper.

McDougall, W. (1908) *An Introduction to Social Psychology,* New York, Methuen.

Moscovici, S., and Zavalloni, M. (1969) 'The group as a polarizer of attitudes', *Journal of Personality and Social Psychology*, vol. 12, no. 2, pp. 125–35.

Murray, H.A. (1938) *Explorations in Personality*, New York, Oxford University Press.

Myers, D.G. and Lamm, H. (1976) 'The group polarization phenomenon', *Psychological Bulletin*, vol. 83, no. 4, pp. 602–27.

O'Connor, S.C. and Rosenblood, L.K. (1996) 'Affiliation motivation in everyday experience: a theoretical comparison', *Journal of Personality and Social Psychology*, vol. 70, no. 3, p. 513.

Postmes, T., Haslam, S.A. and Swaab, R.I. (2005) 'Social influence in small groups: an interactive model of social identity formation', *European Review of Social Psychology*, vol. 16, no. 1, pp. 1–42.

Reicher, S.D. (1984) 'The St. Pauls' riot: an explanation of the limits of crowd action in terms of a social identity model', *European Journal of Social Psychology*, vol. 14, no. 1, pp. 1–21.

Reicher, S.D. (1996) '"The Battle of Westminster": developing the social identity model of crowd behaviour in order to explain the initiation and development of collective conflict', *European Journal of Social Psychology*, vol. 26, no. 1, pp. 115–34.

Reicher, S. and Stott, C. (2011) *Mad Mobs and Englishmen? Myths and Realities of the 2011 Riots*, London, Constable & Robinson Ltd.

Sanders, G.S. and Baron, R.S. (1977) 'Is social comparison irrelevant for producing choice shifts?', *Journal of Experimental Social Psychology*, vol. 13, no. 4, pp. 303–14.

Schachter, S. (1959) *The Psychology of Affiliation*, Stanford, CA, Stanford University Press.

Sherif, M., Harvey, O.J., White, B.J., Hood, W.R. and Sherif, C.W. (1961) *Intergroup Conflict and Cooperation: The Robbers Cave Experiment*, Norman, OK, University of Oklahoma.

Stasser, G., Taylor, L.A. and Hanna, C. (1989) 'Information sampling in structured and unstructured discussions of three- and six-person groups', *Journal of Personality and Social Psychology*, vol. 57, no. 1, pp. 67–78.

Stoner, J.A.F. (1961) *A Comparison of Individual and Group Decisions Involving Risk*, unpublished doctoral dissertation, Cambridge, MA, Massachusetts Institute of Technology.

Tajfel, H. (1982) 'Social psychology of intergroup relations', *Annual Review of Psychology*, vol. 33, no. 1, pp. 1–39.

Tajfel, H. and Turner, J.C. (1979) 'An integrative theory of intergroup conflict', in Austin, W.G. and Worchel, S. (eds) *The Social Psychology of Intergroup Relations*, pp. 33–47, Monterey, CA, Brooks/Cole.

Tajfel, H., Billig, M.G., Bundy, R.P. and Flament, C. (1971) 'Social categorization and intergroup behaviour', *European Journal of Social Psychology*, vol. 1, no. 2, pp. 149–78.

Triplett, N. (1898) 'The dynamogenic factors in pacemaking and competition', *American Journal of Psychology*, vol. 9, no. 4, pp. 507–33.

Tuckman, B.W. and Jensen, M.A.C. (1977) 'Stages of small-group development revisited', *Group and Organization Management*, vol. 2, no. 4, pp. 419–27.

Turner, J.C. (1982) 'Towards a cognitive redefinition of the social group', in Tajfel, H. (ed.) *Social Identity and Intergroup Relations*, Cambridge, Cambridge University Press, pp. 15–40.

Turner, J.C., Wetherell, M.S. and Hogg, M.A. (1989) 'Referent informational influence and group polarization', *British Journal of Social Psychology*, vol. 28, no. 2, pp. 135–47.

Turner, J.C., Oakes, P.J., Haslam, S.A. and McGarty, C. (1994) 'Self and collective: cognition and social context', *Personality and Social Psychology Bulletin*, vol. 20, pp. 454–63.

Williams, K.D., Nida, S.A., Baca, L.D. and Latané, B. (1989) 'Social loafing and swimming: effects of identifiability on individual and relay performance of intercollegiate swimmers', *Basic and Applied Social Psychology*, vol. 10, no. 1, pp. 73–81.

Wilson, R.E., Gosling, S.D. and Graham, L.T. (2012) 'A review of Facebook research in the social sciences', *Perspectives on Psychological Science*, vol. 7, no. 3, pp. 203–20.

Yzerbyt, V., Castano, E., Leyens, J.P. and Paladino, M.P. (2000) 'The primacy of the ingroup: the interplay of entitativity and identification', *European Review of Social Psychology*, vol. 11, no. 1, pp. 257–95.

Zajonc, R.B. (1965) 'Social facilitation', *Science*, vol. 149, pp. 269–74.

Zajonc, R.B., Heingartner, A. and Herman, E.M. (1969) 'Social enhancement and impairment of performance in the cockroach', *Journal of Personality and Social Psychology*, vol. 13, no. 2, pp. 83–92.

Chapter 4

Why don't we like one another? The psychology of prejudice and intergroup relations

John Dixon

Contents

1 Introduction

On 24 April 2013, Pavlo Lapshyn (Figure 4.1) arrived in the United Kingdom from the Ukraine to work at a software firm in Birmingham, a city located in the Midlands of England. Five days later he murdered Mohammed Saleem, an 82-year-old grandfather who lived locally. Mr Saleem was stabbed several times as he returned from evening prayers near his home in the Small Heath suburb of Birmingham. Between this attack and his subsequent arrest on 18 July 2013, Lapshyn planted a series of explosive devices outside mosques in other Midlands towns. Police later found racist literature in his apartment and evidence that he was preparing further bomb attacks using mobile phones as detonators. Asked why he had attacked Mr Saleem, whom he had never met, Lapshyn replied simply: 'I have a racial hatred so I have a motivation, a racial motivation and racial hatred.' He is now serving a life sentence.

Figure 4.1 Pavlo Lapshyn

Lapshyn's behaviour offers an extreme example of what psychologists call *intergroup prejudice*. In one sense, his case provides an appropriate introduction to this chapter because it highlights the importance of answering the question: *Why don't we like one another?* It emphasises that negative thoughts and feelings about members of other groups can have stark consequences in the world. They fuel acts of discrimination.

They sustain wider patterns of inequality. They invite us to mistreat others and sometimes to engage in physical violence against them. Ultimately, they inspire some of the darkest expressions of our inhumanity toward others: slavery, segregation, even genocide.

In another sense, however, Lapshyn's crude racism is a misleading example with which to open this chapter. As you will see, it simplifies the nature of prejudice, particularly as it has evolved and mutated in modern times. It also distances us ('normal people') from those who are 'truly prejudiced'. We can look in horror, perhaps even incomprehension, at the murder of an innocent grandfather, while leaving comfortably uninspected how prejudices shape our own psychology and everyday patterns of behaviour. In short, it confirms our membership of what Billig (1988, p. 99) once called 'the moral community of the unprejudiced'. We are not, after all, like Pavlo Lapshyn.

By the time you have completed this chapter, you should have a richer understanding of the nature of prejudice and how it relates to 'ordinary' human psychology and behaviour, including your own. The vast majority of us are indeed not like Pavlo Lapshyn. We would not murder someone simply because of the colour of their skin, their religious beliefs, or some other superficial marker of group differences. Nor, however, do we stand completely apart from the pattern of thoughts and feelings that drove Lapshyn to attack Mohammed Saleem. The history of research on prejudice does not afford any of us this kind of complacency.

Prejudice
Prejudice is the negative evaluation of members of other social groups.

The chapter opens by defining the concept of **prejudice** and sketching the historical development of the field. It traces shifts over time in how prejudice has been investigated and highlights the concept's importance for understanding both mundane and extreme forms of discrimination. It then discusses a number of psychological explanations of prejudice, addressing directly the question: *Why don't we like one another?* It also discusses what such theories reveal about how to reduce prejudice in order to promote social change, using research on intergroup contact and desegregation as an example. The chapter concludes on a critical note, assessing some potential limitations of work on prejudice and its reduction.

Learning outcomes

On completing this chapter you should:

- have an understanding of the concept of prejudice
- have an understanding of some key psychological studies and explanations of prejudice
- have knowledge of some of the main methods used to study prejudice
- be able to discuss and evaluate the role of intergroup contact in reducing prejudice.

2 The concept of prejudice and its historical significance

The concept of prejudice originally denoted a general distinction between rational thought, based on logic and evidence, and irrational thought, based on religious dogma or superstition (Billig, 1988). It was a product of the liberal enlightenment that swept Europe in the eighteenth century. When it entered social science parlance in the early years of the twentieth century, however, the concept acquired a narrower meaning. 'Prejudice' came to refer more specifically to the dislike of members of other groups purely on the basis that they belonged to such groups. In his classic early text, *The Nature of Prejudice*, the American psychologist Gordon Allport (1954) introduced this narrower conception via a series of anecdotes, including the following (imagined) conversation between 'Mr X' and 'Mr Y' about the 'trouble with Jews'.

> Mr X: The trouble with Jews is that they only take care of their own group.
>
> Mr Y: But the record of the Community Chest campaign shows that they give more generously, in proportion to their numbers, to the general charities of the community than do non-Jews.
>
> Mr X: That shows they are always trying to buy favour and intrude into Christian affairs. They think of nothing but money; that is why there are so many Jewish bankers.
>
> Mr Y: But a recent study shows that the percentage of Jews in the banking business is negligible, far smaller than the percentage of non-Jews.
>
> Mr X: That's just it; they don't go for respectable businesses; they are only in the movie business or run nightclubs.

As this exchange indicates, Allport's definition of prejudice emphasised two key features: its irrationality and its negativity. The *irrationality* of prejudice is captured by Mr X's commitment to his stereotypes about Jews, even in the face of evidence that directly contradicts those beliefs. He simply cannot accept that their actual behaviour disproves that Jews 'think of nothing but money'. He resists and manoeuvres around the evidence presented by Mr Y. The *negativity* of prejudice is captured in the derogatory nature of Mr X's beliefs, which convey the idea that Jews are money-grubbing, intrusive into other groups' affairs, and engaged in dodgy businesses. It is, of course, possible to be prejudiced *in favour of* others, for instance to see one's children as little rays of sunshine who can do no wrong. However, the term is now firmly associated with unfavourable attitudes. Mr X does not like Jews.

These two features were married in Allport's (1954, p. 9) formal definition of prejudice as 'an antipathy based upon a faulty and inflexible generalisation.' Note that this definition allowed for the possibility that we can react negatively towards others *without* harbouring prejudice towards them. For Allport, negative reactions qualified as prejudice only when they were based in delusion, bias and disregard for the facts of social reality. Thus, to adapt another of his anecdotes, to shun others because we rightly believe they may be carrying disease is not to display prejudice: it is to display common sense. Although later commentators have sometimes argued that we should treat all negative attitudes towards other groups as instances of prejudice, many still accept Allport's early definition.

In the decades following the publication of Allport's landmark book, prejudice became a core concept within psychological work on intergroup relations, transforming how social problems such as discrimination and inequality were understood. In the early years of the last century, such problems were mainly seen as the outcome of natural group differences and hierarchies (e.g. see Samelson, 1978). It was assumed that some groups are innately inferior and that this is the main source of intergroup tensions. One of the founding figures of psychology, William McDougall, promoted immigration control as a way of restricting contact between white Americans and other groups, asserting that: '...some blends of human sub-races are eugenically admirable and others disastrous' (McDougall, 1918, cited in Richards, 1997, p. 197).

From the 1920s onwards, however, emphasis shifted away from the study of group differences (e.g. in intelligence) and psychologists became increasingly concerned with the problem of intergroup prejudice. This shift in emphasis had a radical impact on the field. Perhaps most importantly, it reversed the target of research on intergroup relations. The causes of conflict and discrimination were no longer attributed to the psychological inferiorities of the historically disadvantaged; instead, they were attributed to the bigotry of the historically advantaged. As Montagu (1949, p. 176) proclaimed in an early paper: 'It is the discriminators, not the discriminated, the prejudiced, not those against whom prejudice is exhibited, who are the problem.'

Understanding the underlying causes of this problem has preoccupied psychologists for several decades, and it will preoccupy us for the rest of this chapter. To begin with, however, it is worth reminding ourselves why it is important. To conclude, this section will therefore consider an example of research on the effects of prejudice in one arena of social life.

2.1 An opening example: who would you shoot?

On 5 February 1999, four policemen entered the Bronx in New York, searching for a suspected rapist. Around 12:45 a.m. they saw Amadou Diallo (Figure 4.2), a 22-year-old West African immigrant, standing in the doorway of a building, and thought that he matched the suspect's description. They ordered him to stand still. However, when he allegedly moved his hand and attempted to retreat into the building, they shot him 19 times, firing a total of 41 shots. The officers realised their mistake and one of them, Sean Carroll, held Diallo's hand as he died. Although they were acquitted of all charges in the ensuing court case, the event was widely portrayed as an example of racism in the local police force and sparked anti-police demonstrations. Expressing his outrage at the shooting, former New York Mayor David Dinkins stated: 'This will send the wrong message to those members of the Street Crime Unit who walk around saying, "We own the night"' (Fritsch, 2000).

Figure 4.2 Amadou Diallo

The officers involved in this tragedy did not mean to shoot an unarmed suspect, but would Diallo have been gunned down if he was white? In this type of situation, of course, it is always difficult to disentangle the role of the suspect's race from other explanations for what happened. Many factors could have affected the officers' behaviour that night, including the description of the suspect they had been given, how Diallo stood and moved, and their previous experiences working in the Bronx. How can we know that race exerted an influence above and beyond these factors?

Troubled by the Diallo case, Correll et al. (2002) conducted a programme of experimental research designed to address this question. In one of their studies, for example, participants were asked to make 'shoot/no-shoot' decisions in a video-game simulation. They were shown a series of images in which both armed and unarmed suspects appeared in a range of situations and background scenes (see Figure 4.3) and instructed to take a shoot/no-shoot decision as quickly and accurately as possible.

Figure 4.3 Who would you shoot?
(Source: Correll et al., 2002)

Correll et al. (2002) found a consistent racial bias in decision making. Participants were quicker and more accurate when reacting to an armed black male suspect than when reacting to an armed white male suspect.

Conversely, they were quicker and more accurate when reacting to an unarmed white male suspect than when reacting to an unarmed black male suspect (see Figure 4.4). Diallo fell into the latter category and became, in the cold language of cognitive science, a *false positive* – someone wrongly presumed to be armed and thus shot.

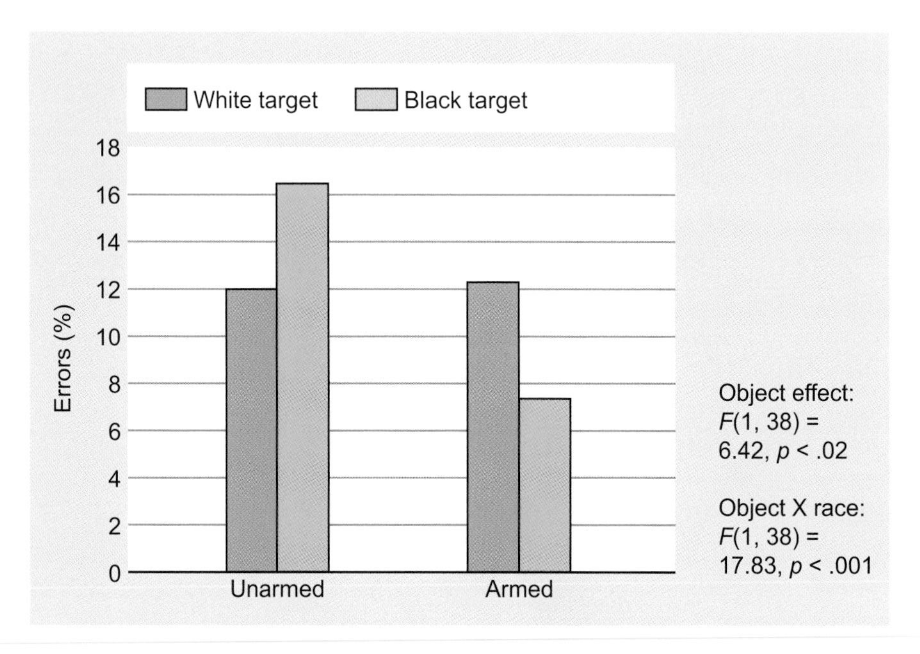

Figure 4.4 Shooter racial bias in accuracy rates in the shoot/no-shoot paradigm (based on Correll et al., 2002)

> ### Pause for thought
>
> Are you convinced by Correll et al.'s (2002) work?
>
> What reservations might you have about generalising their results to actual officer-involved shootings?
>
> What kinds of factors that might play a role in real-life shootings are excluded from, for example, video simulations?

Correll et al. (2002) are themselves cautious about overstating the implications of their findings for understanding what happens during actual police shootings. They acknowledge that numerous contextual and personal variables may shape how officers act in real-life situations, which are difficult to recreate in a laboratory situation (e.g. not least a genuine fear of being shot oneself). Even so, their work allows us to glimpse how racial and other biases may affect decision making in forensic contexts. Their results have now been replicated in over 20 studies. Interestingly, they have been confirmed not only in the responses of white college students, but also among black college students and trained police officers. For the latter group, race of suspect seems to affect the speed more than the accuracy of response (c.f. Correll et al., 2007).

2.2 Summary

This section has introduced the concept of prejudice and discussed its emergence and significance within psychology. It has also illustrated the potential consequences of prejudice in the real world, exemplifying how it may affect decision making in legal and forensic contexts. The next section provides an overview of some key phases in the historical development of the field.

3 Three phases in the development of prejudice research

Prejudice research has developed through three distinct phases (Dovidio, 2001). This section will illustrate and discuss each of these phases, and show not only how the field has evolved methodologically and conceptually, but also how its core image of the 'prejudiced person' has changed over time. The section ends with the suggestion that prejudice research may be entering a fourth phase, focused on the social neuroscience of prejudice. Certainly, growing numbers of psychologists are now crossing disciplinary boundaries to take advantage of developments in neurology and evolutionary biology, as well as brain-imaging technologies such as functional magnetic resonance imaging (fMRI) and **electronencephalography (EEG)**.

Electronencephalography (EEG)
A technique used to explore brain activity by measuring electrical fluctuations along the scalp that arise as a result of neural processes.

3.1 Prejudice as psychopathology

The early phase of prejudice research unfolded under the shadow of the Second World War and was influenced by the (understandable) assumption that there must have been something wrong with those who participated in its atrocities (e.g. working in Nazi death camps). These people were surely aberrations, individuals whose thoughts and feelings were beyond the threshold of ordinary human psychology.

The work of Adorno et al. (1950) on authoritarianism, which you encountered in Brace and Byford (2012), is the most famous example of this approach. Adorno et al. treated prejudice as the product of an abnormal personality that results from a harsh upbringing. The authoritarian's bigotry, they believed, stems from a perversion of the normal course of psychological development, resulting in a maladjusted way of viewing the social world and relating to others (e.g. an obsession with following conventional rules and a tendency to idealise those in authority). Prejudice was thus seen as a symptom of an underlying personality disorder that leads some individuals to irrationally displace negative feelings and beliefs onto scapegoat groups.

Rokeach (1960) provides another example of this type of approach. Rokeach was interested in how some individuals develop a so-called **'dogmatic personality'**, characterised by rigid thought processes and the absolute conviction that their belief systems are correct.

Dogmatic personality
A personality characterised by simplistic thought processes and beliefs that are held inflexibly and with disregard to evidence.

Activity 4.1 illustrates a method used in one of his classic studies (Rokeach, 1948). Try to complete the task yourself.

Activity 4.1: Rokeach's water bottle task

1. Imagine you are given three bottles with capacities of 43 pints, 64 pints and 5 pints. Use these bottles to obtain a measure of exactly 11 pints of water.
2. Now, imagine you are given bottles with capacities of 45 pints, 98 pints and 7 pints. Use these bottles to obtain a measure of exactly 39 pints of water.
3. Next, imagine you are given bottles with capacities of 49 pints, 23 pints and 3 pints. Use these bottles to obtain a measure of exactly 20 pints of water.

These problems can be solved in a number of ways. As you may have worked out, the best solution for the first two problems follows the same basic steps. In problem 1, you should fill the 64-pint bottle with water; then withdraw water using the 43-pint bottle to leave 21 pints; and finally, using the 5-pint bottle, withdraw 5 pints twice to leave exactly 11 pints. The same kind of procedure is also the best solution for problem 2. However, problem 3 has a much simpler solution. Can you see it?

Rokeach (1948) presented his participants with a sequence of such problems. He found that people high in prejudice tended to stick to the (mentally) 'set' solution for longer than people low in prejudice. That is, they tended to persevere with solutions that worked early in a sequence of problems and to be more 'closed minded' to alternative solutions. Such evidence led him to formulate his 'dogmatic personality' theory of the prejudiced person, which proposes that prejudice arises from rigid forms of cognition that are rooted in the individual's personality development.

3.2 Prejudice and the 'normality of prejudgement'

Research conducted in the first wave of prejudice research treated prejudice as an aberration of normal human psychology, proposing a 'rotten apple' (Henriques, 1984) perspective on the problem. In many ways this is a comforting perspective because it allows most of us to divorce our own behaviour from problems such as racism, sexism or xenophobia. Authoritarians and dogmatists may walk among us, but they are not of us. They are the Nazis, Fascists, rednecks, and other bogeymen of populist theories of bigotry. They are the Pavlo Lapshyns of this world. Since the 1970s, however, research on the cognitive foundations of prejudice has challenged this reassuring assumption. It has shown that prejudice is as much a product of 'normal' as it is of 'abnormal' thought processes. In this sense, Fiske (2005) has written of the 'normality of prejudgement'.

Consider, as a simple example, the act of social categorisation. In our everyday lives, we are constantly putting the individuals that we encounter into categories. Indeed, this process is vital – many psychologists would argue *necessary* – if we are to act effectively in the world. Imagine inhabiting a world in which each person we encounter was classified only as an unique individual and not, say, as a shop assistant, teacher, child, doctor, firefighter, neighbour, and so on. That world would be difficult to live in for at least two reasons. First, social categories allow us to make our lives predictable and meaningful and to plan our actions accordingly. We know, for instance, that the woman who is standing at the roadside holding a large lollipop-shaped object is likely to help our children to cross that road. This is a helpful thing to know. Second, categories allow us to filter and organise, and thus render manageable, the massive volume of social information that bombards us each day. Even the most basic activities would become enormously effortful without them. Consider how we would shop without categories such as 'shopper' or 'sales assistant'. How would we cope?

The simple answer is: with great difficulty. We rely on categorisation as a basic psychological tool that allows us to be human beings in the world. The problem is that social categorisation comes at a cost, as Tajfel and Wilkes (1963) illustrated in a classic study. They asked participants to estimate the lengths of various lines that were presented as either grouped or ungrouped (Figure 4.5). Although their study focused on our perception of the physical world, they saw its potential implications for intergroup perception. Just as categorisation distorts our judgements of physical reality (e.g. of differences between lengths of lines), they surmised, so too it distorts our judgements of social reality (e.g. of differences between the social characteristics of people).

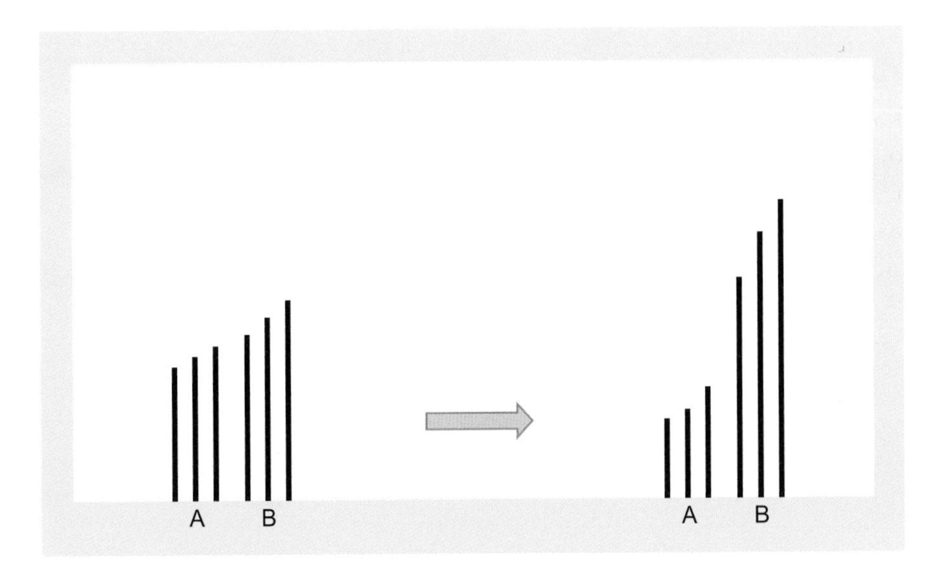

Figure 4.5 How categorisation affects perceptual judgement. Tajfel and Wilkes found that this categorisation produced an accentuation effect in which the mere act of grouping individual elements led participants to exaggerate differences between categories and to underestimate differences within categories

Tajfel and Wilkes's study anticipated a flood of research on how prejudice arises as the by-product of ordinary thought processes. For instance, research on the so-called 'cognitive miser' theory of stereotyping (Fiske and Taylor, 1991) showed how basic 'cognitive mechanisms' can 'lay the foundation for the development of a stereotype belief system' (Hamilton and Trolier, 1986, p. 134). By classifying ourselves and others into categories (e.g. gender, race, religion, occupation) and then attributing category members with shared characteristics (stereotypes), we are able to store and recall information about them more efficiently. We can 'free up' the mental resources required to perform the many other cognitive tasks of everyday life. For this reason, arguably, we rely on stereotypes most heavily when we are 'cognitively busy' and our information processing capacity is under strain (e.g. Crisp et al., 2004). Unfortunately, this normal process of human information processing also produces the kinds of 'faulty generalisations' that are the hallmark of prejudiced thinking. It encourages us to exaggerate group differences and to overlook the complexity and individuality of other people. Moreover, once established as part of our basic cognitive architecture, stereotypes often prove difficult to change. When we encounter individual members who disconfirm a group stereotype, for instance, we tend to treat them as 'exceptions to the rule' rather than adjusting our category representation in light of new information (Richards and Hewstone, 2001).

3.3 Prejudice as an implicit, aversive reaction

Explicit prejudice
An overt, consciously held, negative response towards members of other groups.

The third phase of prejudice research has increasingly emphasised its subtle, often unconscious, nature. Although so-called blatant or **explicit prejudice** is still alive and well (Pettigrew and Meertens, 1995), recent research suggests that this is not its only – or even characteristic – form in many contexts.

The message of this 'third phase' has been summarised in *Blindspot: Hidden Biases of Good People*, a book written by Mahzarin Banajii and Anthony Greenwald (2013). Banajii and Greenwald hold that many of us carry *hidden biases* towards members of other groups. Because we are constantly learning to make implicit, emotionally charged associations between concepts, they argue, we are also learning to be prejudiced in ways we aren't always able to acknowledge. Much of this process occurs, as it were, behind our own backs: it is the legacy of growing up in societies where such associations are subtly communicated all around us (e.g. in popular media, the concept 'black' is regularly associated with the concept 'threat'). We may think we can step outside it, but it leaves a lingering trace in the form of 'blind spots' that then shape our reactions to others (e.g. see Box 4.1).

Box 4.1 Facing prejudice

Hugenberg and Bodenhausen (2003) studied the relationship between implicit prejudice and perceptions of facial threat. White participants watched video images of black and white faces 'morphing' from angry to happy (see Figure 4.6). The experiment measured the time taken to detect the offset of anger (response latency). Results showed that participants high in implicit prejudice viewed anger as lingering longer on black faces than participants low in implicit prejudice.

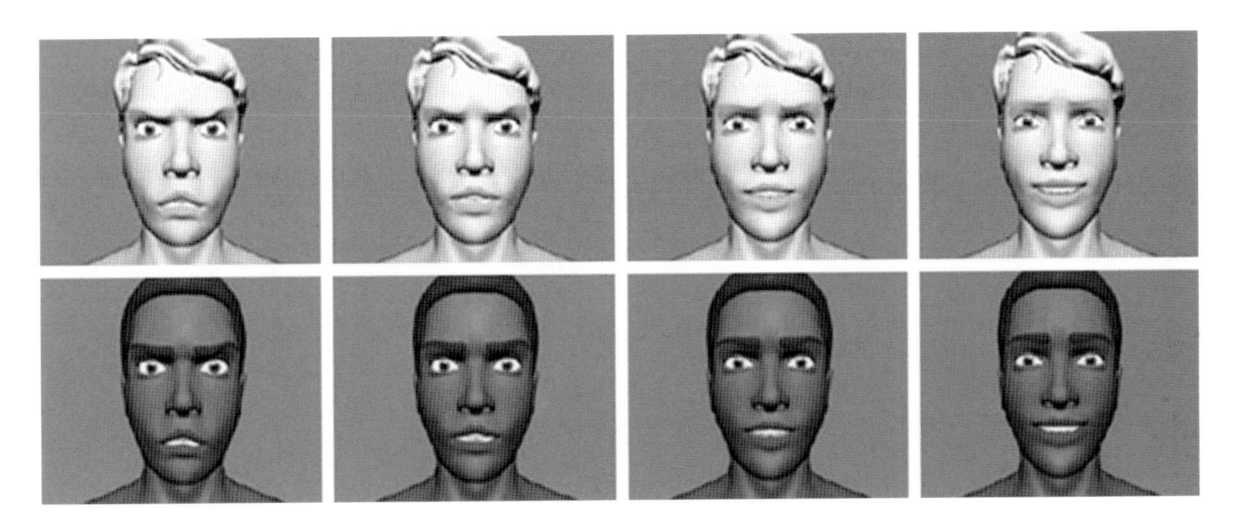

Figure 4.6 Faces 'morphing' from angry to happy

The third phase of research on prejudice has made two main contributions. First, it has generated a sophisticated suite of new methods for revealing **implicit prejudices**. Traditionally, psychologists have measured prejudice using self-report measures (e.g. by having individuals fill in questionnaires), which tap responses that are consciously held and expressed. In recent years, however, they have begun to use methods that tap responses that operate largely outside of conscious awareness. Examples include the implicit association test and the implicit relational assessment procedure. Alternatively, they have exploited techniques for measuring how reactions to others 'leak out' through subtle non-verbal behaviours or through physiological and neurological indicators that are difficult to control. For example, fMRI can detect reactions of fear occurring at a neurological level, which are revealed via patterns of brain activation.

Implicit prejudices
Negative responses towards members of other groups that operate outside of the individual's conscious awareness or intention.

Second, this third phase has generated new theories of the prejudiced person, such as Dovidio and Gaertner's (2004) **aversive racism theory**. Dovidio and Gaertner argue that aversive racists are types of individuals who consciously and sincerely sympathise with the victims of injustice. However, lurking beneath these conscious attitudes of tolerance is a more negative set of unconscious attitudes that are expressed in situations when they are involuntarily elicited or when they can be 'rationalised' as fair. Aversive racists are not individuals who simply hide their 'true' attitudes from the world. Rather, they are individuals who have a *divided and ambivalent response* to other groups, made up of a surface attitude of tolerance and a largely non-conscious attitude of intolerance. Both attitudes are 'true', but they are expressed

Aversive racism theory
Aversive racism theory seeks to explain a complex form of modern prejudice in which individuals express egalitarian attitudes towards other members of other ethnic and racial groups, but also, more subtly and indirectly, behave in ways that express negative feelings about such groups (e.g. avoidance of interaction).

in different ways across different contexts. For example, when they meet a black person, aversive racists may be genuinely concerned about treating that person with respect; at the same time, however, they may display non-verbal behaviours that reveal that, at an unconscious level, they find interacting with that person unpleasant and anxiety-provoking (e.g. increased blinking rates and avoidance of eye contact).

3.4 Crossing boundaries: the social neuroscience of prejudice

This final subsection looks at a potential fourth stage in the development of research on prejudice that focuses on its neurological foundations. Over the past decade or so, the concepts and methodologies of social neuroscience have gradually entered the field, and there now exists a growing body of research. Here a single example is considered, drawn from a research programme being conducted by Harris and Fiske. In this brief treatment, it is not possible to convey adequately the technical details of their work; however, it is possible to convey a few of its central themes. By way of introduction, please complete Activity 4.2.

Activity 4.2: Dehumanising others

Look closely at Figure 4.7, an image of a homeless man.

When you look at the image, what do you think and feel?

What kinds of reactions does it invoke?

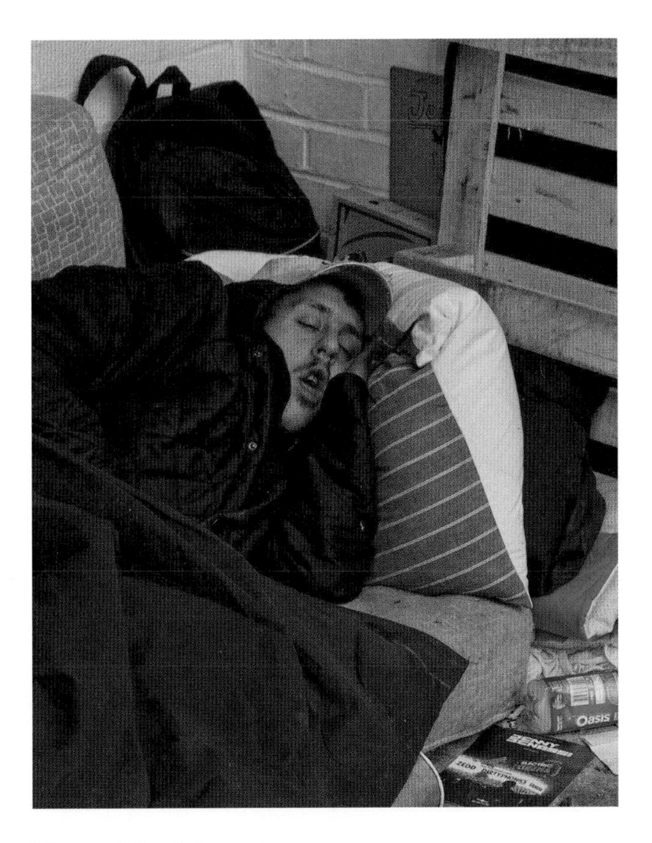

Figure 4.7 A homeless man

Generally, when we look at photos of people, we process information about them in areas of the brain that specialise in social cognition (the psychological processes through which we encode, store and retrieve information about fellow human beings). The location of some of these areas are highlighted in the left part of Figure 4.8, and include the medial prefrontal cortex (mPFC), which is coloured in light grey in this diagram. The mPFC is associated with a variety of forms of social cognition (e.g. moral reasoning), but is particularly central to person perception (the psychological processes through which we form impressions of other people). When we first encounter another person, for example, it tends to be 'switched on' and thus helps us to process information about them.

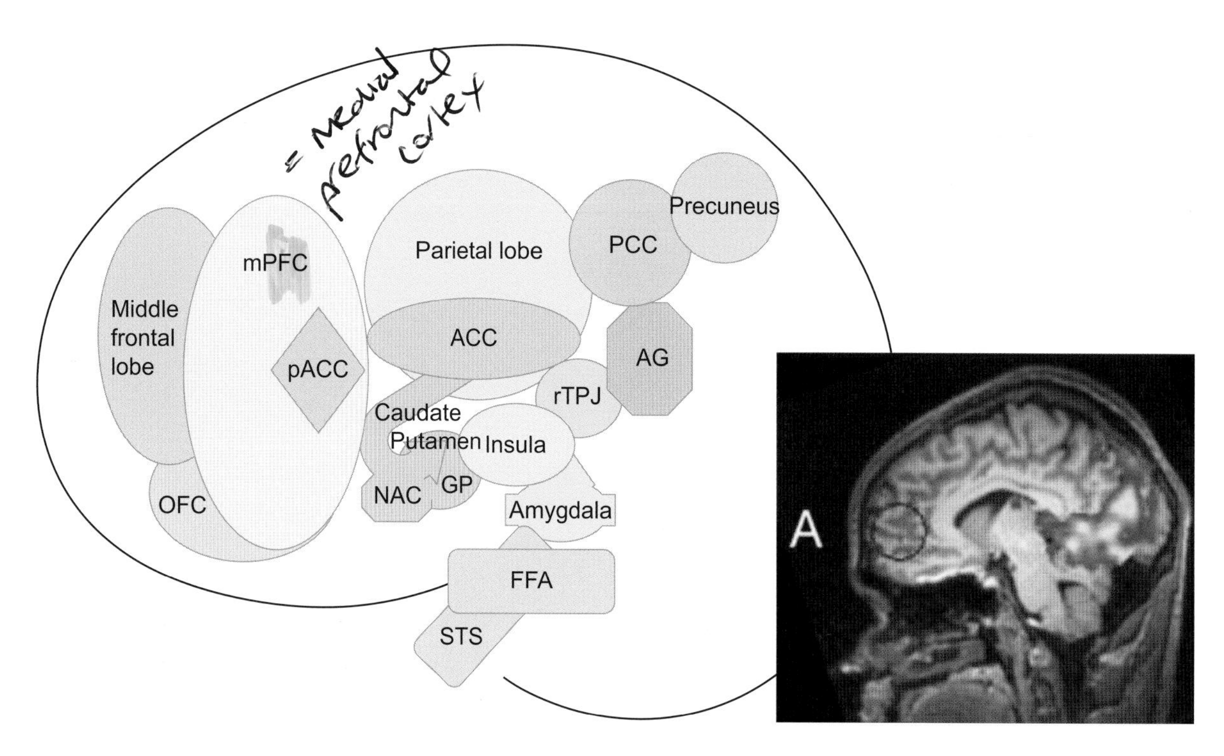

Figure 4.8 Neural regions involved in social cognition
(Source: Harris and Fiske, 2009, p. 196)

The chances are, however, that the mPFC was not fully engaged when you looked at the man in Figure 4.7. If we had used a brain scanning technology to produce an image of how different areas of your brain were activated while you were processing this picture, the resulting pattern would look probably look something like the image produced in the inset labelled A in Figure 4.8. The mPFC is circled in red and, as you can see, there is limited evidence that it has been activated in its normal fashion. Other areas of the brain, indicated in orange, clearly have been activated, however. Why?

In a series of studies, using similar kinds of photographic stimuli and fMRI technology, Harris and Fiske (e.g. 2006) found that certain social groups do not produce the neurological signature of person perception. Instead, these groups are processed mainly by areas of the brain more associated with the perception of non-human objects; i.e. they are literally treated, neurologically, as though they were not, fully, fellow human beings. This reaction is worrying because the 'dehumanisation' of others has been associated with extreme expressions of prejudice (e.g. the willingness to torture, rape or murder other people).

Harris and Fiske also found that such dehumanised groups were attributed with particular kinds of characteristics and evoked particular kinds of emotions. Cognitively, they were evaluated unfavourably on two stereotype dimensions, namely competence (e.g. intelligence) and warmth (e.g. kindness), and this set them apart from other targets of prejudice (e.g. the elderly). Emotionally, they evoked feelings of disgust and were thus, to use Harris and Fiske's phrase, treated as the 'lowest of the low'.

Harris and Fiske's work is intriguing not only because it shows how dehumanised groups may elicit distinctive patterns of psychological and neurological activation, but also because it shows how readily those patterns can be altered. In follow-up research, they found that simply providing humanising information about individuals such as the man in Figure 4.7 (e.g. his food preferences) transformed how participants responded to them neurologically, as evidenced by greater activation of their mPFC brain regions (Harris and Fiske, 2007). This process of (re) humanisation suggests that even 'hard-wired' prejudices are susceptible to social and contextual influences and thus amenable to intervention.

3.5 Summary

This section has discussed several phases in the historical development of prejudice research. As you progressed through it, you may have noticed how the core image of the prejudiced person has shifted over time. In early work, that person was personified by the figure of the right-wing authoritarian, whose prejudices were depicted as a form of mental illness. In the second phase of prejudice research, it was personified by the figure of the individual as 'information processor', with prejudice depicted as the regrettable by-product of ordinary, and otherwise adaptive, thought processes. In the third phase, it was personified by the figure of the 'aversive racist', whose conscious tolerance is offset by a litany of non-conscious biases, anxieties, and blind spots. Emerging work in social neuroscience may signal yet another shift in our core image of the prejudiced individual, as researchers cross the boundaries between psychology and neurology.

4 Three theoretical frameworks

You have already explored the answer to the core question of this chapter, which is: *Why don't we like one another?* Theoretical accounts of the prejudiced personality, the social cognitive basis of stereotyping, aversive racism, and dehumanising patterns of neurological activation undoubtedly contribute part of an answer to this question. Much of the work covered so far, however, is limited by its individualism. By focusing mainly on processes rooted inside the head of the individual, it takes us only so far. Work at this level of analysis, for example, is unable to address some key questions. Why do different forms of prejudice vary in their nature, expression and selection of target groups across different social and historical contexts? How do we account for sudden shifts in such prejudices at a societal scale, such as the rapid decline of anti-Semitism in Germany after the end of the Second World War or of anti-Japanese prejudice in America during the same period? Why do prejudiced feelings, beliefs and behaviours emerge not only within specific individuals, but also, all too commonly, as collectively shared, transmitted and expressed phenomena?

The rest of this section outlines three theoretical frameworks that have attempted to address these kinds of questions, rooted respectively in work on evolutionary psychology, intergroup competition, and social identification.

4.1 An evolutionary psychology perspective

The evolutionary perspective proceeds from a controversial assumption. Prejudice is a biologically evolved response that, however distasteful we may find it from a moral standpoint, has emerged because it has proved adaptive to our survival. To put this point more precisely, prejudiced responses are the legacy of a process of natural selection that occurred many thousands of years ago in response to particular environmental challenges, and they have persisted because they facilitated the successful transmission of genetic material from one human generation to the next. The environmental conditions that shaped this process may be rooted in our species' prehistory, but their traces remain part of our current psychology. We might not like to acknowledge it, evolutionary psychologists argue, but finding members of other groups disgusting, fearing them, avoiding or segregating ourselves from them, or even harbouring murderous desires towards them, does not go against human nature: it is one expression of that nature.

Consider, as an example, the emotion of disgust. The evolutionary perspective on disgust emphasises its role as a disease-prevention mechanism that arose initially as a mechanism for limiting the incorporation of harmful substances (e.g. rotten meat) into our bodies, particularly via our mouths (so-called 'core disgust'). Later it broadened to shape our reactions to contact with other substances (e.g. bodily fluids) that might expose us to disease pathogens (Oaten et al., 2009). As part of this process, we also gradually evolved a tendency to find certain types of individuals disgusting: for example individuals afflicted with visible symptoms of disease; individuals who are dying or already dead; or individuals with deformities, mutations or lesions that remind us of death and disease. In the later stages of this evolutionary process, disgust developed beyond a primitive distaste for putting the wrong things in our mouths: it became a complex moral emotion designed to protect the purity of individuals and the social groups to which they belonged. To adapt Rozin et al.'s (2000, p. 650) elegant phrase: 'A mechanism for avoiding harm for the body' became 'a mechanism for avoiding harm to the soul'. Thus, even people whose practices, beliefs or values were linked only symbolically to contamination and defilement became potentially disgusting.

What is the relevance of this process for understanding negative intergroup reactions? The evolutionary argument goes something like this. In the small hunter–gatherer communities in which we used to live, we evolved immunities to pathogens and parasites in the immediate local environment and to the kinds of diseases that fellow group members were likely to be carrying. However, contact with groups coming from outside this immediate environment posed a greater risk to evolutionary fitness; in fact, it could be deadly. (Consider, for example, how European diseases such as measles, smallpox or even the common cold devastated indigenous peoples in other parts of the world.) Out-group disgust, and related negative behavioural reactions (e.g. avoidance), thus evolved to regulate that risk and limit dangerous forms of exposure.

What evidence supports this kind of argument? First, there are data on the relationship between *perceived* disease vulnerability and intergroup bias. Some studies have established that when individuals feel vulnerable to disease, they also display more negative out-group attitudes (e.g. Navarette and Fessler, 2006). Second, there are data on the effects of *actual* disease vulnerability on such attitudes. For example, when women are in the first trimester of pregnancy – a period when their susceptibility to infections increases – their intergroup biases are elevated (e.g. Navarette et al., 2007). Third, there are data on the specificity of prejudice across different target groups. An evolutionary account would predict that some out-groups are more likely than others to invoke the specific emotional reaction of disgust. This appears to be the case.

Figure 4.9, for instance, presents results from the work of Cottrell and Neuberg (2005) on this topic, depicting the 'emotional profile' of white American prejudice towards three groups: fundamentalist Christians, African Americans and gay men. As you can see, gay men evoked the lowest levels of fear, yet the highest levels of disgust in their study. According to an evolutionary account, this is because the 'threat' they pose is rooted in the disgust-sensitive domain of sexual behaviour, which signals the potential transmission of disease and thus triggers disgust and associated forms of avoidant behaviour. Other groups cue different kinds of threat, triggering different kinds of (evolved) psychological and behavioural reactions. Given the strong cultural association between race and physical violence, for example, the signature reaction of white Americans towards African Americans is not disgust but fear (e.g. see, again, Figure 4.8), and this leads to self-protective responses. Arguably supporting this hypothesis, research shows that such reactions are enhanced under environmental conditions that, in our ancestral past, may have enabled us to avoid successfully the threat of physical attack. For example, they are stronger under conditions of darkness and when out-group targets are male (who generally pose greater physical threat) rather than female (who pose less physical threat) (Neuberg et al., 2010).

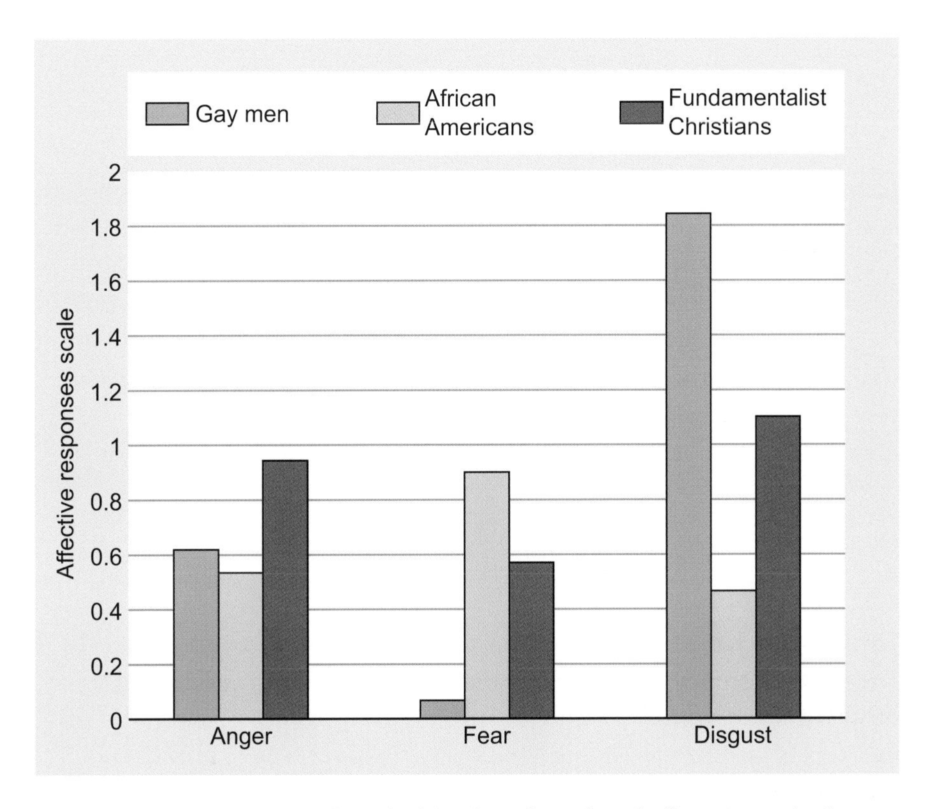

Figure 4.9 Emotional profile of white Americans' prejudices towards three groups

The evolutionary account does not propose a single theory of prejudice. Rather, it offers an overarching framework for understanding how and why different prejudices have evolved, the specific emotional, cognitive and behavioural reactions they entail, the environmental challenges they helped to resolve, and the kinds of environmental and physical cues that elicit them, and so on. Strengths of this framework include its capacity to integrate evidence across a number of different levels of analysis (e.g. historical, cross-cultural, cross-species, environmental and psychological) and to make specific predictions about the kinds of situations that are likely to evoke particular forms of prejudice. Unlike the other frameworks you will consider in this section, moreover, the evolutionary framework is designed to conceptualise the biological bases of prejudiced reactions and is therefore particularly well placed to contribute to the 'fourth' wave of prejudice research. Indeed, as a theory of biological development, evolutionary psychology predicts that our prejudices ultimately have genetic foundations. This need not imply, of course, that they are inflexible or biologically determined. To the contrary, the evolutionary approach predicts considerable variability in the expression of prejudice as it occurs across different environments, types of people, and situations.

The evolutionary approach also has limitations, however. To cite one: it focuses on how current prejudices reflect adaptations that occurred deep in our ancestral past. It thus requires us to make – and evidence – complex inferences about the nature of distant physical environments, the nature of social life there, and how certain responses to contact with out-group members may have conferred evolutionary fitness in response to environmental challenges. Many psychologists prefer to root explanations of prejudice in causes that are more immediate, more tangible and easier to evidence. Work on realistic conflict provides an example.

4.2 A realistic conflict perspective on prejudice

Explaining what first inspired him to understand processes of intergroup conflict and discrimination, Muzafer Sherif noted that as a child it affected him:

> deeply to see each group with a selfless degree of comradeship within its bounds and a corresponding degree of animosity, destructiveness and vindictiveness towards the detested out-group – their behaviour characterised by compassion and prejudice, heights of self-sacrifice and bestial destructiveness.
>
> (Sherif, 1967, p. 9)

Sherif wanted to understand this paradox. He also wanted to produce a theoretical framework that could transform 'the bestial destructiveness' of intergroup relations. Most of his work was produced during the first phase of prejudice research when, as we've seen, social psychologists rooted its causes in abnormal personality development. Sherif felt that this research was guilty of a 'levels of explanation' error. He argued that prejudice – especially prejudice on a collective scale – expresses deeper structural conditions of relations between groups rather than individual-level factors (e.g. high levels of authoritarianism). Change those structural relations, he argued, and you will change the psychology of the individuals who are embedded within them.

Sherif's famous boys' camp studies, which were conducted in the late 1950s and early 1960s, provided the classic demonstration of this idea

(Sherif, 1967). In each of these studies, Sherif divided a sample of boys into two groups, who were then taken away to a 'summer camp', unaware they were about to participate in a field experiment. In the first stage of each study, the groups were segregated and kept unaware of one another's existence. Sherif simply encouraged them to interact with fellow group members, engage in fun activities together (e.g. canoeing), and form a sense of group identity. In the second stage, Sherif brought the groups together and manufactured a relationship of *negative* goal interdependence between them: a specific type of 'zero sum' competition in which one group's victory necessarily comes at the other group's expense. His goal was to explore the effects of this intervention on the boys' social relationships, attitudes and behaviours at the camp.

As he predicted, the intervention had the effect of increasing the boys' sense of in-group solidarity and loyalty. Correspondingly, it created forms of out-group prejudice that had a genuine undercurrent of violence, frequently requiring pacification by Sherif and his team of 'camp counsellors' (mainly psychologists in disguise). The boys formed negative stereotypes of rival groups, segregated themselves from one another, created their own flags and insignia, burned the flags and insignia of the other team, stockpiled weapons, verbally and physically abused one another, and generally behaved in a manner all too reminiscent of real-world conflict.

It was only when Sherif altered the underlying nature of relations between the groups that this pattern began to abate. In the third stage of his study, he put the teams of boys into situations where they had to cooperate to achieve mutually desired goals (establishing *positive* goal interdependence); and he was thus able gradually to change their negative perceptions of one another. Figure 4.10 summarises the key stages of this process and illustrates the basic concepts of what became known as realistic conflict theory.

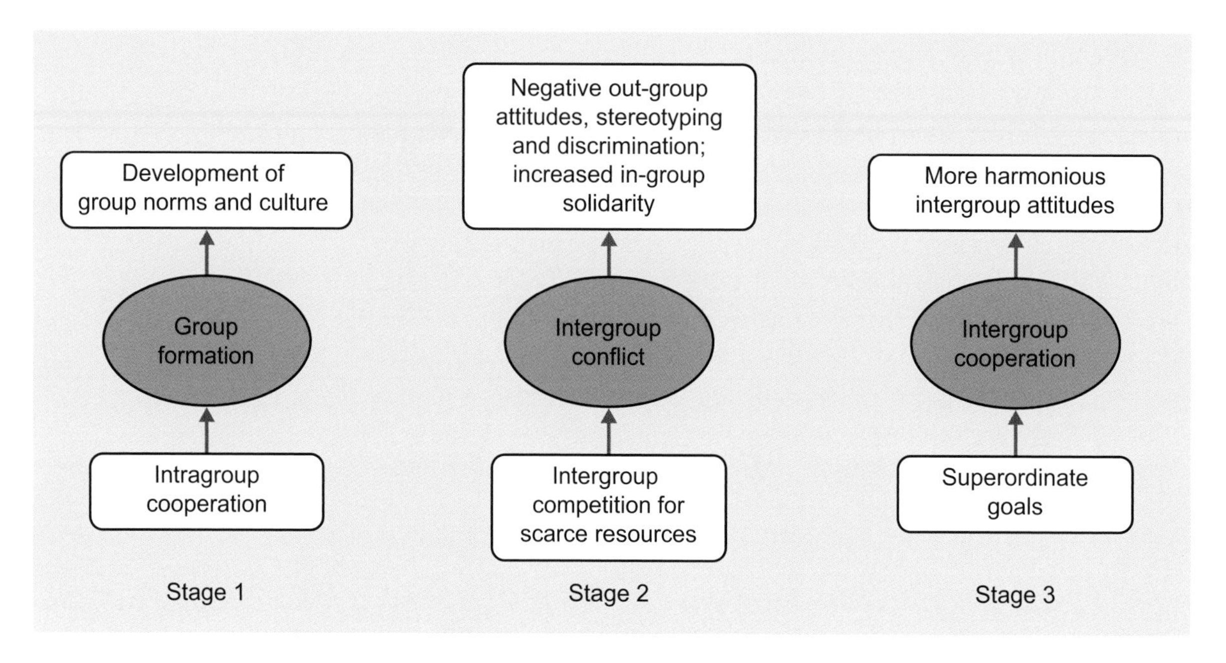

Figure 4.10 A realistic conflict model of intergroup conflict and cooperation

Pause for thought

In selecting participants for their studies, Sherif and his colleagues were careful to screen them for any signs of 'psychopathology', including evidence of heightened levels of prejudice towards others. They were deliberately chosen to be 'normal' children.

Why do you think they used this screening process?

Like many good ideas, the idea that individual prejudice reflects a conflict of interests at an intergroup level is at once simple and obvious. Historically, many conflicts have been waged around a struggle for resources, such as power, wealth and land, and it seems intuitive that these struggles should shape intergroup attitudes. Are any of us surprised to learn, for example, that factory work teams who perceive themselves to be in most direct competition with one another also tend to express higher levels of in-group bias when judging their mutual contributions to a company (Brown et al., 1986)? Or, more grimly, that white-on-black murder rates in the USA are highest in cities where there is greatest economic and political competition between race groups (Jacobs and Wood, 1999)?

According to Sherif and several later commentators, in order to understand these patterns of collective behaviour it is necessary to move beyond analysis of individual psychology. We need to recognise they are a rational response to living in a society where collective 'interests' are organised along intergroup lines. The term 'rational' is used deliberately here. It points to an important distinction between the model of prejudice proposed by work in a Sherifian tradition and the model of prejudice that dominates the rest of psychology. Whereas most psychological research conceives prejudice as an irrational form of 'bias', as you have seen, the realistic conflict tradition emphasises its role in furthering the objective goals of the parties to a conflict. This does not imply that prejudice is morally acceptable, but merely that it has an *instrumental* logic; that is, it expresses a desire to acquire valued resources for the group and reflects 'real' conditions of intergroup competition.

This subsection concludes with an extreme example of the consequences of this process, which echoes Sherif's concern with the 'bestial destructiveness' of groups. In 100 days between April and July in 1994, an estimated 800,000 ethnic Tutsis and moderate Hutus were killed in the Rwandan genocide (Figure 4.11). Killing was conducted both by trained militia and by large numbers of ordinary civilians who often knew their victims. Family members killed other family members, doctors killed their patients, bosses killed their employees and ministers killed members of their own congregation. The speed and scale of the killing and the extent of civilian involvement distinguish Rwandan genocide from similar events.

Figure 4.11 Genocide in Rwanda, 1994

There are many accounts of what happened during these 100 days, and many accounts of why it happened. Jared Diamond (2005) outlines one account in his book *Collapse: How Societies Choose to Fail or Survive*. In this book, Diamond disputes popular explanations of the genocide, which focus, for example, on the role of tribal hatreds between Tutsis and Hutus. He argues that by prioritising such psychological 'symptoms' of the conflict, there is a danger of overlooking the role of wider structural and environmental processes. Rwanda, he points out, is home to more people per square kilometre than any other African country. Much of the population is rural and depends on farming for its livelihood, economy and subsistence. However, this rural population has been growing for decades and in the period preceding the genocide, farmers were being forced to work on smaller and smaller parcels of land. Moreover, that land was of deteriorating quality, and the gap between richer and poorer farmers was increasing. Food shortages and poverty were on the rise. In short, Rwanda was a context of increasing scarcity in which competition for valued resources (e.g. arable land) was becoming ever more intense.

Diamond argues that these environment pressures, and associated competition for resources such as land and food, are central to understanding why the genocide occurred. He points out that land conflicts were increasingly common in the period leading up to the fatal 100 days in 1994. They were resulting not only in inter-ethnic tensions between Hutus and Tutsis, but also in intra-community conflicts, and even conflicts within families. He asks us to consider whether this form of land competition, accentuated by scarcity, did not play as much a role in the genocide as more immediate and obvious factors such as personal prejudices or obedience to political authorities. From a Sherifian perspective, his argument makes sense.

Yet even if we accept that competition is sometimes a *sufficient* condition for the emergence of intergroup prejudice and conflict, is it a *necessary* condition? A potential limitation of the realistic conflict theory is that it deals with only one of several social psychological motivations for prejudice. It may thus be applicable only to a narrow range of contexts; that is, contexts characterised by objective relations of zero sum competition between groups.

4.3 A social identity perspective on prejudice

In the 1970s, Henri Tajfel and John Turner developed the argument about the limits of a realistic conflict model of prejudice, proposing that Sherif's framework did not explain fully the social psychological dynamics of intergroup conflict (Tajfel and Turner, 1986). In a series of experiments, which became known as the **minimal group studies**, they revealed that:

- in-group biases may emerge in the absence of objective relations of competition for material resources
- merely dividing people into different categories is sometimes in itself sufficient to get them to act in ways that are prejudiced
- group members are sometimes more concerned about maximising *status differences* (i.e. choosing ingroup-outgroup reward pairs towards the 'Maximum group difference' end of the scale in Figure 4.12) between their own and other groups than they are about maximising *material rewards* (i.e. choosing reward pairs towards the 'Maximum joint profit' end of the scale in Figure 4.12).

Minimal group studies
A set of studies that demonstrated how even trivial or arbitrary group divisions (e.g. based on art preferences) can be sufficient to create in-group favouritism and discrimination.

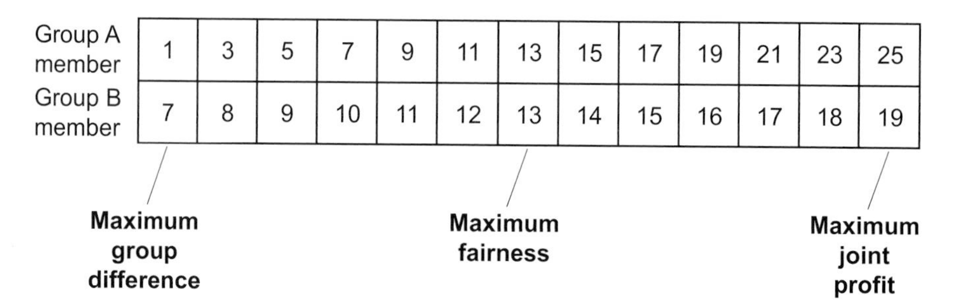

Figure 4.12 The nature of in-group bias in the minimal group studies

Based on such findings, Tajfel and Turner and others argued that objective competition for scarce resources is sufficient but not necessary for intergroup conflict to emerge and a different kind of account is needed to explain conflicts that do not result from material relations of competition. As Hewstone and Greenland (2000, p. 139) later observed: 'many apparently pointless conflicts become more understandable when viewed as, at least in part, attempts to establish, maintain or defend cherished social identities.'

Social identity theory (SIT) was born (see also Chapters 2 and 3). As its name suggests, this theory holds that individuals define themselves in terms of their identification with social groups and that this process has important implications for understanding intergroup relations. As well as being unique personalities, our sense of self derives from our membership of social categories such as community, ethnicity, gender, religion and nationality. When we identify with such categories, we psychologically 'take on board' their defining stereotypes in order to achieve a sense of who we are. Crucially, in any given context, our social identities are formed not in isolation but *relationally*. In Northern Ireland, for instance, the identity 'Catholic' often acquires meaning via its comparative contrast with the identity 'Protestant'. Of course, this process of social comparison does not merely involve a disinterested weighing up of information about who 'we' and 'they' are. Because social identities have emotional implications for our sense of worth, we are generally motivated to emphasise the qualities that positively distinguish 'us' from 'them' (e.g. see Cairns et al., 1995). All too easily this process of differentiation tips over into intergroup prejudice.

When acting in terms of our social identities, our perceptions of social reality also tend to become *depersonalised*. That is, we see ourselves and others not as unique individuals but as representatives of our groups. We interpret the meaning of events through the lens of this group-based identity and in ways that exaggerate group differences. Moreover, the more strongly we identify with the in-group, the more strongly we respond in this kind of 'depersonalised' fashion. Figure 4.13, for instance, is taken from a study conducted by Sahdra and Ross (2007). The study explored historical memories of Sikh–Hindu violence, two groups with a long history of conflict. Sahdra and Ross used a free recall method in which participants were simply asked to remember and write down past acts of violence involving Sikhs and Hindus, and they also measured how strongly participants identified with their own group. As Figure 4.13 records, they found that participants with high levels of identification tended to remember more atrocities in which the in-group were victims and fewer atrocities in which the out-group were victims. This pattern was not found among individuals who did not identify strongly as group members.

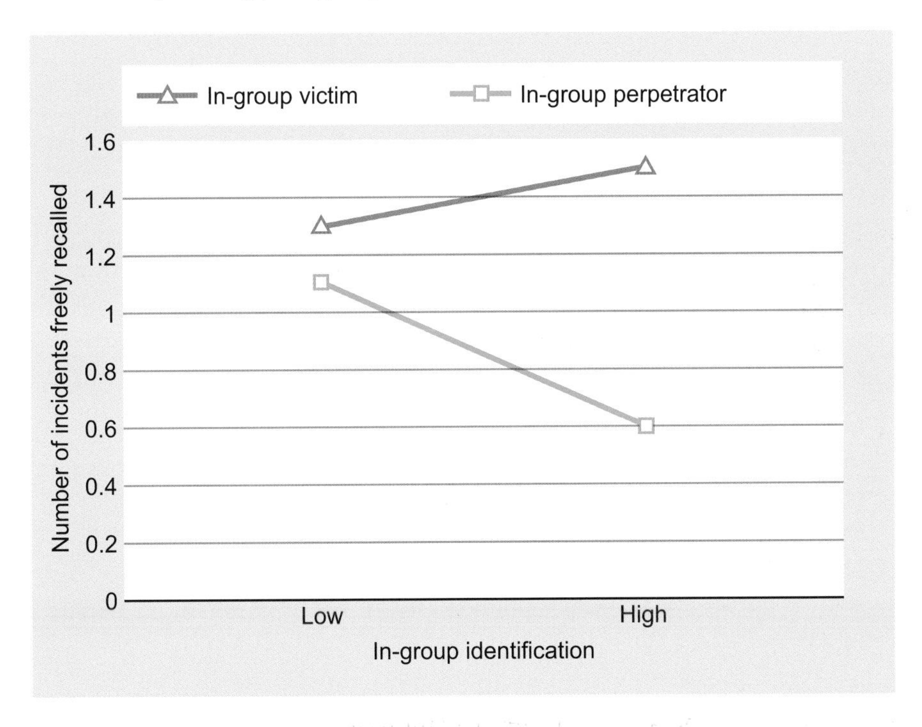

Figure 4.13 Group identification and recall of victim and perpetrator violence

As they developed their theory, Tajfel and Turner (1986) became interested in understanding when and why social identity processes lead to direct conflict between groups. They were particularly interested in relations within hierarchical societies, which are marked by clear status differences. In such societies, they argued, negative social comparisons often have a detrimental effect on the self-esteem of the subordinate group members, leading them to feel inferior or even worthless. Tajfel and Turner believed that the drive to transform this kind of negative social identity had the capacity to alter the social order, but that subordinate groups would only take direct collective action under certain ideological conditions.

What are these conditions? When subordinate group members perceive the status quo as both *unjust* and *unstable*, then overt conflict with dominant groups becomes more likely. Under such conditions, the drive to create a more positive social identity becomes like a fire under the boiler of social change. It impels subordinate groups to take collective action that is designed not only to achieve equality in a material sense, but also to redefine existing status relations. In order to understand the emergence of conflict in places such as Northern Ireland, Palestine and apartheid South Africa, Tajfel and Turner argued, we must also understand how political struggles there have been driven by a growing sense of the illegitimacy and vulnerability of the social order and a growing refusal to accept negative definitions of what it means to be 'Catholic', 'Arab', or 'black'. In each of these societies, members of low-status social groups came to view their status as unfair, recognised the system could be changed and a better one put in its place, and acted together to challenge directly the status quo.

Pause for thought

It has been suggested that the desire for a more positive group identity may, under certain conditions, lead low-status groups to challenge the status quo. This may bring them into relations of conflict with members of higher-status groups. However, is conflict necessarily a bad thing? Do negative intergroup emotions (e.g. anger at being treated unjustly) serve valuable social functions?

It is worth adding that SIT emerged as part of an attempt to move beyond the individualism of early psychological research and, in this sense, it is similar to work in the Sherifian tradition. However, if the 'need' for a positive group identity is conceived as a psychological universal, rooted in the hearts and minds of individuals, do social identity theorists not ultimately reduce collective behaviour to individual psychology? Moreover, does the universal drive to maintain group distinctiveness mean that prejudice and in-group bias are inevitable? Such criticisms open up a complex series of questions and debates that cannot be unpacked here.

Suffice to say that Tajfel (1981) insisted that intergroup relations cannot be understood outside their social context. Just as we do not as individuals invent, for example, what it means to be 'Irish' or 'male' or 'white', so too the contextual processes that generate, channel or reduce intergroup conflict are not reducible to individual psychology.

4.4 Summary

This section has discussed three frameworks for explaining intergroup prejudice and conflict, rooted in work on evolutionary psychology, realistic competition, and social identification. These frameworks offer different perspectives on the problem: *Why don't we like one another?* However, you should not necessarily view them as incompatible with each other. Instead, I hope to have given you sufficient information to think critically about the potential strengths and limits of each framework and to think imaginatively about how they might be compared or contrasted.

5 Reducing prejudice: intergroup contact and social change

Over the long history of prejudice research, psychologists have devised numerous interventions to reduce prejudice and get us to have nicer thoughts and warmer feelings about one another. Such interventions are among the most important applied contributions of psychology: a powerful example of how the discipline can promote a better society. Examples include work on cooperative learning, common identification, re-education, empathy arousal and, perhaps most important, intergroup contact, which is the focus of this section.

5.1 Getting to know you: the 'contact hypothesis'

Contact hypothesis
The hypothesis that positive interaction between members of different groups tends to reduce intergroup prejudice.

The **contact hypothesis** (Allport, 1954) is one of psychology's most influential ideas about how to build a more tolerant society, and it has also generated an extensive literature in companion disciplines such as sociology. Early research focused mainly on race relations unfolding under conditions of institutional desegregation in employment, education, housing and the military (see Activity 4.3). Later work indicated that contact had the potential to improve a wider range of types of intergroup relations, including relations between Catholics and Protestants, Arabs and Jews, gays and heterosexuals, people with and without HIV/Aids, and the young and the elderly (Pettigrew and Tropp, 2011). More recently, studies have shown that even indirect forms of contact (e.g. having friends who have out-group friends) can improve our intergroup attitudes (Dovidio et al., 2011).

Activity 4.3: The desegregation of the American infantry during the Second World War

Star et al.'s (1958) study of white soldiers' responses to the amalgamation of Negro platoons in infantry companies provides a poignant early example of research on contact and desegregation. They studied the experiences of white soldiers brought together with their 'Negro' counterparts in order to fight in a war in which many of them would die (the Second World War). One of the questions they asked concerned soldiers' attitudes towards the process of racial integration: 'Some army divisions have companies that include both Negro platoons and white platoons. How would you feel about it if your outfit was set up like that?' Figure 4.14 presents their findings.

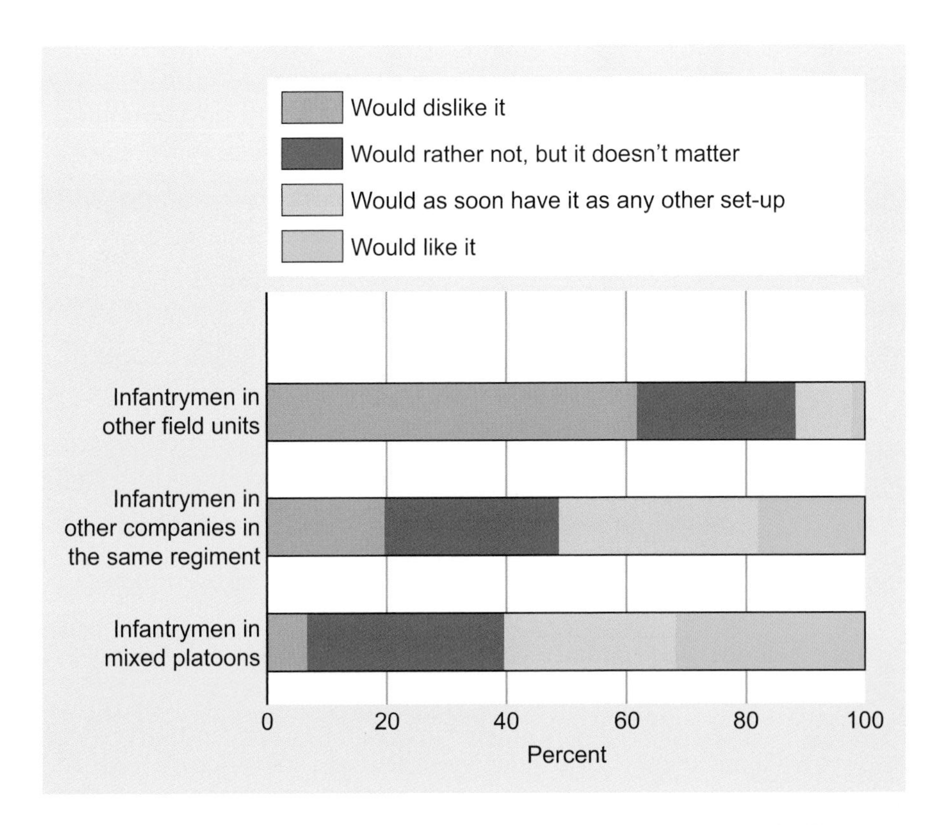

Figure 4.14 Interracial contact and white soldiers' acceptance of military desegregation

Figure 4.14 compares the degree of support for racial desegregation expressed by white infantrymen working in other field units with no black soldiers; white infantrymen working in units that have racially-mixed companies in the same regiment; and white infantrymen fighting in mixed platoons themselves and having regular contact with black soldiers.

What does this figure show? What does it tell us about the relationship between past experiences of interracial contact and acceptance of future racial integration?

The *situational conditions of interaction* between groups, however, are often critical in determining the success of interventions to promote intergroup contact. Indeed, although it is sometimes misrepresented as such, the contact hypothesis does not propose that mere interaction between members of different groups is sufficient to improve relations between them. Its proponents have always recognised that things are more complicated than this. If contact is superficial, marked by competition or unequal status, or lacking institutional support, then it may perpetuate negative stereotypes and feelings about members of another group. Yet if contact is intimate, cooperative, of equal status, and supported by institutional norms and structures, then it may reduce prejudice and dampen the potential for future intergroup conflict.

A great deal of psychological research on the contact hypothesis has explored the role of such ideal conditions for interaction between groups. This research has resulted in a lengthy set of recommendations. For example, contact should ideally:

- be regular and frequent
- occur between individuals who have equal status
- involve a balanced ratio of in-group to out-group members
- have genuine 'acquaintance potential'
- be free from competition
- involve interaction with a 'counter-stereotypic' member of another group
- be organised around cooperation towards the achievement of common goals
- be institutionally supported by authorities.

5.2 Three models for intergroup contact implementation

One problem with this long list of conditions is that it doesn't amount to a coherent explanation of *why* contact works. Initially, positive contact effects were attributed mainly to a vague process of re-education, based on the idea that interaction with others gets rid of (false) stereotypes about them. Recent work has focused on its role in promoting positive emotions such as empathy, while reducing negative emotions such as intergroup anxiety or threat (Pettigrew and Tropp, 2008). The limitations of classic contact theory have also inspired theoretical developments grounded in the social identity theory that was considered in the previous section. Researchers have interpreted the theory's implications in different ways, however.

The decategorisation model: Marilynn Brewer and Norman Miller (1984) have argued that contact works best when it occurs in contexts where group differences are minimised. In such contexts, we may come to know one another as individuals rather than as representatives of social categories. Contact can become personalised, giving us the opportunity for genuine intimacy. Gradually, we can 'attend to information that replaces category identity as the most useful basis for classifying each other' (Brewer and Miller, 1984, p. 288).

The underlying assumption here is that the promotion of group identities is inherently dangerous. It sets in motion processes of social categorisation, comparison and differentiation that lead us to 'depersonalise' ourselves and others and emphasise our differences. In practice, this approach is illustrated by the so-called 'colour blind' approach to integrated education, which is based on minimising references to group differences (e.g. in the school curricula and in school activities) and treating all students as individuals.

The mutual differentiation model: Miles Hewstone and Rupert Brown (1986) have argued that the decategorisation model misinterprets the implications of SIT for understanding contact. In their opinion, it is unrealistic to expect group members to accept the suppression of their collective identities and values. The whole point of SIT, after all, is that group distinctiveness is central to our sense of who we are and what we are worth. Thus, Hewstone and Brown argue that contact is most successful when it is an *intergroup* process in which participants view one another not as individuals but as representatives of their social categories. In practice, this approach translates into a policy of multiculturalism, leading to institutional reforms that favour 'mutual differentiation' – a social climate in which group differences are celebrated as positive phenomena.

This approach is currently applied in many schools in the UK. When schoolchildren are invited to learn and celebrate the history, literature, religious practices or food of another culture, for instance, they are being encouraged to both recognise and 'celebrate their differences'. Figure 4.15 shows schoolchildren from Bradford celebrating intergroup differences. Their school is part of an initiative known as the Linking Schools Project, organised by the Schools Linking Network, which is designed to give school pupils living in ethnically divided cities the opportunity to interact with one another.

Figure 4.15 Celebrating intergroup differences, Bradford

The danger of this approach is that by underlining the importance of groups, even in a sympathetic fashion, we may cue struggles over the comparative value of groups. Mutual differentiation may easily slide into prejudice.

The common identity model: if it is sometimes difficult to break down social divisions, then perhaps some reorganisation of group boundaries might be possible. This idea underlies Gaertner and Dovidio's (2000) model, which holds that contact works best when it promotes a common in-group identity, encouraging members of different sub-groups to see one another as members of a shared in-group. Instead of reducing the importance of group identification, then, re-categorisation attempts to shift category boundaries in the direction of greater inclusiveness, a technique that seems to work in some contexts. Experimental and field studies have confirmed that situations that generate representations of 'we' (rather than 'us' and 'them') can indeed decrease prejudice.

To continue our example of integrated education, the common identity model might seek in practice to build a collective sense of 'we' within a given school, emphasising students' membership of a common category. This need not involve them 'giving up' their other social identities. However, in contexts where the social world beyond the school gates remains deeply divided, the unifying influence of common identities may be fragile and short-lived. The resurgence of sub-group identities and their associated prejudices lingers as a constant threat.

Pause for thought

There are currently several government initiatives to reduce ethnic and racial segregation in the British education system. For example, in towns in the north-west of England, local government has created a number of 'super-schools', designed to provide a more integrated experience of education. Based on the research and theory covered in this section, what measures would you take in order to make such initiatives successful? Under what kinds of conditions would this form of desegregation be most likely, for instance, to improve relations between white and Asian children in historically divided cities such as Burnley, Bradford or Oldham?

5.3 Critical reflections

The contact hypothesis is one of the most successful and long-lived ideas in the history of social psychology. Work in the field has informed public policy in many societies, including the UK. However, the contact hypothesis has also been criticised.

Is the contact hypothesis idealistic? Much psychological research has involved a search for the ideal conditions of intergroup contact, the circumstances under which prejudice is reduced most effectively. As these conditions seldom exist in pure form in the real world, this research has focused on specialised situations in which ideal contact can be easily manufactured, at least for a short period of time (e.g. in the laboratory). The danger here is that we may ultimately produce knowledge that conceals the starker realities of everyday interactions between members of different groups and fails to explain how optimal conditions might be established in the everyday circumstances in which the majority of contact occurs (Dixon et al., 2005).

Optimism about the applied value of the contact hypothesis, for example, must be tempered by an inconvenient truth. In many societies, segregation remains prevalent. Formal interventions to promote desegregation are often offset by informal practices of (re) segregation that maintain intergroup divisions. Relations in many supposedly desegregated contexts such as university lecture theatres, school playgrounds and public spaces may reproduce racial segregation at a micro-interactional scale (see Figure 4.16). For this reason, Pettigrew and Tropp (2011) have called for a better understanding of the so-called 'leading a horse to water' problem. We now know a lot about the nature and consequences of contact between groups and about the conditions under which it facilitates prejudice reduction. We know far less about why, even in the face of institutional pressures to integrate, individuals continue to act in ways that reproduce segregation.

Figure 4.16 Mapping the micro-ecology of segregation on a South African beach. Each red circle = one black person; each blue circle = one white person; each yellow dot = one Indian person; each orange dot = one Coloured person. See Dixon and Durrheim (2003) for a more detailed discussion

Pause for thought

Figure 4.16 depicts where and with whom members of different groups chose to sit on a 'desegregated' beach in post-apartheid South Africa. How might this pattern be relevant to understanding and solving the problem of increasing intergroup contact?

Can interpersonal contact change intergroup relations and perceptions?
Other critics have suggested that the effects of contact on interpersonal relations may not generalise to shape *intergroup* relations, a problem that has been extensively researched in the contact literature. Contact, for example, often leads people to regard particular individuals as 'exceptions to the rule' rather than leading them to

abandon their wider stereotype systems. Other research suggests that contact effects may not generalise beyond the immediate situation in which interaction occurs. For instance, in an oft-cited study of interactions between black and white miners, Minard (1952) found that intergroup relations were positive when miners were working together underground; however, on returning above ground status differences and patterns of racial segregation were quickly re-established.

A related criticism has highlighted a more fundamental limitation of the contact hypothesis. What if the processes that govern conflict between groups are relatively independent of the effects of interactions between individuals? What if, for example, such processes are grounded in wider structural relations of realistic competition (e.g. competition for housing and jobs within a local economy)? This, of course, is one interpretation of the implications of Sherif's work. Although it may be possible to establish cooperative relations within a particular institution (e.g. a school), will such contact have meaningful consequences if relations beyond this immediate situation are characterised by 'realistic' conflict?

5.4 Summary

The contact hypothesis is one psychological approach to prejudice reduction. In their landmark review, Pettigrew and Tropp (2006) distilled over 70 years of evidence into a simple, optimistic message: contact reduces prejudice and it is most effective when it occurs under favourable conditions (e.g. equality of status). There are a number of theories of how and why contact works, including models based on processes of decategorisation, mutual differentiation and common identification. Some critics have suggested that researchers need to think more carefully about how the ideal conditions for contact might be implemented in the real world. They have also questioned whether or not interpersonal interactions can transform intergroup relations and perceptions.

6 Concluding thoughts

This chapter has ended a long way from the opening example of the seemingly mindless brutality of Pavlo Lapshyn. During its course, you have journeyed through the history of different phases of research on intergroup prejudice, examined the complex ways in which prejudice manifests and with what consequences, and encountered a range of methodologies, theories, and studies in the field. You have also seen how psychologists have attempted to develop interventions to reduce prejudice, taking research on the contact hypothesis as an example. Along the way, you should have developed a richer understanding of this area of psychological research and, as importantly, have begun to think critically about what it can contribute to our understanding of: *Why don't we like one another?*

In conclusion, I want to open up two questions that challenge the chapter's overall frame of reference:

- Are negative emotions always the problem?
- Is getting us to like one another more always the solution?

In raising these questions, I will not attempt to provide definitive answers. Rather, I will simply invite you to think about recent debates that are complicating the core idea on which this chapter is based.

6.1 Are negative emotions always the problem?

Men like women. Actually, they often like them rather a lot. They crave their attention, they form deep relationships with them – of friendship, romantic love and familial attachment – they marry and settle down with them, and they spend a lot of their adult lives with them. Even when those relationships fail (or don't get going in the first place), a lot of men spend a lot of their time wishing they could find a woman to love, cherish, be friends with, or simply talk to. Moreover, research shows that men have generally positive intergroup attitudes towards women as a social group. In point of fact, they like them more than they like men, a finding sometimes called the 'women are wonderful' effect (Eagly and Mladinic, 1989).

Yet a lot of evidence suggests that men also discriminate against women. They allow them to participate in relations that are unequal or degrading, fail to support policies designed to create economic equality between the sexes and, more darkly, are physically and emotionally abusive towards them under certain circumstances. Men, in short, are prejudiced against women in terms of their political attitudes and behaviours, but the nature of that prejudice is strange: it mingles affection, desire for contact and even love with discrimination and some of the worst forms of violence (e.g. rape and economic exploitation). Why? If you want you want to find out more about this more complex form of prejudice, here is a reference that will help you to continue your journey through the prejudice literature: Glick and Fiske (2001).

6.2 Is getting us to like one another more always the solution?

The entire message of this chapter has been framed by a common-sense assumption that is worth unpacking now. This assumption is as follows. Disliking other people because they belong to other groups is bad for society, and getting us all to like one another more is thus the solution to problems of intergroup discrimination. In many contexts, this is a valid assumption. Who could possibly defend, for example, prejudice against gay people in Russia or prejudice against Tutsis and moderate Hutus during the Rwandan genocide? Reducing prejudice in these contexts must surely be a good idea.

At the same time, critics have recently highlighted the limits of prejudice reduction as a model of social change in historically unequal societies. Does getting members of historically advantaged groups to like historically disadvantaged groups, for example, motivate them to accept the kinds of political changes that might undermine their advantage or give back the wealth and entitlement they have inherited? Does getting members of historically disadvantaged groups to like the historically advantaged more encourage them to challenge or to accept the status quo? If you want to know more about this debate, then here is a reference that may help you to think critically about the relationship between prejudice reduction and social change: Dixon et al. (2013).

Further reading

- This is the classic text on prejudice and it remains a lively and readable introduction:

Allport, G.W. (1954) *The Nature of Prejudice*, Garden City, NY, Doubleday.

- This is the most systematic and complete review of the field:

Brown, R. (2011) *Prejudice: Its Social Psychology,* 2nd edn, Oxford, Wiley.

- This paper reflects on the strengths and weaknesses of prejudice reduction as an intervention to improve relations between groups:

Dixon, J., Durrheim, K., Kerr, P. and Thomae, M. (2013) 'What's so funny 'bout peace, love and understanding? Further reflections on the limits of prejudice reduction as a model of social change', *Journal of Social and Political Psychology*, vol. 1, pp. 239–52.

References

Adorno, T.W., Frankel-Brunswik, E., Levinson, D. and Sanford, D. (1950) *The Authoritarian Personality*, New York, Harper.

Allport, G.W. (1954) *The Nature of Prejudice*, Garden City, New York, Doubleday.

Banaji, M.R. and Greenwald, A.G. (2013) *Blindspot: Hidden Biases of Good People,* New York, Delacorte Press.

Billig, M. (1988) 'The notion of "prejudice": some rhetorical and ideological aspects', *Text*, vol. 8, pp. 91–111.

Brace, N. and Byford, J. (eds) (2012) *Investigating Psychology*, Oxford, Oxford University Press/Milton Keynes, The Open University.

Brewer, M.B. and Miller, N. (1984) 'Beyond the contact hypothesis: theoretical perspectives on desegregation', in Miller, N. and Brewer, M.B. (eds) *Groups in Contact: A Psychology of Desegregation*, New York, Academic Press.

Brown, R., Condor, S., Matthews, A., Wade, G. and Williams, J. (1986) 'Explaining intergroup differentiation in an industrial organization', *Journal of Occupational Psychology*, vol. 59, pp. 273–86.

Cairns, E., Wilson, R., Gallagher, T. and Trew, K. (1995) 'Psychology's contribution to understanding conflict in Northern Ireland', *Peace and Conflict: Journal of Peace Psychology*, vol. 1, pp. 131–48.

Correll, J., Park, B., Judd, C.M. and Wittenbrink, B. (2002) 'The police officer's dilemma: using ethnicity to disambiguate potentially threatening individuals', *Journal of Personality and Social Psychology*, vol. 83, pp. 1314–29.

Correll, J., Park, B., Judd, C.M., Wittenbrink, B. and Sadler, M.S. (2007) 'Across the thin blue line: police officers and racial bias in the decision to shoot', *Journal of Personality and Social Psychology*, vol. 92, pp. 1006–23.

Cottrell, C.A. and Neuberg, S.L. (2005) 'Differential emotional reactions to different groups: a sociofunctional threat-based approach to "prejudice"', *Journal of Personality and Social Psychology*, vol. 88, pp. 770–89.

Crisp, R.J., Perks, N., Stone, C.H. and Farr, M.J. (2004) 'Cognitive busyness and the processing of evaluative information in intergroup contexts', *Journal of Social Psychology*, vol. 144, pp. 541–4.

Diamond, J. (2005) *Collapse: How Societies Choose to Fail or Succeed*, New York, Penguin.

Dixon, J. and Durrheim, K. (2003) 'Contact and the ecology of racial division: some varieties of informal segregation', *British Journal of Social Psychology*, vol. 42, pp. 1–23.

Dixon, J., Durrheim, K. and Tredoux, C. (2005) 'Beyond the optimal contact strategy: a "reality check" for the contact hypothesis', *American Psychologist*, vol. 60, pp. 697–711.

Dixon, J., Durrheim, K., Kerr, P. and Thomae, M. (2013) 'What's so funny 'bout peace, love and understanding? Further reflections on the limits of prejudice reduction as a model of social change', *Journal of Social and Political Psychology*, vol. 1, pp. 239–52.

Dovidio, J.F. (2001) 'On the nature of contemporary prejudice: the third wave', *Journal of Social Issues*, vol. 57, pp. 829–49.

Dovidio, J.F. and Gaertner, S.L. (2004) 'Aversive racism', *Advances in Experimental Social Psychology*, vol. 36, pp. 1–52.

Dovidio, J.F., Eller, A. and Hewstone, M. (2011) 'Improving intergroup relations through direct, extended and other forms of indirect contact', *Group Processes and Intergroup Relations*, vol. 14, pp. 147–60.

Eagly, A.H. and Mladinic, A. (1989) 'Gender stereotypes and attitudes toward women and men', *Personality and Social Psychology Bulletin*, vol. 15, pp. 543–58.

Fiske, S.T. (2005) 'Social cognition and the normality of prejudgment', in Dovidio, J.F., Glick, P. and Rudman, L.A. (eds) *On the Nature of Prejudice: 50 Years after Allport*, Oxford, Wiley-Blackwell.

Fiske, S.T. and Taylor, S.E. (1991) *Social Cognition*, New York, McGraw-Hill.

Fritsch, J. (2000) 'The Diallo verdict: the overview; 4 officers in Diallo shooting are acquitted of all charges', *New York Times*, 26 February [Online]. Available at www.nytimes.com/2000/02/26/nyregion/diallo-verdict-overview-4-officers-diallo-shooting-are-acquitted-all-charges.html (Accessed 24 April 2014).

Gaertner, S.L. and Dovidio, J.F. (2000) *Reducing Intergroup Bias: The Common Ingroup Identity Model*, Philadelphia, PA, Psychology Press.

Glick, P. and Fiske, S.T. (2001) 'An ambivalent alliance: hostile and benevolent sexism as complementary justifications for gender inequality', *American Psychologist*, vol. 56, pp. 109–18.

Hamilton, D.L and Trollier, T.K. (1996) 'Stereotypes and stereotyping: an overview of the cognitive approach', in Dovidio, J. and Gaertner, S. (eds) *Prejudice, Discrimination and Racism*, pp. 127–63, Orlando, FL, Academic Press.

Harris, L.T. and Fiske, S.T. (2006) 'Dehumanising the lowest of the low: neuroimaging responses to extreme outgroups', *Psychological Science*, vol. 17, pp. 847–53.

Harris, L.T. and Fiske, S.T. (2007) 'Social groups that elicit disgust are differentially processed in mPFC', *Social Cognitive and Affective Neuroscience*, vol. 2, pp. 45–51.

Harris, L.T. and Fiske, S.T. (2009) 'Social neuroscience evidence for dehumanised perception', *European Review of Social Psychology*, vol. 20, pp. 192–231.

Henriques, J. (1984) 'Social psychology and the politics of racism', in Henriques, J., Hollway, W., Urwin, C., Venn, C. and Walkerdine, V. (eds) *Changing the Subject: Psychology, Social Regulation and Subjectivity*, London, Methuen.

Hewstone, M. and Brown, R. (1986) 'Contact is not enough: an intergroup perspective on the "contact hypothesis"', in Hewstone, M. and Brown, R. (eds) *Contact and Conflict in Intergroup Encounters*, Oxford, Basil Blackwell.

Hewstone, M. and Greenland, K. (2000) 'Intergroup conflict', *International Journal of Psychology*, vol. 35, pp. 136–44.

Hugenberg, K. and Bodenhausen, G.V. (2003) 'Facing prejudice: implicit prejudice and the perception of facial threat', *Psychological Science*, vol. 14, pp. 640–3.

Jacobs, D. and Wood, K. (1999) 'Interracial conflict and intergroup homicide', *American Journal of Sociology*, vol. 105, pp. 157–90.

Minard, R.D. (1952) 'Race relations in the Pocahontas coal field', *Journal of Social Issues*, vol. 8, pp. 29–44.

Montagu, M.F. (1949) 'Some psychodynamic factors in race prejudice', *Journal of Social Psychology*, vol. 30, pp. 175–87.

Navarrete, C.D. and Fessler, D.M.T. (2006) 'Disease avoidance and ethnocentrism: the effects of disease vulnerability and disgust sensitivity on intergroup attitudes', *Evolution and Human Behavior,* vol. 27, pp. 270–82.

Navarrete, C.D., Fessler, D.M.T. and Eng, S.J. (2007) 'Elevated ethnocentrism in the first trimester of pregnancy', *Evolution and Human Behavior*, vol. 28, pp. 60–5.

Neuberg, S.L., Kenrick, D.T. and Schaller, M. (2010) 'Evolutionary social psychology', in Fiske, S.T., Gilbert, D. and Lindzey, G. (eds) *Handbook of Social Psychology*, 5th edn, New York, John Wiley & Sons.

Oaten, M., Stevenson, R. and Case, T. (2009) 'Disgust as a disease avoidance mechanism: a review and model', *Psychological Bulletin*, vol. 135, pp. 303–21.

Pettigrew, T.F. and Meertens, R.W. (1995) 'Subtle and blatant prejudice in Western Europe', *European Journal of Social Psychology*, vol. 25, pp. 57–75.

Pettigrew, T.F. and Tropp, L.R. (2006) 'A meta-analytic test of intergroup contact theory', *Journal of Personality and Social Psychology*, vol. 90, pp. 751–83.

Pettigrew, T.F. and Tropp, L.R. (2008) 'How does intergroup contact reduce prejudice? Meta-analytic tests of three mediators', *European Journal of Social Psychology,* vol. 38, pp. 922–34.

Pettigrew, T.F. and Tropp, L.R. (2011) *When Groups Meet: The Dynamics of Intergroup Contact*, Philadelphia, PA, Psychology Press.

Richards, G. (1997) *'Race, Racism and Psychology: Towards a Reflexive History*, London, Routledge.

Richards, Z. and Hewstone, M. (2001) 'Subtyping and subgrouping: processes for the prevention and promotion of stereotype change', *Personality and Social Psychology Review*, vol. 5, pp. 52–73.

Rokeach, M. (1948) 'Generalized mental rigidity as a factor in ethnocentricism', *Journal of Abnormal and Social Psychology*, vol. 43, pp. 259–78.

Rokeach, M. (1960) *The Open and the Closed Mind*, New York, Basic Books.

Rozin, P., Haidt, J. and McCauley, C.R. (2000) 'Disgust', in Lewis, M. and Haviland-Jones, J.M. (eds) *Handbook of Emotions*, 2nd edn, pp. 637–53, New York, Guilford Press.

Sahdra, B. and Ross, M. (2007) 'Group identification and historical memory', *Personality and Social Psychology Bulletin*, vol. 33, pp. 384–95.

Samelson, F. (1978) 'From "race psychology" to "studies in prejudice": some observations on the thematic reversal in social psychology', *Journal of the History of the Behavioral Sciences,* vol.14, pp. 265–78.

Sherif, M. (1967) *Group Conflict and Cooperation: Their Social Psychology*, London, Routledge & Kegan Paul.

Star, S.A., Williams, R.M. and Stouffer, S.A. (1958) 'Negro infantry platoons in white companies', in Maccoby, E.E., Newcomb, T. and Hartley, E.L. (eds) *Readings in Social Psychology*, 3rd edn, New York, Holt, Rinehart & Winston.

Tajfel, H. (1981) 'Social stereotypes and social groups', in Turner, J.C. and Giles, H. (eds) *Intergroup Behaviour*, Oxford, Blackwell.

Tajfel, H. and Turner, J. (1986) 'The social identity theory of intergroup behaviour', in Worchel, S. and Austin, W.G. (eds) *Psychology of Intergroup Relations*, Chicago, Nelson-Hall.

Tajfel, H. and Wilkes, A. (1963) 'Classification and quantitative judgement', *British Journal of Psychology*, vol. 54, pp. 101–14.

Chapter 5
Why do we help one another? Helping, altruism and prosocial behaviour

Rachel Manning and Mark Levine

Contents

1 Introduction

In early 2014, parts of the UK experienced a series of storms and floods that lasted several weeks (Figure 5.1). Daily news reports contained pictures of waterlogged villages and landscapes, accompanied by stories of people attempting to save their homes from impending floods. Media coverage questioned whether the government was doing enough to help people. Stories of helping permeated the coverage in many ways.

Helping, and moral imperatives or implicit assumptions about the worth of helping, often feature in media coverage of natural disasters. You might already be thinking of additional examples of natural disasters in different parts of the world. Does the coverage of such events differ depending on where these events take place? Or the type of disaster? Why might this be?

Figure 5.1 The human cost of flooding in England and Wales

In this chapter you will begin to examine some of the ways in which social psychologists have attempted to answer some of the questions raised by the study of helping. However, the chapter will also point to how assumptions about the 'nature of human nature' can filter through into social psychological theorising about helping. Studying helping allows the examination of a wide range of issues, and also enables consideration of how well social psychological approaches in isolation may account for this variety of experience. You will examine how the notion of helping is itself complex and see how different perspectives can be brought to bear on this topic, not only from within psychology but also from a range of additional disciplines such as philosophy and biology/evolution.

Learning outcomes

On completing this chapter you should:

- have an understanding of the development of different social psychological approaches to the study of helping
- be able to think critically about the phenomenon of 'helping' through the consideration of the nature of different helping behaviours
- be able to evaluate the strengths and limitations of different approaches to helping behaviours
- be able to reflect on the application of social psychology to helping behaviours in everyday life.

2 What is helping?

As you work through this chapter, one of the things that you may notice is the different kinds of 'helping' examined in the research that is presented. In order to help you to think critically about the nature of this helping, first take some time to think about your own perspective on helping.

Activity 5.1: Your perspective on helping

Imagine the following scenarios, and think about how you would react to each one, how you think other people would react, and why. Spend a minute or so on each one, making notes on these issues.

1. You are walking alone through a town centre at night and see a number of young people arguing. They seem to be comprised of two different groups who are facing each other, and one member of one group is beginning to push and shove a member of the other group.
2. You read an advertisement in a newspaper from a charity called Water Aid that states that a child dies every 15 seconds from water-related diseases. The advertisement asks you to sign up to donate £5 a month.
3. You wake up in the middle of the night and think you can hear something happening outside. You think you hear a woman shout. You look out of the window and see a man and woman arguing.
4. You see an older person carrying two big shopping bags up a steep hill. She is walking very slowly.

How do these scenarios differ from one another? Try to note as many differences as possible.

Do you think that other people would react to each of these scenarios in the same way as you think you would? How might we explain differences between people's reactions? Look back at your notes relating to each scenario. Did your own anticipated reactions differ across the different scenarios? Why do you think this is?

These scenarios differ in a number of ways, including the type of need that potential helping might address. In some cases there is a clear need for help (e.g. death from disease) whereas others are more ambiguous (someone walking up a hill). Some situations might seem potentially dangerous. In some situations you, as a potential helper, might be on your own. You might be physically distant from the source of need. The people involved in the situation might be quite different from you. The kind of help that is required might be different, including how long your help might be required for. In addition, your familiarity with these scenarios may be quite different from that of other people. In some cases you may have encountered them before and therefore know what your reaction would be (or at least, what it was on those prior occasions).

The issues involved in deciding which phenomena in the world to study, and how to translate them into social psychological research, is an underlying theme that permeates much research on helping. As Activity 5.1 demonstrates, the possible behaviours that could be investigated are numerous and diverse, presenting a challenge in terms of the development of a coherent, integrated approach to their investigation. Another challenge for studying helping in social psychology is that what we *think* we would do in a helping situation may or may not differ from what we actually *would* do should the situation happen. In examining research in this area, it is useful to bear these issues in mind.

Aside from whether, how and why we might help, there are broader questions of whether we *should*. It can often be assumed that we *should* help, and that to not do so is morally questionable. As moral philosopher Peter Singer (2009) has argued, if you have enough money to buy luxuries (and even bottled water can be considered a luxury if drinkable tap water is available) then you can afford to save the life of someone who might otherwise die of poverty-related causes. Singer argues that we should help others to save a life (Figure 5.2). Singer himself reports that he gives 25 per cent of his earnings to non-governmental organisations (NGOs), most of which help the poor. So why don't we all do the same? Clearly, ideas about what should happen often differ from what does happen. Moreover, you might not agree with Singer's argument – your notion of what should happen might therefore differ.

Figure 5.2 The life you can save

These challenges – our own thoughts on the rights and wrongs of helping, whether helping should happen at all, who should benefit, and who should help (or not) – remind us to examine our own values and thoughts about helping.

2.1 Defining helping

Up until this point, different behaviours have been mentioned that might constitute helping in one form or another. However, you can probably think of additional examples of behaviours that you might consider forms of help. Perhaps not surprisingly, there are various definitions of helping and related terms. 'Helping' has been defined by Bierhoff (2002, p. 9) as a broad term, involving 'all forms of interpersonal support'. 'Prosocial behaviour', on the other hand, is defined as intending 'to improve the situation of the help-recipient, the actor is not motivated by the fulfilment of professional obligations, and the recipient is a person, not an organisation' (p. 9). Bierhoff has suggested that the terms might be organised hierarchically in terms of their breadth, with 'helping' as the more inclusive term, which contains prosocial behaviour, and with 'altruism' – where 'the helper's motivation is characterised by perspective taking and empathy' (p. 9) – as a subset of prosocial behaviour. Macaulay and Berkowitz (1970, p. 3) have alternatively defined altruism as 'behaviour carried out to benefit another without anticipation of rewards from external sources.' Note that this definition usefully doesn't rule out the possibility that there might be a reward for a person who carries out a behaviour that we might consider altruism – it is the *anticipation* of a reward that is important.

In contrast to Bierhoff's (2002) hierarchy, Piliavin et al. (1981, p. 4) have suggested that prosocial behaviour is the more general term: 'defined by society as behaviour generally beneficial to other people and to the ongoing social system', and that 'a great deal of disagreement regarding what is really prosocial can occur depending on where one stands.' Rather than focus on the intention of the helper, as in Bierhoff's definition, Piliavin et al. point to the socially determined nature of what is generally understood to be prosocial behaviour. One example of this is Grzelak and Dergela's (1982) suggestion that, although the pursuit of private self-interest is often translated as selfish, 'private benefits may have a positive effect on society' (p. 10). They additionally claim that there may be positiveness in social behaviour that we might ordinarily consider negative (such as in the productiveness of social conflict).

The issue of whether helping behaviour is necessarily positive will be looked at again later in this chapter. For now, you should note that throughout the literature, terms such as 'prosocial', 'helping' and 'altruism' are often used interchangeably, and there is sometimes a lack of consistency, even by the same authors (maybe even in this module), in the use of these terms.

Researchers often define their target of investigation more specifically, leading to an additional range of terms for helping behaviours. One type of helping behaviour in particular – what Piliavin et al. (1981) termed 'emergency intervention'– has shaped social psychological investigation for decades.

2.2 Summary

You have looked at the notion of helping and how it has been defined, and begun to think about the implications of these issues for the study of helping behaviour in social psychology. You have also begun to see how broad this topic area is, and therefore the wide potential for research. These possibilities bring related challenges. How helping is characterised has implications for how it is studied and theorised. Is it possible to have a single theory or model of helping that allows us to understand these different situations from a social psychological (or any other) perspective? Can social psychology alone, as diverse as it is, explain these phenomena? Moreover, it is difficult to ignore the moral connotations that surround helping, which may differ according to the perspective of the person, helper, or social psychologist involved.

3 The development of social psychologies of helping

Although it might be difficult to agree on a definition of helping, it is easier to identify the development of social psychology's interest in helping itself. In this section we will present some of the early social psychological work on helping behaviours, and use this to begin to consider the kind of knowledge that this work has generated. Understanding the development of research in this area can be helpful in evaluating its utility.

3.1 How did social psychology become interested in helping?

As Penner et al. (2005) have noted, there were several early attempts to examine helping or prosocial behaviours within social psychology (e.g. McDougall, 1908), but one event in particular served as the catalyst for research on helping.

Kitty Genovese was murdered by Winston Moseley in New York on 13 March 1964. On 27 March a story appeared in the *New York Times* reporting that 38 witnesses watched Moseley stab Kitty to death on the street outside their homes, doing nothing until she was dead. Understandably, this story led to debate about why these people reportedly did nothing to help someone who was so clearly in need of help. Bibb Latané and John Darley were two social psychologists who became interested in how to understand the story in social psychological terms (Evans, 1980) and in how they might investigate their hunch that the reported number of witnesses was itself the key to understanding how this happened.

In her critique of social psychological theory, Cherry (1995) has suggested that Latané and Darley's experimental social psychology background informed the manner and content of their subsequent research. Interpreting the Kitty Genovese story in terms of independent variables (e.g. group size) and their effects on dependent variables (e.g. helping behaviour) led to a particular characterisation of the event, where the story of 38 inactive witnesses became part of a broader set of behaviours termed 'bystander intervention'. You may have noticed that so far the story of the 38 witnesses has been referred to as just that: a story. This issue will be returned to later in this chapter.

Latané and Darley therefore conducted a series of laboratory experiments that varied the number of people present at an emergency and observed the reactions of those present. In one of their first studies, Latané and Darley (1968, p. 217) invited college students to participate in an experiment examining 'some of the problems involved in life at an urban university.' Participants were directed to a room that was either empty or that contained two other people, and were asked to fill out a questionnaire. In one condition, the two other people present were also naïve participants; in another condition, they were confederates of the experimenter, instructed to give minimal responses when, as they filled out the questionnaire, a smoke-like substance was piped into the room. Latané and Darley recorded whether participants left the room to obtain help from the experimenter and, if they did, how long it took them to do so. They found the lowest rates of reporting the smoke in the condition where participants were sitting in a room with two passive confederates. In comparison, the highest rate of reporting was found when participants were alone. They suggested that this finding could be explained by a process of 'social influence' (or what Piliavin et al., 1981, termed 'informational social influence'). People look to others in the face of an emergency, and use other people's reactions to help them understand the situation.

= IV

In another early experiment, Darley and Latané (1968) told participants that they were to take part in a discussion with one other person, two other people, or five other people. They couldn't see these people, but could only hear and speak to them via an intercom. While sitting alone in their cubicle, participants heard one of the other people in the discussion choking in a manner that suggested they were having a seizure. The experimenters recorded how many people left the cubicle to fetch help, and the length of time it took them to do so. Again, they found that rates and speed of helping decreased with the number of other people believed to be part of the discussion. As participants couldn't see the other 'bystanders' in this experiment, Darley and Latané suggested that a different process was at work in this situation: **diffusion of responsibility** (and of blame). Their suggestion was that when other people are present in a helping situation, the responsibility for taking action is shared between all of them. The pressure to help is not focused on a single person, and therefore helping is less likely.

Diffusion of responsibility
When other people are present (or believed to be present) in a helping situation, responsibility for taking action is spread out among them.

Based on a series of such experiments, Latané and Darley (1970) formulated a decision-making model of helping behaviour, which suggested that, in order for helping to occur, a bystander must pass through the following stages:

1 notice the event
2 interpret it as an emergency
3 decide they are personally responsible
4 decide how they might help
5 implement that help.

At each stage, decisions are influenced by different social psychological processes. A negative response at any stage would result in no help being given. For example, whether someone decides that an event is an emergency or not is affected by a process of 'pluralistic ignorance' (Latané and Nida, 1981). The more people there are present, who are acting passively (as they themselves are trying to work out what is happening), the less likely a bystander will be to interpret the event as an emergency requiring help. Alternatively, potential interveners may be concerned with how others might evaluate their responses to an emergency. This 'audience inhibition' (Latané and Nida, 1981) serves to prevent helping, as people may decide not to carry out helping behaviour, even though they may know it is needed.

Latané and Darley's finding that people are less likely to respond to emergencies if there are others available (or at least believed to be available) to help has been termed the **'bystander effect'**, and is one of the most robust and replicated effects in social psychology (Latané and Nida, 1981).

Bystander effect
The finding that the more people there are present in an emergency situation, the less likely it is that any one of those people will help. This finding arose from a programme of research conducted by John Darley and Bibb Latané.

Activity 5.2: The influence of Latané and Darley's model

Using a bibliographic database such as Web of Science, try to find some recent studies that have used this model of helping behaviour. To do this, you could locate the record of one of the original studies by Latané and Darley above, and then look at more recent articles that have referred to these sources. Don't limit your search to psychology.

Look at how many academic sources have referred to these studies. Next, note which journals this work is published in. Are they all psychology journals? Are they social psychology journals? You might also look at the abstracts of some of these articles. What is the focus of the research that cites this work? If you can access the full text of the articles, how is Latané and Darley's work used in it? Has the research been used uncritically, or has any evaluation been presented or alternatives argued for?

As you have probably found, the influence of this model is substantial: it continues to be referred to in contemporary research in a range of different areas and applied to a range of different helping behaviours. However, as with any approach, model or theory in psychology, there are inevitably limitations. And, equally inevitably, the approach has been subject to criticism. For example, Bibb Latané himself, in a review article with Steve Nida (Latané and Nida, 1981, p. 322) notes how one limitation of their work is that they had not 'been able to mobilise the increasing store of social psychological understanding accumulated over the last decade to devise suggestions for ensuring that future Kitty Genoveses will receive help.'

Other researchers have pointed to the lack of a specific motivational component in the model that would explain why someone might move from one decision-making stage to the next (e.g. Piliavin et al., 1981; Bierhoff, 2002). Researchers such as Schwartz and Howard (1984) suggested that internalised values, such as feelings of moral obligation, might be usefully added to the model in order to account for this, as well as social and personal norms. John Darley has himself commented that his and Latané's original claim that norms were not a useful explanatory construct was somewhat overstated (Evans, 1980; see also Batson, 1994).

The initial development of research on helping in emergencies illustrates the relationship between research questions and methods, and begins to highlight the ways in which, when analysing the social psychological aspects of helping situations, there is scope for selection by researchers, which, as Cherry (1995) notes, may be based on their academic training. This can have a profound effect on the knowledge social psychologists generate.

3.2 What to explain: why don't people help or why do people help?

Latané and Darley (1970) published the book *The Unresponsive Bystander: Why Doesn't He Help?*, based on their initial series of experiments. The title highlights an additional issue: the focus on situations when helping doesn't happen. This has led some researchers to suggest that we know quite a lot about why people *don't* help, but relatively little about why they *do*.

Piliavin et al. (1981), for example, suggest that the study of positive aspects of social behaviour is rare. In contrast, their own book opens with examples of heroic behaviour. Contemporaries of Latané and Darley, they developed an alternative model of helping in emergencies – the arousal: cost–reward model. This model of helping was the result of a similarly ingenious series of experiments. Researchers staged a series of emergencies on the subway trains of New York. By varying the characteristics of a person in need of help (e.g. Piliavin et al., 1969), they concluded that observation of an emergency creates a state of arousal in bystanders. This arousal becomes more unpleasant the longer it continues, but can be reduced by a response based on a calculation of the relative costs and rewards of that response. Notably, Piliavin et al. (1969) did not find decreased rates of helping when more people were present – a finding they attributed to the setting of their experiments and the size of the groups involved (considerably larger than those in Latané and Darley's experiments).

Such differences illustrate what happens when the focus of research is subtly shifted. In moving from a focus on a lack of helping to a focus on why people do help, different findings were obtained. In addition, Piliavin et al. (1981, p. 57) used a wide range of physiological measures to demonstrate how the arousal response involves a strong emotional component – a 'defence reaction'. Their work thus pointed to the overlap between social, psychological and biological aspects of psychology in the explanation of helping behaviour. The extended model they presented in their 1981 text included additional factors such as victim and bystander characteristics and the notion of 'we-ness', which will be considered later in the chapter.

It is worth noting that Jane Piliavin's work on helping has continued to develop. Her latter work, informed by sociology, has highlighted the importance of role identity, and has examined different forms of helping behaviours, such as blood donation and charitable giving, again illustrating the broad range of disciplines that intersect in the study of helping (see also Piliavin, 2009).

3.3 Summary

In this section, you have begun to see what a social psychological approach brings to the topic of helping. The study of helping shows how explanations of social phenomena can have biological dimensions. In addition, you have seen how events in the world, and the methods of social psychology, impact on the phenomena that are studied. For example, as Cherry (1995) highlights, the influence of the experimental method impacted on initial empirical studies of helping behaviour. Finally, you have also begun to see how subtle differences in focus can alter the knowledge that is produced from research.

4 Explaining helping: so why do we or don't we help?

4.1 Motivations for helping: the egoism/altruism debate

Can helping ever be truly altruistic? You will recall the earlier discussion regarding the nature of altruism as a special subset of helping or prosocial behaviour. It was also noted how these terms are often used interchangeably. In examining 'pure' altruism, however, definitions – and careful experimental manipulations – can be of crucial importance.

> **Pause for thought**
>
> Before you look at this debate, take a minute to think about your personal position on this issue. Do people help selflessly (i.e. is there pure altruism) or are they always self-interested (egoistic)? Your ideas don't need to be backed up with evidence, but think about whether it would be possible to conduct research to test your own ideas.

If you feel that pure altruism does exist, you will enjoy the work of Daniel Batson. Piliavin et al. (1981) have argued that demonstrating pure altruism is almost impossible. This has not, however, deterred Batson, whose academic credentials include PhDs in both psychology and theology. He has for decades been an advocate of the possibility of helping being motivated by pure altruism. If, on the other hand, you think that helping is always in some way self-interested, then you may prefer the work of Robert Cialdini and colleagues, who reject the suggestion that selflessly motivated helping is possible, and instead suggest egoistic motivations.

Batson's empathy–altruism hypothesis (Batson, 1987; Coke et al., 1978) challenges the egoistic bias of much bystander intervention research. It suggests that, while reducing personal distress aroused by another's need serves egoistic motives, perspective taking and empathic concern serve altruistic ones. According to this model, taking the perspective of someone who needs help leads to an increase in empathic emotion, which in turn leads to more helping behaviour. Coke et al. (1978), for example, conducted two experiments using a misattribution of arousal manipulation (where participants are given a pill and told that it will cause arousal, providing an alternative to empathy for any arousal they feel in relation to another's distress) and a false feedback manipulation (where participants were given physiological feedback that falsely suggested they had low levels of arousal in response to someone in need). They reported that feelings of empathy led to increased rates of helping. In response, Cialdini and colleagues (e.g. Cialdini et al., 1997, p. 482) acknowledged the 'credible experimental evidence' in favour of Batson's model, but reinterpreted Batson's results to suggest that altruism can be reinterpreted as egotism due to 'self–other overlap'. That is, when someone takes the perspective of another person, their sense of self becomes incorporated into that other person: the boundaries between the self and another person become overlapped.

Although evidence in this debate comes from carefully crafted experiments, there is more to the debate than research data. The findings from these studies speak to the nature of human beings and to debates beyond psychology. As such, you can begin to see how social psychological research may be motivated by issues other than pure knowledge acquisition and how social psychological findings may have broader moral and philosophical implications. This debate is by no means resolved – although Piliavin (2009) notes that Dovidio et al.'s (1990) research, which was initially intended to demonstrate purely egoistically motivated helping, in fact demonstrated the opposite. The possibility that human beings are capable of pure altruism remains alive.

4.2 It's not you, it's me

Psychologists have also attempted to identify individual characteristics of people to explain helping. While Latané and Darley noted in their original studies that there were no correlations between personality and helping – such was the strength of the situational forces they proposed – this has not meant that personality have been ignored.

Activity 5.3: Identifying prosocial personalities

Can you think of someone you consider to be particularly helpful? This might be someone you know, or someone you know of. What are some of their attributes?

How might we measure people's helpfulness? Might the features that you have identified above constitute items of a scale measuring helpfulness? Try to formulate five questions that might appear on a scale measuring how helpful someone is.

We may be able to identity individuals who seem to help others more than their peers. Such individuals might range from those who undertake one-off helping in emergencies to individuals who undertake long-term, sustained helping behaviours. One example might be Sam Carvalho (see Figure 5.3), who was given a 'Young Person of the Year' award for providing online advice to others. Conversely, it may be difficult to draw out general principles and dimensions of 'being helpful' from our experiences of particular people. The very act of formulating such a scale assumes that helpfulness is a quality of individuals and that some of us have more of it than others. You might like to compare your list with the list provided in Box 5.1, which comes from the 'helpfulness' factor on Lou Penner's prosocial personality battery (PSB). Scores on the PSB have been found to correlate with a number of behaviours, such as the speed of response in simulated emergencies, everyday acts of helping, helping co-workers, and the willingness to be an organ donor (Penner, 2002).

Figure 5.3 Sam Carvalho

Note: Sam Carvalho founded Stand Up, Stay Strong: an advice website for young people experiencing social and psychological problems, which provides free and confidential advice.

Box 5.1 Penner's prosocial personality battery (PSB)

The PSB (Penner, 2002) consists of a number of scales including personal distress and self-reported altruism. Items on the self-reported altruism scale require a response from 1, 'never', to 5, 'very often'. Items on the personal distress scale require a response from 1, 'strongly disagree', to 5, 'strongly agree'. The combination of responses on the personal distress and self-reported altruism scales gives a person's score on a 'helpfulness' factor (the other factor is 'other-oriented empathy'). The items relating to this 'helpfulness' factor are reproduced below. (The item marked with an 'R' is individually reverse scored before all personal distress items are added together and reversed by subtracting the total from 18.)

Self-reported altruism scale

26. I have helped carry a stranger's belongings (e.g. books, parcels, etc.).

27. I have allowed someone to go ahead of me in a line (e.g. supermarket, copying machine, etc.).

28. I have let a neighbour whom I didn't know too well borrow an item of some value (e.g. tools, a dish, etc.).

29. I have, before being asked, voluntarily looked after a neighbour's pets or children without being paid for it.

30. I have offered to help a handicapped or elderly stranger across a street.

Personal distress scale

14. I am usually pretty effective in dealing with emergencies. (R)

17. I tend to lose control during emergencies.

19. When I see someone who badly needs help in an emergency, I go to pieces.

In reviewing previous research that had failed to find personality correlates of prosocial actions, Penner notes:

> Most researchers did not, in fact, search for the 'prosocial personality'; rather they studied how a very specific personality trait related to a very specific kind of helping. When significant findings were obtained, attempts to 'replicate' them often involved a quite different kind of helping. Most of these replications failed, but not because personality is unrelated to helping, but rather because the salient characteristics of the criterion measure had changed. Thus, perhaps what the null results really showed is that one relatively specific personality trait is unlikely to be related to a wide range of helping behaviours.
>
> (Penner, 2002, p. 450)

Penner points to some of the issues that have been considered so far in this chapter: the wide range of possible helping behaviours, and the way in which the type of helping behaviour studied can impact on the findings obtained – and in this case how this can result in universal claims (e.g. that there is no link between personality and helping) that others would challenge.

In contrast to this personality approach, but illustrating how different features of individual helpers may help us to understand helping behaviour, Huston, Geis and colleagues (Geis and Huston, 1983; Geis et al., 1976; Huston et al., 1981) carried out interviews with people who had intervened in dangerous criminal incidents. They did not find any personality differences between this group of people and a group matched for age, sex, education and ethnic background. Instead, they found that interveners were taller and heavier than non-interveners, and had greater previous exposure to violence, as witnesses and victims. Interveners commonly felt confident that their intervention would be successful.

These contrasting approaches to the study of helpers point to further debates about the nature of humans; e.g. is helpfulness a product of our experiences or part of our essential nature? As such, they lead us to cross the frontiers of social psychology into biological and developmental psychology.

4.3 It's my genes

How much of our helping behaviour is determined by our genes? In popular culture, this version of the nature/nurture debate has been shaped by Richard Dawkins' famous book *The Selfish Gene* (1976). Dawkins described humans as 'survival machines – robot vehicles blindly programmed to preserve the selfish molecules known as genes … this gene selfishness will usually give rise to selfishness in individual behaviour' (Dawkins, 1976, p. 1). However, biological anthropologists and economists have discovered that, unlike other animals, humans frequently cooperate with genetically unrelated strangers in large groups, with people they will never meet again and where there is no personal benefit (Richerson and Boyd, 2005; Fehr and Gächter, 2002). So how do we explain helping if humans are inherently selfish? Just as some psychologists have highlighted the evolutionary origins of negative behaviours, such as intergroup prejudice and conflict (Chapter 4), this puzzle has led others to formulate possible evolutionary explanations of prosocial behaviours, such as helping and cooperation.

When considering some of the existing explanations of the effect of genes on helping we are not talking about the proportion of genes we share with others. This is because humans share 99 per cent of their genes (and there is a 98 per cent genetic overlap between humans and chimpanzees). Genetically we are remarkably similar to one another and to other primates. When it comes to the effect of genes on

Inclusive fitness theory
A concept drawn from the area of evolutionary biology, which attempts to account for the existence of altruism (behaviour that was troubling for evolutionary theory). Helping others (particularly those with a higher degree of genetic relatedness to themselves) is suggested to enhance the survival or propagation of an organism's genes, and therefore becomes understandable from an evolutionary perspective. According to inclusive fitness theory, then, fitness could be enhanced by means other than reproduction.

Cost-benefit analysis
A cost-benefit analysis compares the costs and benefits of a particular course of action. So, Hamilton's cost-benefit analysis compares the costs (c) of altruism with the benefits (b). The benefits are weighted by the coefficient of relatedness (r). Altruism may evolve when $r \times b > c$.

helping, we are talking about the effect of something that might be called the *altruism gene*. All our remaining genes are irrelevant.

One of the first explanations of how genes might influence helping came in the form of Hamilton's (1964) **inclusive fitness theory** (in this context altruism refers to behavioural effects rather than motives or intentions; Dawkins, 1979). Hamilton extended Darwin's classic version of natural selection to understand the emergence of altruism using a **cost-benefit analysis** that includes a 'coefficient of relatedness'. Given that we receive half of our genome from each of our parents, the likelihood of passing on a gene or genes for altruism to an offspring would be 50 per cent (25 per cent for grandchildren, 12.5 per cent in a great grandchild, 50 per cent for siblings, etc.). We can determine these coefficients of relatedness between any combination of family members. Hamilton suggested that natural selection will favour an altruism gene if the benefits of the altruism it causes, weighted by the 'coefficient of relatedness' between helper and helped, outweigh the costs. Thus, in the past, natural selection may have favoured a gene for parental care for children, even at cost to itself, as it ensured the survival of that gene (which the child has a 50 per cent likelihood of inheriting from its parent). Hamilton's rule helps us understand why altruism towards kin might come to exist in a population and become an evolutionary stable strategy.

Another way in which genetic explanations have been used to explain helping, specifically of non-kin, is the idea of **reciprocal altruism** (Trivers, 1971). Trivers argues that altruism towards strangers could have evolved if there was a chance of being in a situation where someone who had been helped would then reciprocate. For example, sharing of food with strangers during times of plenty could be a useful strategy to ensure that others help you in times of famine. By helping unrelated others (and temporarily reducing your own genetic 'fitness' while promoting theirs) you take a risk. Those you have helped could refuse to reciprocate at a later date (known as 'defection'). Thus, for reciprocal altruism to exist, the same individuals must come into regular contact. Finally, there must be a way to detect 'cheating' or defection in order to dissuade people from doing so. Reciprocal altruism stops happening if defection occurs.

More recent experimental research has revealed what Gintis (2000) calls strong reciprocity: the human predisposition to cooperate with others and to punish non-cooperators, even when punishment is costly for the punisher. This costly punishment has been termed altruistic punishment (Fehr and Gächter, 2002). For example, people will give up their own money to ensure a selfish player loses money – or even pay a fine, just so they can have the opportunity to punish a stranger who has behaved selfishly. Fehr and Gächter argue that these findings cannot be explained by kin selection or reciprocal altruism. In dissuading individuals from behaving selfishly, altruistic punishment helps the group to remain cooperative and seems to be designed to promote group interest. An alternative group-level approach to helping will be looked at later in this chapter.

Reciprocal altruism
An alternative theory of altruistic behaviour from evolutionary biology that suggests people may help others (at an immediate cost to themselves) so that person will be able to help them in return in the future.

4.4 It's my parents

An alternative perspective on why we help, and in particular why some people might help more than others, comes from work that looks at the development of prosocial behaviour and the role of parenting.

> ### Pause for thought
>
> How might you examine the influence of parenting on the development of helping behaviour in children? What aspects of parenting, or parents, might be important? What might a relevant research question be?

In examining the development of helping behaviour, there is evidently an overlap between social and developmental psychology. Research has suggested that, while there is evidence that helping behaviour may ordinarily increase with age (Zahn-Waxler et al., 2001), empathy is relatively stable through childhood, after an increase from 14 months to 36 months (Knafo et al., 2008). However, there is also evidence that differences in the rewards given to children can have an impact on helping behaviours. Grusec and Redler (1980) conducted a study in which children were induced to give some of the marbles they won in a game to poor children. Eight-year-old children who were told that they were a 'nice person' after they had donated marbles scored more highly on a subsequent measure of generalised altruism than children who were told that their marble donation was a 'nice thing to do' (Grusec and Redler, 1980, p. 527).

Box 5.2 discusses an additional study that has examined prosocial behaviour in children, looking specifically at the promotion of prosocial value and the reduction of aggression in young boys.

Box 5.2 Crossing boundaries: Reducing boys' aggression

Ervin Staub's career has revolved around the examination – and promotion – of prosocial behaviours. This has included a lifelong investigation of the development of prosocial behaviour in children (indeed, this is the title of one of his early books: Staub, 1975). It has also involved a range of applied or field activity, where Staub has drawn on this wide-ranging research to inform the production of, for example, workshops and radio dramas in Rwanda to promote reconciliation and prevent violence (Figure 5.4), and teacher training to promote non-violent classrooms.

Spielman and Staub (2000) conducted an intervention study in which they explored the role of a 'prosocial value orientation' personality measure in boys' aggression, and used an intervention methodology to examine changes in hostile attributions.

Figure 5.4 Interventions to promote prosocial behaviour in Rwanda

Speilman and Staub argue that **prosocial value orientation** (PVO), a personality characteristic associated with a number of different forms of helping other people, would be a likely inhibitor of aggressive behaviour. Theoretically informed by cognitive, developmental and social psychology, these researchers set out to find out whether, as they predicted, an aggression–reduction intervention they had developed would be more effective with boys with a higher PVO, as they might be more open to the treatments provided in the intervention. Speilman and Staub developed an intervention to do this, involving discussion and role play that enabled the participants to learn ways of constructively fulfilling their needs. The intervention was based on research suggesting that 'aggressive boys lack the cognitive tendencies and social skills to fulfil their goals in prosocial ways' (Spielman and Staub, 2000, p. 165). Using measures of PVO, hostile attribution bias, disciplinary records and teacher evaluations, they found their intervention reduced the level of hostile attributions the boys made to others, as well as evidence of PVO being negatively associated with aggressive behaviour.

This study, and Staub's work more generally, highlights how a practical focus is often less concerned with the maintenance of (sub-)disciplinary boundaries and, conversely, how effective action may necessitate an approach that is informed by a broad range of perspectives.

Prosocial value orientation
Proposed by Ervin Staub, prosocial value orientation (PVO) is a personality characteristic that includes a concern for the welfare of others, and is associated with a range of helping behaviours.

4.5 Actually, it *is* you

As you saw above, Piliavin et al. (1981) included the characteristics of both bystanders and victims in their expanded version of the arousal: cost-reward model. Similarly, other approaches have highlighted how our perception of others may influence helping. Lerner's (1970) **just-world hypothesis**, for example, points to how potential helpers' perceptions of victims can influence helping behaviour. Lerner suggests that both rejection of victims and compassion towards them arise from the same underlying psychological process: a need for justice (Lerner, 1970, p. 207). Thus work in this area tends to look at different scenarios, often presented in questionnaire studies, to examine attribution of blame. Similarly, research has examined the ways in which people attribute the causes of behaviour (Lodewijkx et al., 2001) and suggested that if a victim is perceived as responsible for their

Just-world hypothesis
Coined by Lerner, this term describes the belief that people deserve what they get and get what they deserve.

situation, then help will be withheld. If, however, the cause of the situation is uncontrollable, then help is more readily given.

The work of Zagefka et al. (2011) on charitable donation also illustrates the role of blame in helping behaviour. Focusing on donations to disaster victims, their work shows that when people perceive disasters as naturally caused rather than caused by people, donation rates are higher. They have argued that this difference is due to people perceiving victims of natural disasters as less blameworthy for their situation. Victims of natural disasters are also perceived as making more of an effort to help themselves. In another study, Zagefka et al. (2013) examined people's willingness to donate – termed 'donation proclivity' – in response to the Asian tsunami of 2004 and the Chinese earthquake of 2008. In this study they found that if the victims and places where they live are well known to participants, they are more likely to identify with them. This identification with victims, in turn, leads to a greater willingness to donate.

4.6 Summary

In this section you have looked at a range of different approaches that have attempted to explain why people help. You have been introduced to some key debates in the area, including whether or not pure altruism exists. Although this debate seems unlikely to be resolved (empirical findings might point in one direction or the other, but beliefs about the character of human nature that underlie the motivation for conducting the research may be less receptive to change), we might also question the practical contribution of the debate. Would resolving the debate lead to more helping? Are the issues it raises resolvable – by social psychology, or even psychology as a whole? Does it matter whether or not the ultimate motivation of helping is altruistic or selfish? Is it perhaps more important to consider how we can increase or encourage helping?

The section has also introduced biological approaches that assume helping and cooperation are genetically driven. Alternatively, developmental approaches offer the potential for understanding how a person's prosociality may result from their childhood experiences. The issue of how the characteristics of people involved in helping situations might influence the likelihood of helping will be visited again in the following section.

5 Groups and helping

Groups and group processes have had, until recently, a rather bad press when it comes to explaining helping. As you have seen, in research on helping in emergencies it has been argued that group processes have a negative impact on the willingness of individuals to intervene because of processes such as diffusion of responsibility, pluralistic ignorance or audience inhibition (Section 3.1). However, the 'rediscovery' of the social group in European social psychology, and the theoretical frameworks that subsequently developed (e.g. social identity theory, Tajfel, 1978, 1982; and self-categorisation theory, Turner et al., 1987) have provided a platform for rethinking helping behaviour (see Chapters 2, 3 and 4 for further discussion of these frameworks).

5.1 Rethinking the bystander effect

As you saw in Section 3, the bystander effect is one of the most robust findings in social psychology. A recent meta-analysis by Fischer et al. (2011) confirms that individuals are more likely to help when on their own than when in the presence of other bystanders. However, Fischer et al. (2006) also show that the bystander effect does not hold in cases of dangerous or violent emergencies. They argue that this may be because dangerous or violent emergencies lead to greater arousal, which in turn leads to a swifter cost–reward analysis through which the presence of others can reduce the costs of intervention.

However, Levine and colleagues (Levine, 1999; Manning et al., 2007; Levine and Crowther, 2008) offer an alternative explanation based not simply on whether the emergency is dangerous or others are present. They explore the social identity relationships between all those present at a violent emergency – including bystanders, victims and perpetrators. By revisiting the story of the 38 witnesses – the event that prompted research in the emergency helping tradition – they show that, contrary to the traditional understanding of events surrounding the murder of Kitty Genovese, there is no evidence that 38 witnesses watched Winston Moseley carry out her murder over a half-hour period without intervening. In fact, the evidence suggests that only a few witnesses saw Moseley and Genovese together and the murder itself took place inside a stairwell where few people could see. There was also evidence that some people tried to call the police. Manning et al. (2007) argue that the continued fixation on the apparent failure of 38 witnesses to act has meant that other important features of the Kitty Genovese murder have been ignored.

For example, Cherry (1995) points out that social psychologists have ignored the gendered nature of this attack: the fact that this incident involved a man being violent towards a woman did not translate into much of the research that followed. She argues that, in the late 1960s, we were yet to become sensitised by the feminist movement to the social problem of male violence towards women. As a consequence of the way in which social psychologists at the time commonly analysed events in the world and translated them into objects of psychological investigation – what Cherry terms 'culturally embedded theorising' – psychologists did not explore gender or violence in their experimental work. Had they gone beyond being interested simply in the numbers of bystanders who were present, they might have developed a richer understanding of why bystanders sometimes intervene and sometimes do not.

The social identity approach to helping asks questions about the kinds of identities that are relevant to bystanders when they are faced with intervention decisions. For example, Levine (1999) shows that the failure of bystanders to intervene successfully during the abduction of the toddler James Bulger by two ten-year-old boys (Robert Thompson and Jon Venables) in Liverpool in 1993 was not because of the bystander effect. Bystanders failed to intervene because they assumed that the three boys were brothers. By invoking an identity of 'the family', the two abductors prevented adult bystanders from 'interfering' in what they understood to be 'family business'. This either normalised the relationship between the older boys and the crying toddler – or made bystanders feel that, as 'strangers', they had neither the right nor the responsibility to intervene in another family's concerns.

Levine and Crowther (2008) also show that the effect of the presence of others is qualified by who we think bystanders are and how we think they will act. In a study that showed CCTV footage of gendered violence (an attack by a man on a woman) to male and female participants who either sat on their own or in groups of three, they demonstrated that women were more likely to say they would intervene when they sat with other women rather than on their own, which is counter to the bystander effect. However, men were more likely to say they would intervene when on their own rather than in a group, supporting the bystander effect. When a woman sat with two men, she was least likely to indicate that she would intervene – but when a man sat with two women he was most likely to do so. Levine and Crowther suggest that this latter finding might be explained by norms of 'chivalry' that lead both men and women to expect men to intervene in violence.

5.2 How group identities can influence helping

Levine and colleagues (Levine et al., 2002; Levine and Thompson, 2004; Levine et al., 2005; Reicher et al., 2006; Hopkins et al., 2007; Levine and Manning, 2013) have drawn on the social identity tradition to outline four key elements of an approach that demonstrates the impact of social identity on helping behaviour. These elements include the salience of social identity, the boundaries of social identity, the contents of social identity and the strategic interests of social identity.

5.2.1 The salience of social identity

A social identity approach argues that identities can change as a function of changes in social context. Sometimes we can see ourselves in terms of our personal identities (which we think of as unique) while at other times we see ourselves in terms of our social identities (which we can share with others). We don't have to be alone to see ourselves in terms of a personal identity, nor do we have to be with others to experience a social identity. Take for example commuters on the London tube system. They might be crammed in together with other strangers which, despite the close physical proximity, might make them feel profoundly individualised. However, under some circumstances, these strangers can come to identify as common category members. When a social identity becomes salient, then the presence of others can lead to feelings of social solidarity and support. This leads in turn to greater helping behaviour. This is precisely what John Drury and colleagues found (Drury et al., 2009; Drury and Reicher, 2010) in studying the behaviour of people who were on the tube during the London bombings of 7 July 2005. Rather than act in a selfish or self-serving manner in the aftermath of the bombs – and despite still being in danger – people went out of their way to help others (Figure 5.5). Survivors described feeling a sense of unity with others in the emergency situation. It was the emergence of this collective identity that bound them together at the psychological level and led to the increased helping of strangers.

Figure 5.5 Passengers leaving the London tube system following one of the London bombings of 7 July 2005

5.2.2 The boundaries of social identity

When a social identity becomes salient, the limits of helping are shaped by the boundaries of that identity. We are more likely to help those who fall inside the boundaries of the group than those left outside. Identities with more inclusive boundaries will mean that a greater number of people are likely to be helped. Take for example the 'football shirt' study by Levine et al. (2005). In two studies using Manchester United football fans, Levine et al. asked participants to think of themselves as either 'football fans' or 'Manchester United fans'. A confederate, who was dressed in either a Manchester United shirt, a Liverpool FC shirt or an ordinary unbranded sports shirt, fell in front of the individual participants in the study. When the participants were thinking about themselves as Manchester United fans, they only helped when the victim wore the Manchester United shirt. When participants thought about themselves as football fans, however, they were equally likely to help the victim when he wore the Liverpool shirt or the Manchester United shirt – but not the unbranded sports shirt.

5.2.3 The content of social identity

It is important to remember that a social identity approach does not imply that the salience of social identity always results in in-group favouritism. Rather, it is necessary to take into account the content of the specific identity being made salient. Some identities may contain injunctions to 'look after our own'. Others may use out-group helping as a way of differentiating their own group from others (Jetten et al., 1996; Reicher et al., 2005). For the most part this will mean that people are more likely to be helped when they are seen as members of the in-group than when they are not. However, it can sometimes also lead to helping the out-group as an expression of the norms and the values of the in-group. Take, for example, the Christian fundamentalist movement in the USA and its support for Israel. A key element of this particular worldview is the central theological importance of Israel in Christian eschatology. Group members believe that the survival of Israel is key to the moments before the end of the world (and their own salvation), and thus work to support and preserve the Israeli state.

5.2.4 The strategic interests of social identity

In addition to the importance of the salience of social identity and the contents of that identity, helping can sometimes be a function of strategic concerns that are related to in-group interests. For example, Hopkins et al. (2007) showed how helping behaviour can be used to counter negative or unflattering stereotypes of the group. In experiments with Scottish participants, Hopkins et al. showed that when Scots were told that the English had a stereotype of Scots as being mean, they resented the stereotype and were motivated to refute it. Thus, when they were subsequently given the opportunity to help they did so by helping out-group members more than in-group members. Hopkins et al. argued that this was because helping others who are not part of your group is the most effective way to counter the idea that you are mean. They suggest that helping in-group members could be perceived as self-interest, but helping out-group members can in contrast be more easily attributed to generosity.

5.3 Is helping always good?

At first glance the answer to this question seems obvious. Most research on the psychology of helping tries to understand it in order to increase the incidence of helping. The logic of this is that helping behaviour is a clear public good. However, the work of Arie Nadler and colleagues (Nadler, 2002; Nadler and Saguy, 2004; Halabi et al., 2008; Nadler et al., 2009) shows that, under some conditions, helping behaviour can be experienced negatively by its recipients.

Nadler argues that, almost by definition, helping occurs between unequals: a person or group who has superior resources directs them towards others (at least presumed to be) in need. Helping can signal generosity, but it can also remind the recipient of their dependence or weakness. In other words, helping is related to power and status relations. Even when the motives of the helper are good, they can have negative consequences on the recipient of help, fostering a sense of dependency, inferiority or even helplessness. Alternatively, motives may appear good, but the help offered is strategically intended to keep the less powerful in their place.

For example, Nadler shows how powerful groups can assume they know best about what kind of help might be needed, and deliver it without involving the recipient in the decision. He calls this 'assumptive help'. Its consequences can be seen in examples of famine relief, where donor countries make decisions about what kind of help is required, or how the help should be delivered, without consulting the people in need of the help. This can have unintended consequences or lead to locals appearing to be rather ungratefully 'refusing' help.

Nadler also identifies two other different kinds of helping: **dependency-orientated help** and **autonomy-orientated help**. Dependency-orientated help treats recipients as though they are unable to contribute towards solving their problems. Autonomy-orientated help, on the other hand, treats recipients as resourceful, and tries to provide recipients with the tools to solve the problem on their own (Nadler and Halabi, 2006).

Nadler (2002) has developed the 'intergroup helping as status relations' (IHSR) model to illustrate the ways in which groups can preserve or challenge their status relative to relevant out-groups using helping behaviours. For example, when power and status relationships between groups are perceived as stable and legitimate, low-status groups are happy to receive dependency-orientated help from high-status groups. However, when power relations start to become unstable, the helping is more problematic. Low-status groups start to reject dependency-orientated help because they feel it keeps them in a socially devalued

Dependency-orientated help
This is where the helper assumes that the person being helped cannot help themselves. The helper provides a 'full solution'.

Autonomy-orientated help
The helper provides partial and temporary help to the person being helped. The underlying assumption of autonomy-oriented helping is that, given the right tools, a person can help themselves.

position. However, high-status groups become more reluctant to offer autonomy-orientated help; they prefer dependency-orientated helping as a way of countering the threat to their position by the low-status group. Nadler refers to this as 'defensive helping'. Nadler's sensitivity to the politics of helping shows that helping behaviour is not always good, and must be understood in terms of the power and status relations between the helper and the helped.

5.4 Future perspectives

In the past ten years, researchers interested in group processes have begun to explore the role of emotions in shaping helping behaviours. For example, Stürmer and colleagues (Stürmer et al., 2005; Stürmer et al., 2006) have shown that while liking or attraction was a strong predictor of helping when those needing help were out-group members, it was feelings of empathy that predicted helping when they were in-group members.

This interaction between emotions and identities has been developed in a recent review by Thomas et al. (2009). They take three primary prosocial emotions (guilt, sympathy/empathy and anger/outrage) and look at how these emotions interact with three elements of the social identity model of helping (boundaries of identity, contents of identity, and strategic interests of identity; see Section 5.2). For example, they argue that, because guilt is primarily a self-focused emotion, it maintains boundaries between groups – and is thus more likely to lead to top-down, tokenistic forms of helping. Similarly, they suggest that we should distinguish between sympathy and empathy at the group level. Sympathy maintains boundaries between in-group and out-group ('feeling sorry for them'), while empathy suggests the merging of boundaries into a single common category ('feeling the things they feel'). Thus the former might be prone to the problems of paternalistic helping identified by Nadler, while the latter might lead to genuine attempts at mutual cooperation. Of course, they don't just argue that empathy between groups will always produce cooperation. The norms and values of the group and the way emotions play a role in the content of the particular group identities are equally important.

By integrating the social identity and the intergroup emotions literature in this way, Thomas et al. (2009) are beginning to argue for a more dynamic approach to the identity–emotion relationship. Rather than the more traditional social identity approach that tends to place a salient identity as causally prior to an experienced emotion (c.f. van Zomeren et al., 2008), they suggest that emotions can equally give rise to social identities or shape group norms. Deepening the understanding of the relationship between social identities and intergroup emotions is thus one of the key challenges in future work on helping behaviour.

5.5 Summary

This section has briefly explored how a developed theoretical framework – the social identity tradition – can broaden our understanding of helping behaviour. In examining the story that captured social psychology's initial interest in helping behaviours, this work has pointed to different ways of understanding helping. Using a group level of analysis, for example, can lead to findings that challenge the bystander effect. In highlighting the role of the salience, boundaries, content and strategic interests of social identity, this approach has begun to illustrate the importance of group memberships in the study of helping. Moreover, the recent integration of intergroup emotions with a social identity approach to helping offers the potential for an additionally sophisticated group-level understanding of helping.

6 Concluding thoughts

> **Pause for thought**
>
> At this point you might find it useful to look back at Activity 5.1. Have any of the approaches that you have now looked at provided additional insight into your reactions? Which of the approaches did you find the most convincing? Were any of these approaches similar to your initial explanations?

This chapter has attempted to set out some of the challenges in studying helping behaviour. Examining the definition of helping enabled us to see some of the fundamental issues in this area: a lack of consistency in the use of terms points to a broader lack of integration of the wider field and presents potential problems for explaining helping at a general level. Do all the various types of behaviour that we might consider to be 'helping' share enough common features to be explained by one theory?

The more recent use of the social identity approach to studying helping behaviour offers potential to integrate the study of helping within a broader theoretical framework. However, we might additionally question whether a 'pure' social psychological approach can account for all of these behaviours. As you have seen, social psychological approaches have often drawn from different disciplines in understanding helping. Moreover, it is evident from attempts to engage at a practical level with helping that a broadly informed perspective has utility. As noted by Penner et al. (2005, p. 385) in their review of theory and research on prosocial behaviour, it is because of the breadth of research in the area that it 'is able to contribute to connections between psychology and other social science disciplines and can facilitate the development of interdisciplinary and multidisciplinary collaborations and perspectives for both theory and application.'

Further reading

Dovidio, J.F., Piliavin, J.A., Schroeder, D.A and Penner, L.A. (2006) *The Social Psychology of Prosocial Behaviour*, Mahwah, NJ, Lawrence Erlbaum Associates.

Fischer, P., Krueger, J., Greitemeyer, T., Vogrincic, C., Kastenmüller, A., Frey, D., Heene, M., Wicher, M. and Kainbacher, M. (2011) 'The bystander effect: a meta-analytic review on bystander intervention in dangerous and non-dangerous emergencies', *Psychological Bulletin*, vol. 137, pp. 517–37.

Levine, M. and Manning, R. (2013) 'Social identity, group processes and helping in emergencies', *European Review of Social Psychology*, vol. 24, pp. 225–51.

Penner, L.A., Dovidio, J.F., Schroeder, D.A. and Piliavin, J.A. (2005) 'Prosocial behaviour: multilevel perspectives', *Annual Review of Psychology*, vol. 56, pp. 365–92.

Stürmer, S. and Snyder, M. (eds) (2010) *The Psychology of Prosocial Behaviour: Group Processes, Intergroup Relations, and Helping*, Chichester, Wiley-Blackwell.

References

Batson, C.D. (1987) 'Prosocial motivation: is it ever truly altruistic?' in Berkowitz, L. (ed.) *Advances in Experimental Social Psychology,* vol. 20, pp. 65–122, New York, Academic Press.

Batson, C.D. (1994) 'Looking back at "The Unresponsive Bystander": Camelot or the Golden Age?', *Contemporary Psychology*, vol. 39, pp. 941–3.

Bierhoff, H.-W. (2002) *Prosocial Behaviour*, Hove, Psychology Press.

Cherry, F. (1995) *The Stubborn Particulars of Social Psychology*, London, Routledge.

Cialdini, R.B., Brown, S.L., Lewis, B.P., Luce, C. and Neuberg, S.L. (1997) 'Reinterpreting the empathy–altruism relationship: when one into one equals oneness', *Journal of Personality and Social Psychology*, vol. 73, pp. 481-94.

Coke, J.S., Batson, C.D. and McDavis, K. (1978) 'Empathic mediation of helping: a two-stage model', *Journal of Personality and Social Psychology*, vol. 36, pp. 752–66.

Darley, J.M. and Latané, B. (1968) 'Bystander intervention in emergencies: diffusion of responsibility', *Journal of Personality and Social Psychology*, vol. 8, pp. 377–83.

Dawkins, R. (1976) *The Selfish Gene*, Oxford and New York, Oxford University Press.

Dovidio, J.F., Allen, J.L. and Schroeder, D.A. (1990) 'The specificity of empathy induced helping: evidence for altruism', *Journal of Personality and Social Psychology*, vol. 59, pp. 249–60.

Drury. J. and Reicher, S. (2010) 'Crowd control', *Scientific American Mind*, November/December, pp. 58–65.

Drury, J., Cocking, C. and Reicher, S. (2009) 'The nature of collective resilience: survivor reactions to the 2005 London bombings', *International Journal of Mass Emergencies and Disasters*, vol. 27, pp. 66–95.

Evans, R.I. (1980) 'John McCannon Darley', in Evans, R.I. (ed.) *The Making of Social Psychology: Discussions with Creative Contributors*, New York, Gardner Press Inc., pp. 214–25.

Fehr, E. and Gächter, S. (2002) 'Altruistic punishment in humans', *Nature*, vol. 415, pp. 137–40.

Fischer, P., Greitemeyer, T., Pollozek, F. and Frey, D. (2006) 'The unresponsive bystander: are bystanders more responsive in dangerous emergencies?', *European Journal of Social Psychology*, vol. 36, pp. 267–78.

Fischer, P., Krueger, J.I., Greitemeyer, T., Vogrincic, C., Kastenmüller, A., Frey, D., Heene, M., Wicher, M. and Kainbacher, M. (2011) 'The bystander effect: a meta-analytic review on bystander intervention in dangerous and non-dangerous emergencies', *Psychological Bulletin*, vol. 137, pp. 517–37.

Geis, G. and Huston, T.L. (1983) 'Bystander intervention into crime: public policy considerations', *Policy Studies Journal*, vol. 11, pp. 398–408.

Geis, G., Huston, T.L. and Wright, R. (1976) 'Compensating good Samaritans', *Crime Prevention Review*, vol. 5, pp. 28–35.

Gintis, H. (2000) 'Strong reciprocity and human sociality', *Journal of Theoretical Biology*, vol. 206, pp. 169–79.

Grusec, J.E. and Redler, E. (1980) 'Attribution, reinforcement, and altruism: a developmental analysis', *Developmental Psychology*, vol. 16, pp. 525–34.

Grzelak, J. and Derlega, V.J. (1982), 'Cooperation and helping behaviour: an introduction', in Derlega, V.J. and Grzelak, J. (eds) *Cooperation and Helping Behaviour: Theories and Research*, New York, Academic Press.

Halabi, S., Dovidio, J.F. and Nadler, A. (2008) 'When and how high status groups offer help: effects of social dominance orientation and status threat', *Political Psychology*, vol. 29, pp. 841–58.

Hamilton, W.D. (1964) 'The evolution of social behavior', *Journal of Theoretical Biology*, vol. 7, pp. 1–52.

Hopkins, N., Reicher, S., Harrison, K., Cassidy, C., Bull, R. and Levine, M. (2007) 'Helping to improve the group stereotype: on the strategic dimension of prosocial behaviour', *Personality and Social Psychology Bulletin*, vol. 33, pp. 776–88.

Huston, T.L., Ruggiero, M., Conner, R. and Geis, G. (1981) 'Bystander intervention into crime: a study based on naturally occurring episodes', *Social Psychological Quarterly*, vol. 44, pp. 14–23.

Jetten, J., Spears, R. and Manstead, A.S.R. (1996) 'Ingroup norms and intergroup discrimination: distinctive self-categorization and social identity effects', *Journal of Personality and Social Psychology*, vol. 71, pp. 1222–33.

Knafo, A., Zahn-Waxler, C., van Hulle, C. , Robinson, J. and Rhee, S.H. (2008) 'The origins and development of empathy', *Emotion*, vol. 8, pp. 735–52.

Latané, B. and Darley, J.M. (1968) 'Group inhibition of bystander intervention in emergencies', *Journal of Personality and Social Psychology*, vol. 10, pp. 215–21.

Latané, B. and Darley, J.M. (1970) *The Unresponsive Bystander: Why Doesn't He Help?,* New York, Appleton-Century-Crofts.

Latané, B. and Nida, S. (1981) 'Ten years of research on group size and helping', *Psychological Bulletin*, vol. 89, pp. 308–24.

Lerner, M.J. (1970) 'The desire for justice and reactions to victims', in Macaulay, J. and Berkowitz, L. (eds) *Altruism and Helping Behaviour: Social*

Psychological Studies of Some Antecedents and Consequences, New York and London, Academic Press.

Levine, R.M. (1999) 'Rethinking bystander non-intervention: social categorisation and the evidence of witnesses at the James Bulger murder trial', *Human Relations*, vol. 52, pp. 1133–55.

Levine, M. and Crowther, S. (2008) 'The responsive bystander: how social group membership and group size can encourage as well as inhibit bystander intervention', *Journal of Personality and Social Psychology*, vol. 96, pp. 1429–39.

Levine, M. and Manning, R. (2013) 'Social identity, group processes, and helping in emergencies', *European Review of Social Psychology*, vol. 24, pp. 225–51.

Levine, M. and Thompson, K. (2004) 'Identity, place, and bystander intervention: social categories and helping after natural disasters', *Journal of Social Psychology*, vol. 144, pp. 229–46.

Levine, M., Cassidy, C., Brazier, G. and Reicher, S. (2002) 'Self-categorisation and bystander intervention: two experimental studies', *Journal of Applied Social Psychology*, vol. 7, pp. 1452–63.

Levine, M., Prosser, A., Evans, D. and Reicher, S. (2005) 'Identity and emergency intervention: how social group membership and inclusiveness of group boundaries shapes helping behaviour', *Personality and Social Psychology Bulletin*, vol. 31, pp. 443–53.

Lodewijkx, H.F.M., Wildschut, T., Nijstad, B.A., Savenije, W. and Smit, M. (2001) 'In a violent world a just world makes sense: the case of "senseless violence" in The Netherlands', *Social Justice Research*, vol. 14, pp. 79–94.

Macaulay, J. and Berkowitz, L. (eds) (1970) *Altruism and Helping Behaviour: Social Psychological Studies of Some Antecedents and Consequences*, New York and London, Academic Press.

Manning, R., Levine, M. and Collins, A. (2007) 'The Kitty Genovese murder and the social psychology of helping: the parable of the 38 witnesses', *American Psychologist*, vol. 62, pp. 555–62.

McDougall, W. (1908) *Social Psychology*, London, Metheun.

Nadler, A. (2002) 'Intergroup helping relations as power relations: helping relations as affirming or challenging intergroup hierarchy', *Journal of Social Issues*, vol. 58, pp. 487–502.

Nadler, A. and Halabi, S. (2006) 'Intergroup helping as status relations: effects of status stability, identification, and type of help on receptivity to high-status group's help', *Journal of Personality and Social Psychology*, vol. 91, pp. 97–110.

Nadler, A. and Saguy, T. (2004) 'Trust building and reconciliation between adversarial groups: a social psychological perspective', in Langholtz, H. and Stout, C.E. (eds) *The Psychology of Diplomacy*, New York, Praeger, pp. 29–47.

Nadler, A., Harpaz-Gorodeisky, G. and Ben-David, Y. (2009) 'Defensive helping: threat to group identity, ingroup identification, status stability, and common group identity as determinants of intergroup help-giving', *Journal of Personality and Social Psychology*, vol. 97, pp. 823–34.

Penner, L.A. (2002) 'Dispositional and structural determinants of volunteerism: an interactionist perspective', *Journal of Social Issues*, vol. 58, pp. 447–67.

Penner, L.A., Dovidio, J.F., Piliavin, J.A. and Schroeder, D.A. (2005), 'Prosocial behaviour: multilevel perspectives', *Annual Review of Psychology*, vol. 56, pp. 365–92.

Piliavin, J.A. (2009) 'Altruism and helping: the evolution of a field: the 2008 Cooley-Mead presentation', *Social Psychology Quarterly*, vol. 72, pp. 209–25.

Piliavin, I.M., Rodin, J. and Piliavin, J.A. (1969) 'Good Samaritanism: an underground phenomenon', *Journal of Personality and Social Psychology*, vol. 13, pp. 289–99.

Piliavin, J.A., Dovidio, J.F., Gaertner, S.L. and Clark, I.R.D. (1981) *Emergency Intervention*, New York, Academic Press.

Reicher, S., Hopkins, N., Levine, M. and Rath, R. (2005) 'Entrepreneurs of hate and entrepreneurs of solidarity: social identity as a basis for mass communications', *International Review of the Red Cross*, vol. 860, pp. 621–37.

Reicher, S., Cassidy, C., Wolpert, I., Hopkins, N. and Levine, M. (2006) 'Saving Bulgaria's Jews: an analysis of social identity and the mobilisation of social solidarity', *European Journal of Social Psychology*, vol. 36, pp. 49–72.

Richerson, P. and Boyd, R. (2005) *Not By Genes Alone: How Culture Transformed Human Evolution*, Chicago, IL, University of Chicago.

Schwartz, S.H. and Howard, J.A. (1984) 'Internalized values as motivators of altruism', in Staub, E., Bar-Tal, D., Karylowski, J. and Rykowski, J. (eds) *Development and Maintenance of Prosocial Behaviour*, pp. 229–55, New York, Plenum.

Singer, P. (2009) *The Life You Can Save: How to Play Your Part in Ending World Poverty*, London, Picador.

Spielman, D. and Staub, E. (2000) 'Reducing boys' aggression. Learning to fulfil basic needs constructively', *Journal of Applied Developmental Psychology*, vol. 21, no. 2, pp. 165–81.

Staub, E. (1975) *The Development of Prosocial Behaviour in Children*, Morristown, NJ, General Learning Press.

Stürmer, S., Snyder, M. and Omoto, A.M. (2005) 'Prosocial emotions and helping: the moderating role of group membership', *Journal of Personality and Social Psychology*, vol. 88, pp. 532–46.

Stürmer, S., Snyder, M., Kropp, A. and Siem, B. (2006) 'Empathy-motivated helping: the moderating role of group membership', *Personality and Social Psychology Bulletin*, vol. 32, pp. 943–56.

Tajfel, H. (ed.) (1978) *Differentiation Between Social Groups: Studies in the Social Psychology of Intergroup Relations*, London, Academic Press

Tajfel, H. (ed.) (1982) *Social Identity and Intergroup Relations*, Cambridge, Cambridge University Press and Paris, Editions de la Maison des Sciences de l'Homme.

Thomas, E.F., McGarty, C. and Mavor, K.I. (2009) 'Transforming "apathy into movement": the role of prosocial emotions in motivating action for social change', *Personality and Social Psychology Review*, vol. 13, pp. 310–33.

Trivers, R.L. (1971) 'The evolution of reciprocal altruism', *The Quarterly Review of Biology*, vol. 46, pp. 35–57.

Turner, J.C., Hogg, M.A., Oakes, P.J., Reicher, S.D. and Wetherell, M.C. (1987) *Rediscovering the Social Group: A Self-Categorisation Theory*, New York, Basil Blackwell.

Van Zomeren, M., Postmes, T. and Spears, R. (2008) 'Toward an integrative social identity model of collective action: a quantitative research synthesis of three socio-psychological perspectives', *Psychological Bulletin*, vol. 134, pp. 504–35.

Zagefka, H., Noor, M. and Brown, R. (2013) 'Familiarity breeds compassion: knowledge of disaster areas and willingness to donate money to disaster victims', *Applied Psychology: An International Review*, vol. 62, pp. 640–54.

Zagefka, H., Noor, M., Brown, R.J., de Moura, G. and Hopthrow, T. (2011) 'Donating to disaster victims: responses to natural and humanly caused events', *European Journal of Social Psychology*, vol. 41, pp. 353–63.

Zahn-Waxler, C., Schiro, K., Robinson, J.L., Emde, R.N. and Schmitz, S. (2001) 'Empathy and prosocial patterns in young MZ and DZ twins: development and genetic and environmental influences', in Emde, R.N. and Hewitt, J.K. (eds) *Infancy to Early Childhood: Genetic and Environmental Influences on Developmental Change*, New York, Oxford University Press, pp. 141–62.

Chapter 6

Why would I hang around with you? The psychology of personal relationships

Simon Watts and Vicki McDermott

Contents

1 Introduction

Psychology, in common with most Western cultures, typically assumes that individual people are self-contained (Sampson, 1989). This means we should all strive to be complete 'in isolation' and to operate and make decisions independently, free from the supposedly contaminating influence of other people and social groups. This image of relationships as potential contaminants influenced many of the important early studies in social psychology, from Le Bon's (1895) work on 'crowd psychology' to Asch's (1952, 1956, 1959) seminal studies on conformity and Milgram's (1963) infamous treatment of obedience. Contact with other people, it seems, can really mess you up!

The assumption of self-contained **individualism** has also led psychology to prioritise approaches that study people in isolation and to see relationships as an optional extra. In fact, **personal relationships** only became part of the British Psychological Society curriculum about 15 years ago. Critical social psychologists have nonetheless continually challenged this position (Stainton Rogers et al., 1995). As Ian Burkitt puts it:

Individualism
The ways that people identify themselves and focus their goals, with an emphasis on personal freedom and achievement.

Personal relationships
Voluntary interdependence between two people intended to facilitate the socio-emotional goals of the participants over time.

> The view of human beings as unitary individuals who carry their uniqueness deep inside themselves ... is one that is ingrained in the Western tradition of thought. It is the vision of the person as a monad ... a self-contained being whose social bonds are not primary in its existence ... suppose [however, that] we tried to understand human beings from a different perspective, as social selves rather than self-contained individuals. From such an angle, we would try to see human beings inside their essential connections to other people.
>
> (Burkitt, 1993, p. 1)

This is what the study of personal relationships tries to do. Two prominent names in the field, Ellen Berscheid and Anne Peplau, have described relationships as 'the foundation and theme of the human condition' (1983, p. 19). The implication is that, far from being optional extras, relationships are both necessary and fundamental to the making of ourselves and that they are, as such, of central importance for people and for psychology.

It is symptomatic, therefore, that the study of personal relationships has gradually found a home in many of psychology's sub-disciplines, including physiological, clinical, evolutionary, developmental, counselling, cognitive and social psychology. Nor is this an exhaustive list. Personal relationships blur the boundaries in psychology very effectively and this makes the topic ideally suited to a volume of this type. The study of personal relationships, or relationship science (Fletcher et al., 1999), also extends into many other disciplines including, but not limited to, sociology, communication studies, gender studies, anthropology and history. This makes the subject very interesting, but equally something of a nightmare when the literature reviewing starts! It also means there is a pressing need to define and delineate the parameters and aims of this chapter at the earliest opportunity, so this is addressed in the next section.

Learning outcomes

On completing this chapter you should:

- have an understanding of the importance of studying personal relationships in psychology
- be familiar with the main psychological theories around processes of attraction
- be able to appreciate why communication and self-disclosure are so important for personal relationships
- have an understanding of the concept and process of friendship and the main theories of love
- have an understanding of the role of conflict and the dangers of violence in personal relationships, as well as the process of relationship dissolution.

1.1 Useful definitions and chapter aims

Many subtly different definitions of personal relationships exist, but we particularly like this one: 'voluntary interdependence between two persons over time that is intended to facilitate the socio-emotional goals of the participants' (Hays, 1998, p. 395). In truth, this is actually a definition of friendship, but it serves our purpose because it allows us to quickly distinguish personal from both family and impersonal relationships.

Family relationships obviously have personal aspects since they typically facilitate the socio-emotional goals of the participants, but the interdependence of the two parties is not completely voluntary. You do not choose your biological parents, nor your brothers and sisters. For this reason, this chapter will not deal with family relationships. Conversely, impersonal relationships typically demand some sort of voluntary interdependence, usually one participant is fulfilling a role or practical function in the life of the other, but this function is not expected to facilitate anyone's socio-emotional goals. This lack of emotional content leaves impersonal relationships outside the current remit.

What remains is a focus on voluntary and reciprocal relationships, relationships in which we choose to engage, ordinarily inspired by mutual feelings of attraction, friendship and/or love. Beyond this emotional attachment, personal relationships are also characterised by high levels of behavioural interdependence and by their capacity to satisfy many of the social and psychological needs of the parties involved. The aim of this chapter is to guide you through the life cycle of a typical personal relationship. Starting with the processes involved in attraction, you will look at issues of relational communication and self-disclosure, friendship, love, as well as conflict and violence. The chapter concludes by considering the main theories of relationship 'break-up' or dissolution.

Pause for thought

Section 1.1 suggests that the main focus of this chapter will be voluntary and reciprocal relationships. This excludes family relationships, and also excludes arranged marriages. Arranged marriage is, and always has been, the most common type of marital relationship in the world, so consider for a moment the reasons for excluding it from the chapter. The answer is that relationship science and the personal relationships literature has a Westernised and individualistic focus. In other words, it contains something of a cultural bias. Material on arranged marriage (and other typically non-Western approaches to relationships) can be found in a separate and almost distinct cross-cultural literature. Likewise, material focused exclusively on lesbian and gay relationships is largely to be found in a separate literature focused on issues of sexuality. Both represent limitations of the mainstream relationship literature which are worth you knowing about.

2 Processes of attraction

Attraction represents a typical first stage in the life cycle of a personal relationship. It is the phenomenon that draws friends and intimate partners together. In the sections that follow, the key factors that influence attraction will be outlined, including proximity, familiarity, physical appearance and similarity.

2.1 The question of choice

People in individualistic cultures expect a free choice when it comes to personal relationships, but our freedom is actually somewhat restricted (Sprecher and Duck, 1993). This is because our so-called *field of desirables*, i.e. the range of people that we might seriously consider as a friend or intimate partner, is considerably smaller than our *field of eligibles*, i.e. the range of people who we can feasibly befriend or love (because of our own demographic characteristics, such as our age, ethnicity, socio-economic status, physical appearance, intelligence, religion, and so on); and the number of people who are eligible is itself far smaller than our *field of availables*, i.e. the range of people who are, in principle, available for a personal relationship.

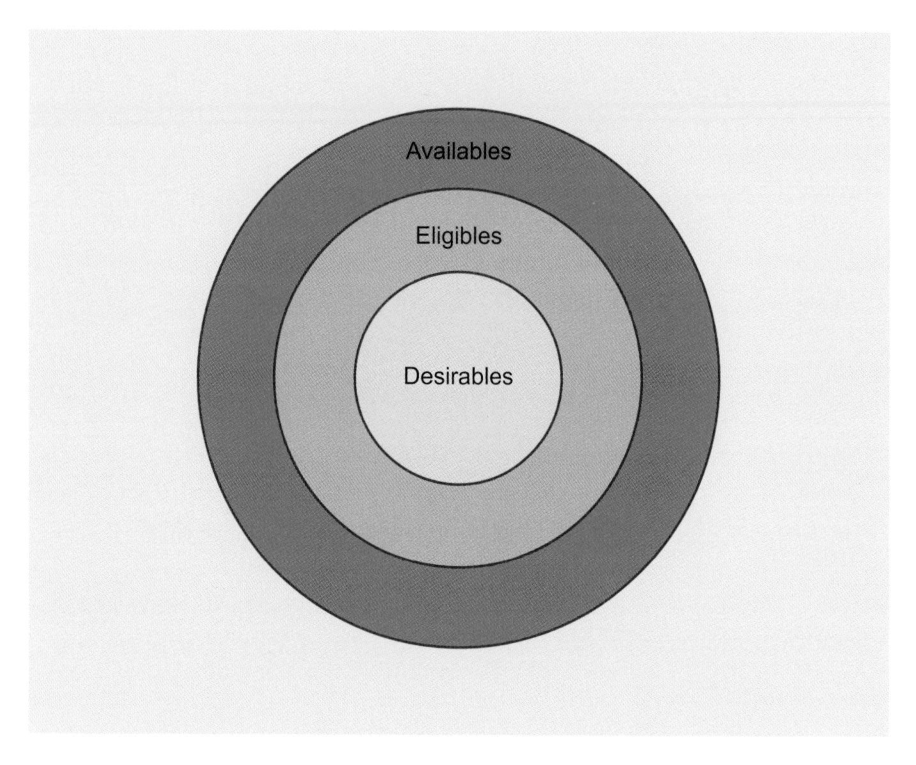

Figure 6.1 Sprecher and Duck's (1993) concentric fields of available, eligible and desirable people

While 'desirability' is undoubtedly a matter of personal choice, therefore, such choice can only be applied relative to those who are eligible, and eligibility is always, to a large extent, predefined and delimited by our cultural circumstances and a host of pertinent demographic characteristics. As we are about to see, personal relationships require the establishment of **proximity**, and this is often difficult to achieve across social, cultural and demographic boundaries.

Proximity
Being near in space, time, order, occurrence or relation.

2.2 Attraction factor 1: proximity or 'propinquity'

Festinger et al. (1950) is a seminal study in social psychology that demonstrates the importance of physical proximity (or 'propinquity') for the establishment of personal relationships. The study took place in a particular housing project and aimed to ascertain the impact of physical distance on the likelihood of residents forming friendships. Sixty-five per cent of best friends, it turned out, were located within the same building block, 41 per cent lived next door to each other, 22 per cent lived two doors apart, and only 10 per cent were at opposite ends of the hallway. Basically, friendship was aided by proximity and handicapped by distance. Indeed, the people who reported the most friends lived adjacent to the stairwell, apparently because this location afforded them proximity to the greatest number of passers-by!

The world has clearly changed since 1950 such that proximity can now be established not just physically, but also online and in a 'virtual' fashion. There is much research in this area, which considers, among other issues, the establishment of friendships in an online setting (Tang, 2010), the differences between online and offline friendships (Chan and Cheng, 2004) and the merits of online dating (Finkel et al., 2012).

Pause for thought

Take a moment to consider the role of social media in personal relationships. Do you use Facebook or some other form of social media? If so, do you find it useful for maintaining friendships? Have you established new friendships in this way?

Box 6.1 The growing role of e-technology in establishing and maintaining personal relationships

The internet is undoubtedly having a profound influence on personal relationships. Social networking sites like Facebook have proved themselves a very useful vehicle for maintaining friendships (Ellison et al., 2011). Many online dating sites also exist, such as eHarmony.com and match.com, and the establishment of intimate relationships over the internet has become a billion-dollar industry. Cacioppo et al. (2013), for example, in a paper published in the *Proceedings of the National Academy of Sciences of the United States*, have recently concluded, following a survey of a nationally representative sample of 19,131 respondents who married between 2005 and 2012, that slightly more than one-third of marriages in the USA now begin online. Interestingly, this paper also proposed that marriages that began online delivered slightly higher levels of marital satisfaction and were slightly less likely to break up or end in divorce than more traditional offline alternatives. This led the authors to suggest that the internet was implicated, not just as a means of establishing personal relationships, but also in the very dynamics and outcomes of marriage.

A look at the small print of this study nonetheless demonstrates that the survey was commissioned by eHarmony.com, which clearly has a vested interest in promoting online dating and relationships. It is clear, however, that Cacioppo et al. (2013) followed procedures outlined by the *Journal of the American Medical Association*; independent statisticians reviewed their data, and the stated proportion of online marriages broadly agrees with the findings of an earlier review of the scientific data conducted by Finkel et al. (2012). This earlier review also agrees that online dating can offer some important advantages over offline approaches. It allows easy and convenient access to a wide range of potential partners, for example, as well as all the personal information necessary to make well-informed decisions about who to meet face to face.

Finkel et al. (2012) do conclude, however, that little evidence exists to suggest online approaches improve romantic outcomes, and that they may well undermine them in some circumstances. Easy access to a wide range of potential partners, it is suggested, might easily lead to an 'assessment-oriented' and judgemental approach to dating and to the objectification of potential partners. It may also make people reluctant to commit to a single relationship. Either way, the role of the internet in personal relationships will undoubtedly continue to provoke a lot of interesting research in the coming years.

2.3 Attraction factor 2: familiarity

Familiarity
A subjective feeling of recognition provoked by a situation, event, place, person or object we recognise from memory.

People show a definite preference for things to which they have previously been exposed (Zajonc, 1968). This phenomenon is called the *mere exposure* or **familiarity** *effect*. It is a robust and reliable effect that appears to reach its peak at somewhere between 10 and 20 exposures. This suggests that the more often you see a particular person, up to a point at least, the more pleasing they are likely to appear. If, however, you are now inspired to 'get seen' more often by someone you like, a note of caution is probably in order. Seeing too much of someone can reduce and even reverse this preference (Bornstein, 1989). Some studies actually suggest that repeated exposure to people or stimuli we didn't initially like only serves to make us dislike them even more (Ebbesen et al., 1976; Perlman and Oskamp, 1971).

Moreland and Beach (1992) nonetheless provide a powerful demonstration of familiarity at work. This study used four female confederates who entered a classroom either 5, 10 or 15 times, or not at all, across the course of a single term. They did not interact with the other students. At the end of term, the students were asked to provide ratings of the confederates across a range of social and personality dimensions. Amazingly, the more often a confederate had entered the classroom the more positively she was rated. Of even more interest, however, is that these ratings occurred despite the majority of students reporting no awareness that the confederates had even been in their class! Familiarity, it seems, is a very important factor in attraction (Reis et al., 2011).

2.4 Attraction factor 3: physical attractiveness

Pause for thought

Before reading this section, make a list of the physical and personality characteristics that you would or do find most attractive in a long-term intimate partner. Try to list them in order of importance. Would the list/order/balance of physical and personality characteristics change in the context of a short-term liaison? For your information, intelligence, a good sense of humour, outgoing, considerate, trustworthy, honest, interesting and understanding often feature highly as personality characteristics on lists of this type. Physical attractiveness nonetheless tends to feature highly and is typically considered to be very important, although most studies are too polite to list what this means in practice!

A lot of research has been carried out on the sort of facial characteristics people tend to find attractive. First, we seem to like symmetrical faces. Little and Jones (2003) demonstrated that this preference for symmetry only occurs for faces, not for other objects or even for inverted or 'upside-down' faces. This, they concluded, suggests that symmetry is only attractive in the context of stimuli relevant to our partner choices, not because we have a general perceptual bias for symmetrical objects (i.e. because they are easier for our perceptual systems to process). In addition, the attractiveness of symmetrical faces may be because it signals a healthy set of genes and a possible evolutionary advantage for the individual in question. The latter is certainly an interesting and plausible hypothesis, although it remains a matter for speculation.

A second facial quality we appear to like is averageness. This seems surprising. Very attractive people are surely anything but average? People do, however, typically rate composite faces (a single face created through the merging of many faces) as more attractive than the constituent faces from which they were created. Perrett et al. (1994) nonetheless demonstrates that the situation is more complex. They created three faces (while controlling for other factors such as symmetry): a first composite face constructed from photographs of 60 young women, a second from photographs of the 15 young women rated as the most attractive (of the original 60), and a third face, based on the second one, which exaggerated or enhanced the facial features typically considered to be the most feminine and attractive for women (the eyes were slightly increased in size, for example, the lips made fuller, and so on); see Figure 6.2. This third face was rated as most attractive by the study participants even though it was the *least average* of the three from a mathematical perspective. The conclusion was drawn, therefore, that highly attractive faces are not average per se, but that they do tend to deviate systematically from an average shape.

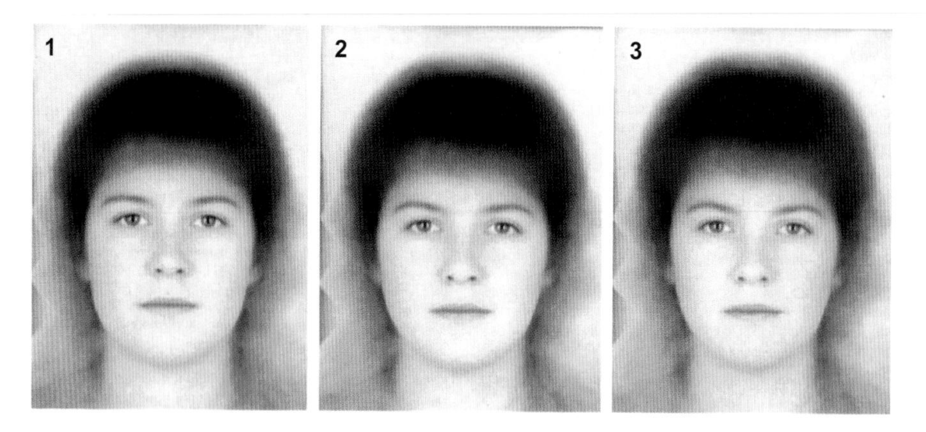

Figure 6.2 Three faces created by Perrett et al. (1994)

It is also noteworthy that the faces of both women *and* men are considered to be more attractive (by both men and women) when their facial features are feminised (Perrett et al., 1998). This may be because typically feminine facial features are associated with more positive personality characteristics such as warmth, good parenting, trustworthiness, and so on, than are typically male facial features such as pronounced brow ridges and square jawlines. Again, however, this suggestion is open to question. Penton-Voak et al. (1999) have also found that women not taking oral contraception preferred more masculine faces at the point in their menstrual cycle when their fertility was at its peak. The reason for this altered preference is not yet clear.

There are other contextual factors, such as facial expression and gaze direction, which influence facial attractiveness (Jones et al., 2006). Regardless of context, however, the literature suggests that men tend to value physical attractiveness more highly than women (Feingold, 1991). They are more likely to choose an intimate partner based on their youthfulness and physical appearance, while women are more likely to concentrate on the resources a potential partner might offer (Miner and Shackleford, 2010). Evolutionary psychologists suggest this difference is a result of natural selection and the pursuit of different sexual strategies by women and men (Buss and Schmitt, 1993). Men, they argue, who need not invest heavily in the upbringing of a child, have simply developed a short-term sexual strategy that maximises their potential to reproduce. Female fertility typically peaks around the age of 25, so a focus on young and attractive women has a certain adaptive logic. Women, on the other hand, who typically invest heavily in a child's upbringing, have developed a long-term strategy that focuses attention on a partner's resources and their potential to provide adequate support.

Of course, such evolutionary explanations can only ever be postulated as 'likely stories', and it is clear that reported gender differences of this type may equally be a reflection of power dynamics, socialisation and comparative access to material resources (Howard et al., 1987). Either way, the personal relationships literature suggests that men are typically more preoccupied with physical attractiveness than women. Greitemeyer (2005), for example, demonstrated that men are always more willing than women to accept hypothetical sexual offers from a stranger, across a range of short- and long-term scenarios, and that this receptivity increases with the stranger's physical attractiveness. Women also showed some preference for physical attractiveness in this study, in the context of short-term liaisons, but the socio-economic status of the stranger carried far greater weight in the long term.

Dunn and Searle (2010) also presented evidence to demonstrate the importance of socio-economic status for women. In their study the socio-economic status of men was manipulated by presenting photos of them in a low-status car (the neutral-status condition) and in a prestige car (the high-status condition). Women were then asked to rate the physical attractiveness of the men, either in the neutral- or high-status condition. The results showed that the same men were rated as more physically attractive when pictured with an expensive car (Figures 6.3 and 6.4).

Figure 6.3 Rating attractiveness in different status conditions

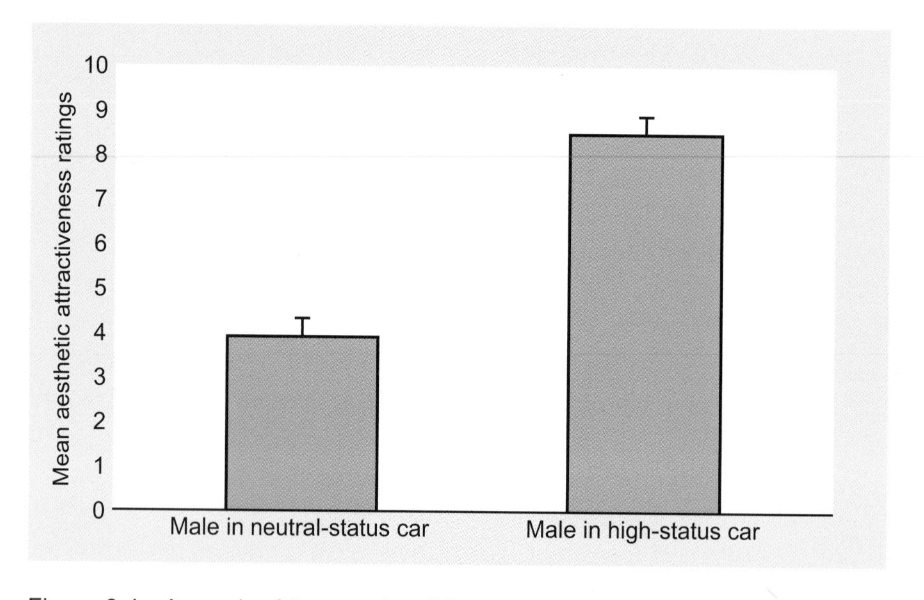

Figure 6.4 A graph of the results of Dunn and Searle (2010)

Halo effect
Attributing positive traits and characteristics to a person we like, even when we have little or no evidence to support these attributions.

Perhaps the most concerning aspect of the relationships literature, however, is our widespread tendency to conflate physical attractiveness with positive personal and social characteristics. Dion et al. (1972) called this the 'what is beautiful is good hypothesis'. In actuality, however, it is an example of a wider phenomenon known as 'the **halo effect**'. Basically, the halo effect leads us to attribute positive traits and characteristics to people we find attractive, even where we have little or no evidence to support these attributions. As Dion et al. (1972, p. 289) put it, 'not only are physically attractive persons assumed to possess more socially desirable personalities than those of lesser attractiveness ... it is [also] presumed that their lives will be happier and more successful.'

One possible reason for these assumptions is, as Langlois (1986) suggests, that our desire to engage with attractive people and tendency to react positively in their company may actually help them to develop the enhanced personalities and social skills we expect. In other words, the perceived connection between beauty and goodness may actually be a self-fulfilling prophecy (for example, Chaiken, 1979; Reis et al., 1980).

2.5 Attraction factor 4: similarity (and complementarity)

Partner similarity (or homogamy) is one of the best predictors of longevity in friendship and marriage and its role in attractiveness is well established (Berscheid and Reis, 1998). Long-term friends and intimate partners tend to have similar backgrounds and demographic characteristics (physical health, age, religion, level of education, etc.), similar cognitive abilities, similar attitudes, values, personality traits, and so on. Berscheid et al.'s (1971) '**matching hypothesis**' also concludes that we are drawn to people possessing similar levels of physical attractiveness to our own.

Matching hypothesis
The idea that we are attracted to people with similar physical attractiveness to our own.

There are various possible explanations for this preference, which go beyond the obvious conclusion that similar people are likely to like us, to reinforce us and to approve of many of our thoughts and actions. The first is that similarity is not a preference as such, but a by-product of the need for proximity. We tend to live near, be educated with, and work alongside people who are similar to us in terms of their backgrounds, socio-economic status, levels of intelligence, interests, and so on. This means that similar people are simply more accessible to us. The second explanation, which is related to the first, is that similarity is easier to obtain and maintain. There are simply greater risks involved in pursuing a partner who is more attractive than we are, for example, or much younger, or from a different culture. Many theories of relationship dynamics suggest that personal relationships exist most comfortably in a balanced or equitable state, and a preference for similarity conforms to this model (Homans, 1974; Thibaut and Kelley,

1959; Adams, 1965). Studies have also shown that dissimilarity is actually our preferred option, provided we know in advance that the 'different' person likes us and wants to have a relationship (Aron et al., 2006). This suggests that an evaluation of risks and costs is almost certainly involved in our general preference for similarity.

The final explanation is that similarity is not a cause of attraction, but its *effect*. In simple terms, we admire the qualities of people to whom we are attracted (and they admire us) and in the process of mutual relationship and admiration we gradually become more and more alike. Morry's (2005) '**attraction-similarity hypothesis**' also suggests that while similarity can cause attraction, levels of attraction (and consequent levels of relational satisfaction) also influence our *perceptions* of similarity. This means the more satisfied we are with a particular friend or partner, the more attractive we find them, and the more similar we consider them to be!

Attraction-similarity hypothesis
This hypothesis suggests that similarity can cause attraction but levels of attraction can also influence our perceptions of similarity.

All things considered, there is little doubt that similarity is strongly implicated in processes of attraction. The only powerful counter-argument involves our potentially being attracted to people who possess many of the key characteristics (skills or abilities) that we lack. This is known as *complementarity* (Winch et al., 1954). Murstein's (1972) '**beauty–money trade off**' proposes, for example, that attractive men and women tend to marry people possessing higher levels of wealth and resources than themselves and that, reciprocally speaking, affluent people tend to marry partners who are more attractive. The beauty of one partner, in other words, is taken as a fair and complementary trade for the wealth of the other. Complementary *behaviour* has certainly been shown to positively influence measures of satisfaction in personal relationships, but ultimately that satisfaction seems only to reinforce the perception that we and our partner are very similar indeed (Dryer and Horowitz, 1997).

Beauty–money trade off
The beauty–money trade off proposes that attractive men and women tend to marry people who have higher levels of wealth and resources than themselves. Reciprocally speaking, affluent people tend to marry partners who are more attractive.

> **Pause for thought**
>
> In what ways (if any) are you similar to or different from your friends/intimate partner? In what ways (if any) are your personality characteristics and/or behaviours complementary to those of your friends/intimate partner? Make a list for each person. In doing so, consider how each of them fits into your life and how and where they make their particular contribution to your well-being. This is an important process that can help you to appreciate your friends and intimate partner that little bit more.

2.6 Summary

This section has considered the main factors that influence attraction, including proximity, familiarity, facial and physical attractiveness, similarity and complementarity. It has also considered some of the important hypotheses and effects that characterise the attractiveness literature, including the mere exposure effect, the 'what is beautiful is good hypothesis' (or 'halo effect'), the 'matching hypothesis', the 'attraction-similarity hypothesis' and the 'beauty–money trade off'.

3 Communication and self-disclosure

3.1 Communication in relationship, communication as relationship

In 1999, the online survey company Roper Starch asked 1001 Americans to tell them what they considered to be the main reason for divorce. Among other answers, 3 per cent cited children, 5 per cent sexual problems and 29 per cent financial difficulties, yet a majority of 53 per cent opted for ineffective communication. Communication quality is indeed a very good predictor of relational satisfaction and endurance when it functions well and an equally good predictor of dissatisfaction and dissolution when it doesn't (Dindia and Fitzpatrick, 1985). Markman (1981) also showed that 'communication-impact' was the only measure to successfully predict marital adjustment at 2.5 and 5 years after marriage. This is not surprising, however, given that many researchers see communication not just as a part of personal relationships, but as constituting the relationship itself. In other words, relationships are conceived as *communications* (Baxter, 2004). Understood in this way, it becomes obvious that a breakdown in communication must, almost by necessity, signal a concomitant breakdown in relationship.

3.2 Content and style of communication

Alberts et al. (2005) provides an interesting summary of the things we typically talk about in our relationships and when we talk about them most. This was done by 'listening in' to couples over an extended period of time in their home environments (with their knowledge and consent!). The results suggested that people spend the most time talking about themselves. Self-report of this type accounted for 27.5 per cent of relational communication. General observations accounted for a further 14.9 per cent of conversation, while people focused on their partner's concerns and experiences only 10.3 per cent of the time. That's about the same amount of time (10.5 per cent) they spent talking about television programmes. Interestingly, two-thirds of all conversation took place at the weekend, which led to satisfaction with relational communication and conflict issues being highest on a Monday and lowest on a Wednesday.

Fletcher (2002) highlights three typical styles or models of relational communication. The first is the **good communication model**. This model encourages open and honest reflection and communication about problems, as well as the mechanics and progress of the relationship itself. Love and admiration are to be freely expressed, the relationship nurtured, with the personal growth of both partners being the ultimate relational goal. The **good management model**, by contrast, avoids problems and conflict and rarely makes 'the relationship' a central topic of conversation. Well-managed relationships are described as warm and affectionate while cohering to a quite rigid, traditional and gendered structure. Interactions are generally rather predictable and the closeness and interdependency of the partners is implicitly accepted without concern being expressed about personal freedoms. The third style is the **volatile model**, which brings argument to the fore. The partners say exactly what they think, whenever they think it, and express all things (including their love) in an uninhibited and passionate fashion. They come into conflict regularly, perhaps even becoming physical as they argue, but they also enjoy regular 'make-up' sex. This approach finds appeal in emotion-laden and essentially unpredictable patterns of communication.

Good communication model
In this model, love and admiration are freely expressed. The ultimate relational goal is the personal growth of both partners through open and honest reflection and communication about problems and the inner workings and progress of the relationship.

Good management model
With this model, problems and conflicts are avoided and the relationship itself is rarely a central topic of conversation.

Volatile model
In this model, communication is emotion-laden and unpredictable. Partners say exactly what they think whenever they think it and express all things in an uninhibited and passionate way.

Fletcher (2002) concludes that women typically prefer the good communication model and men the good management model, although generalisations of this type are probably best avoided. It is also clear that other models and approaches are possible and that the above only touches the surface of a very large literature focused on matters of communication.

Pause for thought

The literature on communication implies that men and women differ in their standard patterns of communication or 'communication styles' (do an internet search for 'Gender differences in communication' to illustrate this point), with men supposedly preferring a more instrumental or factual style of communication and women a more affective or feeling-oriented style. Do you observe such a difference in your own experiences and, if so, how might this impact on the ways in which men and women communicate with each other? If not, do people tend to communicate factually or affectively for the most part or, in your experience, is the style of communication adopted more dependent on the individual and/or the social context?

> Some of the literature, particularly much of the popular psychology literature, implies that women tend to interpret men as cold, inflexible and emotionally inarticulate as a result of their preference for instrumental communication and men to interpret women as changeable and overly emotional on the basis of their preference for affective communication. Why might this be the case?

3.3 Self-disclosure

Self-disclosure
The sharing of personal information and feelings.

Self-disclosure, which involves the sharing of personal information and feelings, is an *expectation* in personal relationships. It is, in many ways, what makes a personal relationship personal. Self-disclosure is positively correlated with self-esteem, relational esteem and responsiveness within relationships, as well as relationship quality, satisfaction, love and commitment (Sprecher and Hendrick, 2004). Pennebakker (1980) also suggests that self-disclosure has positive psychological benefits. In other words, it has many advantages.

Telling someone your secrets nonetheless demands trust. Self-disclosure increases relational intimacy and security, but it also increases personal risk and potential threat. Having intimate knowledge about someone can enable you to provide help and support, but it also allows you to hurt them in conflict situations. For this reason, self-disclosure usually operates according to a 'norm of reciprocity' at the start of a relationship. This means if I say something intimate, perhaps 'I love you', you are expected, at the very least, to say something positive in return! Evidence nonetheless suggests that a sensible balance between disclosure and personal privacy must be struck if a relationship is to last (Baxter, 1988). Tailoring the amount of self-disclosure to prevailing circumstances is also important (Derlaga et al., 1993). Berg (1984), for example, showed that students who reported the highest levels of self-disclosure two weeks into their relationship liked each other considerably less after six months. As we have said, self-disclosure is an expectation in personal relationships, but care is required: telling your life story straight away is probably too much!

3.4 Summary

Communication is very important, to the extent that some researchers understand personal relationships as *communications*. This section highlighted three typical models of relational communication, before observing that self-disclosure was both an *expectation* in personal relationships and one of the key mechanisms for rendering a relationship personal.

4 Friendship

4.1 Problems of definition

Friendship
A voluntary interdependence between two people over time which facilitates the socio-emotional goals of the participants.

Friendship is actually a rather vague and nebulous concept, in individualistic cultures at least, which means different things to different people at different times in their lives (Brownlow, 2012). It involves a voluntary interdependence between two persons over time, but the nature and style of that interdependence can vary enormously. The main goal of friendship is to facilitate the socio-emotional goals of the participants, but there are also no rules prescribing how that should be achieved. As the literature suggests, this makes friendship one of very few relationships that is not definable by the *content of its interactions* (Hinde, 1997).

Activity 6.1: Defining friendship

How do you define friendship? Make a list of the ten most important features of friendship from your perspective. Consider how your friendships 'measure up' to those standards and if/how the most important features vary across different friendships.

According to the literature, good friends are supposed to stand up for you when you're not around, share and take pleasure in your successes, give emotional support, be trustworthy and capable of protecting confidences, provide help when you need it, respect your privacy and make you feel good when you're together. There are a lot of things they shouldn't do as well, but it's probably best to stick with the positives!

4.2 The progress and maintenance of friendship

Rawlins (1981) presents a six-stage model that explains how friendships form and develop (Figure 6.5). At the first or *role-limited* interaction stage you meet another person and make initial, tentative contact. Conversation is limited by social convention to polite exchanges, and the relationship, while affable, remains largely impersonal. The *friendly relations* stage sees questions being asked about potential shared interests and the possibilities for further shared interaction. Only in the *moving towards friendship* stage, however, does genuinely personal information begin to be shared. The potential friends spend more time together and begin to interact in new and different contexts. Decisions are made at this stage about the chances of establishing a genuine and deep friendship.

Figure 6.5 Rawlins' six-stage model of friendship development
(Source: Rawlins, 1981)

The *nascent friendship* stage sees friendship proper get underway. The friends see each other regularly and become very relaxed in each other's company. They also start to develop their own personal and distinctive patterns of interaction and rules of communication. By the time a *stabilised friendship* emerges, the relationship is characterised by mutual trust, the sharing of intimate information and emotional support, as well as a shared sense of reliance and interdependence. The long-term nature of the relationship and future interaction is taken for granted. This taken-for-granted status nonetheless comes into question in the *waning friendship* stage, perhaps because changes in family, life or work circumstances have made shared interactions with a particular friend seem less comfortable and relevant to our everyday lives, or simply because one or both friends fails to satisfy the expected patterns of interaction that previously characterised the relationship.

Friendships also compete against the demands of work commitments, romantic relationships, children, and so on, all of which can leave comparatively little available time (and/or energy) to spend with our friends. Friends having contradictory needs can also be problematic (Baxter, 1988). Despite these observations, however, friendships are generally very resilient. This is because the positive aspects of such relationships typically outweigh the negatives, making the outright abandonment of even a troubled relationship seem rather drastic (Bushman and Holt-Lundstat, 2009). A sense of obligation also plays a part in maintaining long-term friendships, as do mutual connections with various social groups, continued physical proximity, and personal values such as forgiveness and a self-identity which sees 'many friends' as a desirable quality (Hess, 2000, 2002, 2003). In the end, however, friendship has no real rules or role obligations other than the ones we create for ourselves. This is a positive benefit in times of crisis because it allows the relationship to respond flexibly to new demands and to easily redefine itself according to any agreed set of parameters.

4.3 Cross-sex friendship

A preference for same-sex friendships begins in childhood (Turner et al., 1993). Women's friendships, the literature suggests, are typically characterised by intimacy and emotional expression, whereas men's tend to revolve around shared activities (Fuhrman et al., 2009). Cross-sex friendships are rarer and less stable. This is primarily because the sexual and/or romantic interests of the friends require careful management. Men, for example, tend to consider sexual attraction and a desire for sex as important reasons for initiating cross-sex friendships and the absence of sex as a good reason for their dissolution (Bleske-Rechek and Buss, 2001). This situation is further complicated, it appears, by a male tendency to over-perceive the sexual interest of their cross-sex friends and for women to under-perceive the sexual interest of theirs (Koenig et al., 2007).

Evidence also suggests that expectations of cross-sex friendships shift along with people's relational status, such that more is expected of our cross-sex friends when we are not in a romantic relationship and less when we are (Fuhrman et al., 2009). Shifting expectations, of course, can be difficult to manage and this difficulty is only exacerbated when one friend is involved in an intimate relationship and the other is not. Cross-sex friends often appear as a threat to intimate relationships and, primarily for this reason, successful cross-sex friendships typically draw very clear sexual and romantic boundaries (Monsour et al., 1993).

Box 6.2 The potential complications of cross-sex friendship

As you have seen above, cross-sex friendships suffer more internal and external pressures than same-sex friendships and are consequently rarer and less stable. The potentially damaging impact of sexual and romantic attraction is a particular problem. Indeed, these themes are often picked up by the media and in popular television programmes like *Friends*. The cross-sex friendships that form the main storylines in these programmes are continually being shaped and endangered by underlying physical attractions and sexual tensions.

In *Friends*, for example, four of the six main characters were actually in romantic relationships with one another by the end of the series and it is worth considering the message this sends about the potential trajectory of cross-sex friendships. The real situation is certainly complicated. Reeder (2000), for example, suggests that attraction in cross-sex friendship is highly variable and subject to change. In the end, she concludes that while cross-sex friends may often be asked if they are attracted to each other, 'there is not a [simple] yes or no answer to this question. Indeed, cross-sex friends would have to reply, "Which one of us, at what point in the friendship, and what kind of attraction?"' (Reeder, 2000, p. 346).

4.4 Summary

Friendship cannot be defined by the content of its interactions and that makes it a rather vague and nebulous concept. Rawlins' six-stage model of friendships was included in this section to show how friendships form and develop, before cross-sex friendship was briefly considered. Cross-sex friendships are rarer and less stable than same-sex friendships, a situation that starts in childhood and is exacerbated in adult life by the need to manage the romantic and sexual interests of both the friends.

5 Love

As you have seen already, personal relationships are supposed to facilitate each partner's socio-emotional goals. There is perhaps no better way of fulfilling such goals than to love and to be loved. Yet, as the following sections will demonstrate, love can mean many different things to different people at different times in their lives and psychological theory has had to work hard to reflect this.

5.1 Definitions and important distinctions

Rubin (1970, 1973) concluded that love involves a need for affiliation and dependence, a predisposition to help and a sense of exclusiveness and absorption into a single relationship. Exclusiveness and absorption are precisely what distinguish 'being in love' from mere loving (Meyers and Berscheid, 1997). We are capable of loving many people (and things) simultaneously, but the expectation is that we should be 'in love' with only one.

Two further distinctions are worth knowing at this stage. The first is Maslow's (1962) distinction between *deficit* and *being* love. Deficit love, he suggested, was motivated by feelings of personal deficiency. This meant a partner was pursued primarily as a source of security and need satisfaction and hence as a means of making someone feel safe and complete. Being love, by contrast, was a love in which two complete individuals would join together to facilitate the personal growth and well-being of the other.

The second distinction is between *passionate* and *companionate* love (Hatfield and Walster, 1978). **Passionate love** is described as a powerful and changeable emotional state, closely tied to feelings of sexual arousal, while **companionate love** describes calmer and more stable feelings, more overtly related to affection and friendship than sex. This distinction also maps nicely on to our cultural tendency to define love as both a *feeling* and as a *relationship* (Watts and Stenner, 2005). In 'settling down' with a partner, there is a clear expectation that our turbulent and changeable passions will also settle down, over time, into the more stable and reliable feelings of affection typically associated with long-term companionship. This temporal relationship that sees passion convert slowly to companionship is

Passionate love
A powerful and changeable emotional state which is closely tied to feelings of sexual arousal.

Companionate love
Calm, stable feelings more overtly related to affection and friendship than to sex.

precisely what most people expect to experience when in love (Hatfield, 1988).

5.2 Theories of love

Box 6.3 Crossing boundaries in psychology: the difficult case of love

The main theories of love are drawn from very different areas of psychology. This is not surprising given that love is an activity of the whole organism, involving the coordination of cognitive appraisals, subjective feelings, physiological processes, action tendencies and instrumental behaviours in various measures (Hatfield and Rapson, 1993). These areas clearly offer psychologists a wide range of research opportunities. By the mid-1980s, however, the highly variegated nature of love, combined with several rather disconnected strands of research (and attempts by each strand to define love according to its own interests), had left the literature 'marked with conflict, confusion and disagreement' (Fehr, 1988, p. 557). Indeed, by the time the first major collection of social scientific research into love was published in the latter part of that decade (Sternberg and Barnes, 1988), Zick Rubin was forced to conclude that:

> *The investigators in this volume share so little of a common vocabulary … many of the contributors have [simply] developed their own taxonomies of love. Each categorising scheme differs from the next, and there are no ready translation rules from one chapter's formulation to another. Just as partners with different views of love may find themselves talking past each other … I suspect that some of the contributors to this volume may find it difficult to relate to other's perspectives.*
>
> (Rubin, 1988, p. ix)

This sense of disconnection is not uncommon in psychology, but it is precisely what a volume of this type (and the attempt to cross boundaries in psychology) is trying to overcome. With that in mind, the theories of love presented in Sections 5.2 and 5.3 can, and should, be read as attempts to resolve the disconnection. As you will see, they are drawn from different areas of psychology, but they all share the view that many definitions of love are both possible and acceptable. They also acknowledge, to a greater or lesser extent, that people's personal and subjective definitions should be the primary focus of research in the area. In so doing, they demonstrate how knowledge emanating from different areas of psychology can ultimately come together in a complementary fashion, blurring sub-disciplinary boundaries and giving us a more rounded picture of a particular phenomenon.

Robert Sternberg's (1986) 'triangular theory of love' and his subsequent (1996) 'theory of love as a story' (see below and Section 5.3) provide a nice example of this approach. The triangular theory understands love as a combination of affect (intimacy), physiology (passion) and cognition (decision/ commitment). In other words, it acknowledges and combines three distinct areas of psychology within a single umbrella theory. Recognising, however, that love may be an even more variable and personal experience than this umbrella framework will allow, Sternberg proposes the theory of love as a story as a complement to his earlier work. Bringing the two theories together under the name the 'duplex theory of love', Sternberg (2006) ultimately suggested that the triangular theory was designed to deal with the *structural* aspects of love, and that while it does so adequately, the theory of love as a story was added as a means of better appreciating love's *process* and *development* and the many different stories of love that emerge as an outcome.

The *attachment theory* of adult love (Hazan and Shaver, 1987) finds its inspiration in evolutionary principles and a developmental theory proposed by John Bowlby (1969). This theory was originally designed to account for the relationship between an infant and their primary caregiver. Bowlby nonetheless suggested that the nature of this initial attachment would be characteristic of a person's relational behaviour throughout their lifetime. According to the attachment theory, romantic love is understood as 'a biological process designed by evolution to facilitate attachment between adult sexual partners who, at the time love evolved, were likely to become parents of an infant who would need their reliable care' (Hazan and Shaver, 1987, p. 523).

The theory proposes three major attachment styles, namely *secure, anxious/ambivalent* and *avoidant* (Ainsworth et al., 1978). Bartholomew (1990) subsequently created a fourth style, however, by dividing the avoidant style into two sub-categories, in order to discriminate between individuals who were *dismissive* or *fearful* of personal relationships. Securely attached individuals are confident and open and describe their personal relationships in terms of friendship, trust and happiness. Anxious/ambivalent individuals lack self-confidence, typically fall in love easily and find others unwilling to commit to the same extent. Their relationships are characterised by jealousy, intense sexual desire, demands for reciprocation and emotional turbulence. Avoidant individuals see themselves as independent and unpopular and consider romantic love hard to find. They typically fear or dismiss the possibility of closeness and their love relationships are marked by jealousy and a lack of mutual acceptance.

Attachment theory has inspired a lot of research. Kirkpatrick and Davis (1994), for example, examined 354 'seriously dating' couples and found no avoidant–avoidant or anxious–anxious couples at all. They also found that avoidant individuals tended to be with anxious partners and felt more comfortable being so. Madey and Rogers (2009) showed that the more secure a person's attachment, the more intimate and committed their main love relationship was likely to be. These enhanced levels of intimacy and commitment were also shown to be predictive of relationship satisfaction.

The *prototype theory* of love (Fehr, 1988) has its background in cognitive psychology. Following Rosch's (1973, 1978) prototype theory of concepts, Fehr proposed that love could be grasped in terms of its prototypical structure, i.e. the clearest case or best examples of the concept, and that other exemplars of love would then 'be ordered [in people's minds] in terms of their degree of resemblance to the prototypical case' (Fehr, 1988, p. 558). Participants in prototype studies of love are duly asked to rate various possible exemplars of the concept for their centrality and importance in order to discover the ones that are considered 'most prototypical'.

Using this approach, Fehr and Russell (1991) demonstrated that maternal love was rated as the prototypical love, followed by parental love and friendship. Romantic love was rated in fifth place and infatuation was considered the least prototypical of 93 exemplars. Regan et al. (1998) found trust, honesty and happiness to be central to the prototype of romantic love, while trust, sexual attraction, acceptance and tolerance were mentioned most frequently by study participants. Negative features such as submission, obedience and deception occupied the periphery of the prototype.

Sternberg's (1986) *triangular theory* of love (Figure 6.6) has its background in social psychology. It proposes that love can be understood in terms of three basic components: *intimacy*, *passion* and *decision/commitment*. Intimacy refers to the feelings of closeness and connectedness that typify loving relationships. Passion draws attention to the physiological aspects of love and the drives that lead to physical attraction, sex and romance. And finally, decision/commitment deals with the cognitive and rational aspects of love, our decision to enter a relationship and our subsequent commitment to maintain it. Intimacy is considered the most fundamental of these components, forming the central core in all types of love relationships, while passion and decision/commitment become important far more selectively and only in the context of particular relationships.

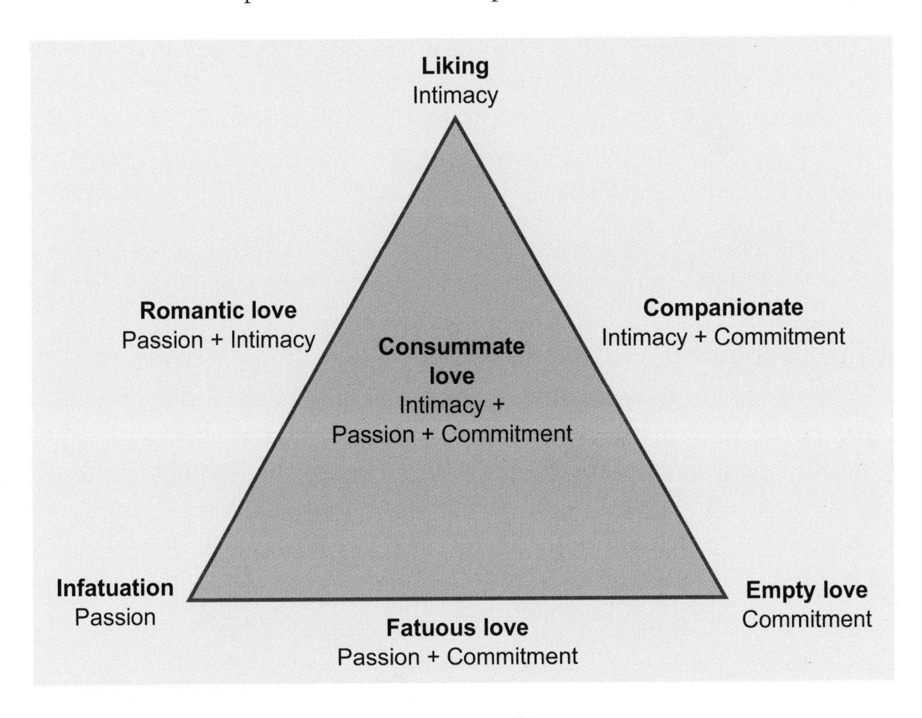

Figure 6.6 Sternberg's triangular theory of love

The theory suggests that these three components, interacting at different levels and in different combinations, come together to produce different kinds of love. Feelings of intimacy only, for example, would produce 'liking'. Decision/commitment, without feelings of intimacy or passion, would lead to an 'empty love' of the type that can occur in long-term relationships that have somewhat stagnated. Romantic love is understood as a combination of intimacy and passion (without much commitment), companionate love as a combination of intimacy and commitment (without much passion), and so on. Sternberg also concluded that consummate love, which involves roughly equal proportions of intimacy, passion and commitment, is a goal towards which most relationships strive, although no evidence is provided to support this proposal.

The triangular theory nonetheless provides a comprehensive framework for understanding love and corresponds well with people's everyday experiences (Aron and Westbay, 1996). What it does not claim to do, however, is define or capture love in a singular or timeless fashion. On the contrary, the theory explicitly recognises that love is a variable and complex experience, and hence that the proposal to understand love in terms of intimacy, passion and commitment, while sensible and potentially useful, may not be valid for all purposes. There are, in other words, other possible stories that might be told about love, and this idea will be explored further in the next section.

5.3 Styles, stories and social constructions (of love)

Barthes (1990) suggests that any pretensions to find a single definition of love should be replaced with a concern about its affirmation and what people actually say and do in love's name. This has led many researchers to focus on people's personal definitions and experiences of love. Lee (1977) was the first to exemplify this approach, studying love as a problem of competing ideologies about the optimum arrangement for intimate adult partnering. Citing six central ideologies or love styles, which variously promoted love as passionate/erotic, as game-playing, as friendship, as practical and calculating, as altruistic, and as an obsession, Lee (1988) suggested that people would simply 'buy into' one or more of these styles at different times and in different contexts and relationships. The various styles might also be combined in an almost infinite number of ways, such that Lee (1988, p. 45) ultimately concluded it would be 'pointless to attempt to say how many love styles there are'.

Sternberg's (1995, 1996, 1998) *theory of love as a story* extends this emphasis on personal definition. It proposes that each person's experiences of love coalesce to form their own love story. Although this story is personal, it is nonetheless always derived as a person interacts with their culture and environment. A person's culture, Sternberg suggests, places them under 'continual, although usually subtle, pressure to create only those stories which are socio-culturally acceptable' (1995, p. 544). Sternberg (1996) reports a preliminary taxonomy of 24 love stories, including the 'love as science' story (which proposes a rational approach to love), the 'love as art' story (which emphasises the physical attractiveness and appearance of a partner), and the 'love as war' story (which envisages love relationships as a constant series of battles). The theory nonetheless suggests, along similar lines to Lee, that the number of possible love stories is probably infinite.

The love styles and stories approaches are connected by their treatment of **love as a social construction** (Averill, 1985). Loosely speaking, this means that different societies, cultures, social groups, and so on, have their own, often unique, definitions of love and that these serve as a kind of behavioural resource and interpretative blueprint for people interacting within the group. As Beall and Sternberg (1995, p. 419) put it, social constructionism argues that 'part of the experience of love is its definition and that when cultures have different definitions of love, they [i.e. the people within that culture] experience love differently' (p. 419). The implication, of course, is that all answers to the question 'What is love?' must inevitably be a function of time and place and that no single answer to the question could ever suffice.

Love as a social construction
Definitions of love differ across and between societies, cultures and social groups. These different definitions act as a behavioural resource for people interacting within a particular collective.

Box 6.4 On the stories of love captured in Watts and Stenner (2005, 2013)

Watts and Stenner (2005, 2013) provide a nice example of love being studied as a social construction. These papers also evidence the abundant variability of love. Watts and Stenner (2005), for example, discovered a predominant story that emphasised the need for a continual effort to deliver *mutual trust, recognition and support*, alongside the belief that a healthy love relationship should serve to maximise the life potential of both individuals. Love was not viewed primarily in romantic terms, but as a mundane and effortful relationship, which requires great honesty, patience, compromise, excellent communication and no little personal sacrifice before it can deliver the promised benefits.

Other stories included *hedonistic love*, in which love was viewed as a simple and hedonistic by-product of sexual attraction closely tied to the pursuit of personal pleasure, happiness and excitement, and *ultimate connection and profound feeling*, which viewed love as the most profound and meaningful feeling a person can have and as the foundation of the ultimate connection between two people. This feeling and connection, it was suggested, must be experienced before life could ever be considered complete or fulfilled.

Watts and Stenner (2013) highlight six different stories of love being told by a sample of 59 British women. For example, the story *attraction, passion and romance* saw these three elements as the catalysts of an all-consuming chemistry between two people and as the keys to a happy and worthwhile relationship, while *unconditional love* promoted the expectation that love would endure 'whatever happens' and be given without expectation of receiving anything in return. Love was likened, on this account, to both sibling and maternal love. *Sex and fun*, by contrast, presented love as an antidote to the mundane existence delivered by everyday companionship. The latter was seen as containing and oppressive, whereas love should be driven by sex, fun and the pursuit of excitement.

Hopefully it is clear, even via presentation of these few examples, that there really are many acceptable answers to the question 'What is love?'

5.4 Summary

This section considered some useful distinctions between loving and 'being in love', deficit and being love, and passionate and companionate love. It also outlined the attachment, prototype and triangular theories of love, as well as Lee's (1977) 'love styles' research and the 'theory of love as a story'. The latter two were presented as examples of work adhering to the principles of social constructionism. Social constructionism suggests that different societies, cultures, social groups, and so on, have their own definitions of love and that these serve as a kind of behavioural resource and interpretative blueprint for people interacting within the group.

6 Conflict and violence in personal relationships

Fortunately, violence in personal relationships remains relatively rare. When it does occur, however, and when conflict gets out of control, the results typically have a destructive and potentially catastrophic impact on personal relationships. These issues will be the subject of the next section.

6.1 Conflict as destructive, conflict as constructive

Some degree of conflict in a personal relationship is almost inevitable and often arises because of a mismatch in the short- and long-term goals of the partners (Hinde, 1997). Jealousy can also lead to conflict, initiated by a belief that our partner is attracted to someone else or by our partner's time involvement with other activities (White and Mullen, 1989). The most important thing to realise, however, is that conflict can have positive as well as negative consequences for a relationship, depending on its focus and conduct (Hinde, 1997). According to Duck (1991), constructive or *beneficial conflict* typically focuses on 'who does what' in a relationship and serves to clarify role-performance issues, whereas *destructive conflict* is generally unfocused and involves argument, verbal abuse and threats. The former can pave the way for the future success of a relationship, while the latter makes it less likely to survive.

In a similar vein, Canary and Cupach (1988) identified three alternative strategies for dealing with conflict:

- *Integrative strategies* involve the pursuit of common ground, expressing trust and seeking to satisfy the interests of both parties. Such strategies are constructive.
- *Distributive strategies*, by contrast, involve sarcasm, threats, and so on, and are duly destructive. They tend to produce an escalation of relational conflict.
- *Avoidance strategies*, such as denying the existence of relational problems, using indirect aggression and deliberately provoking a partner's jealousy, are also commonly used. Such strategies prevent

a couple from dealing directly with issues in their relationship and can lead to problems building up.

Only integrative strategies actually *resolve* conflict issues, and it is worth remembering that their use can promote both the maintenance and the development of a personal relationship.

6.2 Relational violence: causes and consequences

Violence
A phenomenon that can include physical, emotional and sexual abuse and a wide range of coercive, intimidating and controlling behaviours.

Sometimes **violence** is used as a strategy in conflict (Jewkes, 2002). Violence is a wide-ranging phenomenon that can include both physical and sexual threat, but also refers to a number of coercive, intimidating and controlling behaviours (Harne and Radford, 2008). While research has found high levels of conflict to be strongly associated with physical violence, it is widely recognised that the causes of relational violence are complex (Stith and McMonigle, 2009; Hoffman et al., 1994; Jewkes et al., 2002; Jones et al., 1999; Stets, 1990). Jewkes (2002) nonetheless identified two main risk factors, which were the subordinate positioning of women within a particular relationship and perceptions that violence is a 'normal response' to conflict. The interaction of these two factors greatly increases the risk of relational violence occurring.

Such violence crosses class, ethnic and social boundaries. Across the spectrum, however, violence appears highly gendered, with men typically being reported as the perpetrator and women as the victim (Hester et al., 2007; McCarry, 2009; Burman and Cartmel, 2005). The British Crime Survey indicates that women are likely to experience both more and a wider range of violence and abuse than men, and that young women aged between 16 and 24 are the demographic most at risk (Smith et al., 2011). Of course, this doesn't mean that men do not experience relational violence: they certainly do, but the evidence suggests they typically feel far less threatened by female violence and often consider it unworthy of serious attention (Sinclair and Frieze, 2000).

Research also indicates that female victims of violence report a wider range of both short- and long-term consequences (Harne and Radford, 2008). These include minor and severe physical injuries, an increased risk of sexually transmitted diseases and unplanned pregnancy, chronic pain and even death (Bowen, 2011). In the UK, every week, at least two women are either killed by their intimate partner or attempt suicide as a result of their violence (Povey, 2005;

Harne and Radford, 2008). Psychological consequences include depression, post-traumatic stress disorder, self-harm, anxiety and low self-esteem (Bowen, 2011; Campbell et al., 2009). A number of research studies suggest that it is psychological not physical violence – intimidation, emotional abuse, and so on – that is most strongly associated with negative mental health outcomes and that some victims may also become dependent on drugs or alcohol as a consequence (Bowen, 2011; Harne and Radford, 2008).

This may make you wonder why people in violent relationships don't just leave. As you will see in the next section, however, the ending of relationships can be a lengthy and emotionally arduous process, even in reasonable circumstances, and violence typically creates an environment from which it is difficult to escape. Strategies of power and control, threats, intimidation, constant surveillance, humiliation and semi-imprisonment can all be employed to prevent a person from leaving. Fear of repercussions, as well as practical reasons, such as potential job loss, financial insecurity, having nowhere to go and concerns about children, can also play a part. Sadly, the evidence also suggests that leaving may not, in itself, resolve the problem. Violence is actually quite likely to continue, and in some cases to get worse, after a relationship has been ended (Harne and Radford, 2008).

6.3 Summary

Some degree of conflict in a personal relationship is inevitable, but it need not be a negative phenomenon. Integrative conflict strategies can help to promote the maintenance and development of personal relationships. Relational violence was also considered in this section. This is defined in terms of both physical and sexual threat, but also refers to a range of coercive, intimidating and controlling behaviours. The conclusion was drawn that women are more likely to experience relational violence than men (and a wider range of violence) and that men often consider female violence to be unworthy of serious attention.

7 Relationship dissolution

7.1 Reasons for dissolution

Despite the unhappy ending to the previous section, violence is not typically associated with personal relationships or their dissolution. In fact, Baxter (1986) suggests that personal relationships usually end because one or more of eight basic *expectations* has not been satisfied. These involve one or both partners feeling:

- they lack sufficient personal freedom and autonomy
- their partner is not sufficiently similar
- their partner is not supportive of their self-esteem and feelings
- their partner is not sufficiently loyal or committed to the relationship
- the relationship lacks in openness and honesty
- the partners do not spend enough time together
- the distribution of effort and resources being invested in the relationship are neither equal nor equitable
- the relationship lacks a certain 'magical quality'.

Pause for thought

Baxter (1986) suggests that one of the main reasons people cite in dissolving intimate relationships is the lack of a certain 'magical quality'. But what is it that makes a relationship magical? Think about the features of an intimate relationship that differentiate it from friendship and the additional things you might expect an intimate partner to make you feel. Is love the magical quality? Is it sex? Does it require romance (and what is romance anyway)? If it's one of the main reasons for relationship dissolution, it's clearly worth thinking about. There's no right or wrong answer here though, because that would clearly spoil the magic!

7.2 Theories of dissolution

Relationship 'break-up' or dissolution is often an extended process, involving repeated attempts at reconciliation and a relatively slow and gradual decline in intimacy. The evidence also suggests that the greater our attraction to someone and the more time and resources we have invested in the relationship, the longer and more emotionally painful the dissolution process is likely to be. As a result of this extended nature, psychologists (and others) have usually described the dissolution process as progressing through a series of distinct stages.

As an example, Duck's (1982) theory of relationship dissolution highlights four phases, each successive phase being entered when a specific threshold has been reached. In the *intra-psychic* phase, someone starts to feel as though they 'can't stand the current situation any more'. They focus on their partner's behaviour and role performance, evaluate the plusses and minuses of the relationship and consider the personal costs of withdrawal. At the culmination of this phase, they face an 'express or repress' dilemma. If the person still feels they'd be 'justified in getting out', a second threshold is passed and the dissolution process enters the *dyadic* phase. Concerns are then shared with a partner, negotiations begin about the state of the relationship and the possibilities for repair and reconciliation are considered (along with the joint costs of reduced intimacy and potential withdrawal).

In the absence of an acceptable resolution, one (or both) partners decide that they 'mean it this time' and the *social* phase begins. Negotiations are now made public, matters are discussed within the couple's immediate social network, friends and family either promote the break-up and/or try to resurrect it and a series of face-saving and blame-placing accounts starts to emerge. The focus shifts to the negotiation of an acceptable post-dissolution state. The final, so-called *grave-dressing* phase begins when the break-up is perceived as inevitable. The partners then immerse themselves in 'getting over' activities while engaging in retrospective and reconstructive post-mortem attributions about the relationship (and its failure). The break-up story is publicly distributed, but this often has different versions depending on who is telling it!

7.3 Summary

Baxter (1986) suggests that personal relationships usually end because one or more of eight basic *expectations* has not been satisfied. This section outlined those expectations and highlighted that relationship break-up or dissolution is often an extended process, involving repeated attempts at reconciliation and a relatively slow and gradual decline in intimacy. As a result, psychologists (and others) have usually described the dissolution process as progressing through a series of distinct stages. Duck's (1982) theory of relationship dissolution was presented as an example.

8 Concluding thoughts

The chapter followed the life cycle of a typical personal relationship. It considered the factors involved in initial attraction, talked of communication, self-disclosure, friendship and love, examined what happens when conflict and relational violence come to the fore, and finally described the process of relationship dissolution.

The chapter also started with the assumption that people might be self-contained and that this might mean they don't need personal relationships, but the intention is to end the chapter with the opposite thought. Loneliness occurs when there is a discrepancy between the number or kind of personal relationships that you *desire* and the ones you actually have in your life. The evidence also tells us that loneliness has dramatic psychological and physical repercussions, including increased depression and stress, lower subjective well-being, raised blood pressure, lower immunity, and the list goes on. Lonely people are nearly twice as likely to die prematurely as people with a satisfactory history of personal relationships. *The Lonely Society*, a report commissioned by the Mental Health Foundation in 2010, surmised a clear and direct link between our individualistic society and the rise of mental health disorders over the past 50 years. Arguing that individual people should consider themselves self-contained, therefore, which psychology often has, is not only wrong: it is positively damaging. Personal relationships really are the foundation and theme of the human condition; they define our lives, and we would do well to remember that.

Further reading

Duck, S. (ed.) (1982) *Personal Relations 4: Dissolving Personal Relationships*, New York, Academic Press.

Fletcher, G.J.O. (2002) *The New Science of Intimate Relationships*, Oxford, Basil Blackwell.

Goodwin, R. (2013) *Personal Relationships Across Cultures*, London, Routledge.

Hinde, R.A. (1997) *Relationships: A Dialectical Perspective*, Hove, Psychology Press.

Sternberg, R.J. and Weis, K. (eds) (2006) *The New Psychology of Love*, New York, Yale University Press.

References

Adams, J.S. (1965) 'Inequity in social exchange', in Berkowitz, L. (ed.) *Advances in Experimental Social Psychology*, vol. 2, pp. 267–99, New York, Academic Press.

Ainsworth, M., Blehar, S., Waters, M.C. and Wall, E. (1978) *Patterns of Attachment: A Psychological Study of the Strange Situation*, Hillsdale, NJ, Erlbaum.

Alberts, J.K., Yoshimura, C.G., Rabby, M. and Loschiavo, R. (2005) 'Mapping the topography of couples' daily conversation', *Journal of Social and Personal Relationships*, vol. 22, no. 3, pp. 299–322.

Aron, A. and Westbay, L. (1996) 'Dimensions of the prototype of love', *Journal of Personality and Social Psychology*, vol. 70, no. 3, pp. 535–51.

Aron, A., Fisher, H.E. and Strong, G. (2006) 'Romantic love', in Perlman, D. and Vangelisti, A. (eds) *The Cambridge Handbook of Personal Relationships*, Cambridge, MA, Cambridge University Press.

Asch, S.E. (1952) *Social Psychology*, New York, Prentice-Hall.

Asch, S.E. (1956) 'Studies of independence and conformity: I. A minority of one against a unanimous majority', *Psychological Monographs: General and Applied*, vol. 70, no. 9, pp. 1–70.

Asch, S.E. (1959) 'A perspective on social psychology', in Koch, S. (ed.) *Psychology: A Study of a Science*, vol. 3, *Formulations of the Person and the Social Context*, New York, McGraw-Hill, pp. 363–83.

Averill, J.R. (1985) 'The social construction of emotion: with special reference to love', in Gergen, K.J. and Davis, K.E. (eds) *The Social Construction of the Person*, New York, Springer-Verlag.

Barthes, R. (1990) [1978] *A Lover's Discourse* (trans. R. Howard), London, Penguin Books.

Bartholomew, K. (1990) 'Avoidance of intimacy: an attachment perspective', *Journal of Social and Personal Relationships*, vol. 7, no. 2, pp. 147–78.

Baxter, L.A. (1986) 'Gender differences in the heterosexual relationship rules embedded in break-up accounts', *Journal of Social and Personal Relationships*, vol. 3, no. 3, pp. 289–306.

Baxter, L.A. (1988) 'A dialectical perspective on communication strategies in relationship development', in Duck, S. (ed.) *Handbook of Personal Relationships*, pp. 257–74, London, Wiley.

Baxter, L.A. (2004) 'Relationships as dialogues', *Personal Relationships*, vol. 11, no. 1, pp. 1–22.

Beall, A.E. and Sternberg, R.J. (1995) 'The social construction of love', *Journal of Social and Personal Relationships*, vol. 12, no. 3, pp. 417–38.

Berg, J.H. (1984) 'Development of friendship between roommates', *Journal of Personality and Social Psychology*, vol. 46, no. 2, pp. 346–56.

Berscheid, E. and Peplau, L.A. (1983) 'The emerging science of relationships', in Kelley, H., Berscheid, E., Christensen, A., Harvey, J.H., Huston, T., Levinger, G., McClintock, E., Peplau, L.A. and Peterson, D.R. (eds) *Close Relationships*, New York, W.H. Freeman.

Berscheid, E. and Reis, H.T. (1998) 'Attraction and close relationships', in Gilbert, D.T., Fiske, S.T. and Lindzey, G. (eds) *The Handbook of Social Psychology*, 4th edn, vol. 2, pp. 193–281, New York, McGraw-Hill.

Berscheid, E., Dion, K., Walster, E. and Walster, W.G. (1971) 'Physical attractiveness and dating choice: a test of the matching hypothesis', *Journal of Experimental Social Psychology*, vol. 7, no. 2, pp. 173–89.

Bleske-Rechek, A.L. and Buss, D.M. (2001) 'Opposite-sex friendships: sex differences and similarities in initiation, selection, and dissolution', *Personality and Social Psychology Bulletin*, vol. 27, no. 10, pp. 1310–23.

Bornstein, R.F. (1989) 'Exposure and affect: overview and meta-analysis of research', *Psychological Bulletin*, vol. 106, no. 2, pp. 265–89.

Bowen, E. (2011) *The Rehabilitation of Partner Violent Men*, Chichester, Wiley-Blackwell.

Bowlby, J. (1969) *Attachment and Loss, Vol. 1: Attachment*, New York, Basic Books.

Brownlow, C. (2012) 'Making friends', in Brace N. and Byford J. (eds) *Investigating Psychology*, Oxford, Oxford University Press/Milton Keynes, The Open University.

Burkitt, I. (1993) *Social Selves: Theories of the Social Formation of Personality*, London: Sage.

Burman, M. and Cartmel, F. (2005) *Young People's Attitudes Towards Gendered Violence*, Edinburgh, NHS Scotland.

Bushman, B.B. and Holt-Lunstad, J. (2009) 'Understanding social relationship maintenance among friends: why we don't end those frustrating friendships', *Journal of Social and Clinical Psychology*, vol. 28, no. 6, pp. 749–78.

Buss, D.M., and Schmitt, D.P. (1993) 'Sexual strategies theory: an evolutionary perspective on human mating', *Psychological Review*, vol. 100, no. 2, pp. 204–32.

Campbell, J.C., Baty, M.L., Laughton, K. and Woods, A. (2009) 'Health effects of partner violence: aiming toward prevention', in Whitaker, D.J. and Lutzker, J.R. (eds) *Preventing Partner Violence: Research and Evidence-based Intervention Strategies*, Washington, DC, American Psychological Association.

Canary, D.J. and Cupach, W.R. (1988) 'Relational and episodic characteristics associated with conflict tactics', *Journal of Social and Personal Relationships*, vol. 5, no. 3, pp. 305–25.

Cacioppo, J.T., Cacioppo, S., Gonzaga, G.C., Ogburn, E.L. and VanderWeele, T.J. (2013) 'Marital satisfaction and break-ups differ across on-line and off-line meeting venues', *Proceedings of the National Academy of Sciences*, vol. 110, no. 25.

Chaiken, S. (1979) 'Communicator physical attractiveness and persuasion', *Journal of Personality and Social Psychology*, vol. 37, no. 8, pp. 1387–97.

Chan, D.K.S. and Cheng, G.H.L. (2004) 'A comparison of offline and online friendship qualities at different stages of relationship development', *Journal of Social and Personal Relationships*, vol. 21, pp. 305–20.

Derlega, V.J., Winstead, B.A., Wong, P.T.P. and Hunter, S. (1985) 'Gender effects in an initial encounter: a case where men exceed women in disclosure', *Journal of Social and Personal Relationships*, vol. 2, no. 1, pp. 25–44.

Dindia, K. and Fitzpatrick, M.A. (1985) 'Marital communication: a comparison of three approaches', in Duck, S. and Perlman, D. (eds) *Understanding Personal Relationships: An Interdisciplinary Approach,* Beverly Hills, Sage Publications.

Dion, K., Berscheid, E. and Walster, E. (1972) 'What is beautiful is good', *Journal of Personality and Social Psychology*, vol. 24, no. 3, pp. 285–90.

Dryer, D.C. and Horowitz, L.M. (1997) 'When do opposites attract? Interpersonal complementarity versus similarity', *Journal of Personality and Social Psychology*, vol. 72, no. 3, pp. 592–603.

Duck, S. (ed.) (1982) *Personal Relations 4: Dissolving Personal Relationships*, New York, Academic Press.

Duck, S. (1991) *Understanding Relationships*, New York, The Guilford Press.

Dunn, M.J. and Searle, R. (2010) 'Effect of manipulated prestige-car ownership on both sex attractiveness ratings', *British Journal of Psychology*, vol. 101, no. 1, pp. 69–80.

Ebbesen, E.B., Kjos, G.L. and Konecni, V.J. (1976) 'Spatial ecology: its effects on the choice of friends and enemies', *Journal of Experimental Social Psychology*, vol. 12, no. 6, pp. 505–18.

Ellison, N.B., Steinfield, C. and Lampe, C. (2007) 'The benefits of Facebook "friends": social capital and college students' use of online social network sites', *Journal of Computer-Mediated Communication,* vol. 12, no. 4, 1143–68.

Fehr, B. (1988) 'Prototype analysis of the concepts of love and commitment', *Journal of Personality and Social Psychology*, vol. 55, no. 4, pp. 557–79.

Fehr, B. and Russell, J.A. (1991) 'The concept of love viewed from a prototype perspective', *Journal of Personality and Social Psychology*, vol. 60, no. 3, pp. 425–38.

Feingold, A. (1991) 'Sex differences in the effects of similarity and physical attractiveness on opposite-sex attraction', *Basic and Applied Social Psychology*, vol. 12, no. 3, pp. 357–67.

Festinger, L., Schachter, S. and Back, K.W. (1950) *Social Pressures in Informal Groups: A Study of Human Factors in Housing*, New York, Harper.

Finkel, E.J., Eastwick, P.W., Karney, B.R., Reis, H.T. and Sprecher, S. (2012) 'Online dating: a critical analysis from the perspective of psychological science', *Psychological Science in the Public Interest*, vol. 13, no. 1, pp. 3–66.

Fletcher, G.J.O. (2002) *The New Science of Intimate Relationships*, Oxford, Basil Blackwell.

Fletcher, G.J.O. Simpson, J.A., Thomas, G. and Giles, L. (1999) 'Ideals in intimate relationships', *Journal of Personality and Social Psychology*, vol. 76, no. 1, pp. 72–89.

Furhman, R.W., Flannagan, D. and Matamoros, M. (2009) 'Behavior expectations in cross-sex friendships, same-sex friendships, and romantic relationships', *Personal Relationships*, vol. 16, no. 4, pp. 575–96.

Greitemeyer, T. (2005) 'Receptivity to sexual offers as a function of sex, socioeconomic status, physical attractiveness, and intimacy of the offer', *Personal Relationships*, vol. 12, no. 3, pp. 373–86.

Griffin, J. (2010) *The Lonely Society?*, London, The Mental Health Foundation.

Harne, L. and Radford, J. (2008) *Tackling Domestic Violence: Theories, Policies and Practice*, Maidenhead, Open University Press.

Hatfield, E. (1988) 'The passionate love scale', in Davis, C.M., Yaber, W. and Davis, S.L. (eds) *Sexuality-related Measures: A Compendium*, Lake Mills, IA, Graphic Publishing.

Hatfield, E. and Rapson, R.L. (1993) *Love, Sex, and Intimacy: Their Psychology, Biology, and History*, New York, Harper Collins.

Hatfield, E. and Walster, G.W. (1978) *A New Look at Love*, Lanham, MD, University Press of America.

Hays, R.B. (1988) 'Friendship', in S. Duck (ed.) *Handbook of Personal Relationships: Theory, Research, and Interventions*, California, John Wiley, pp. 391–408.

Hazan C. and Shaver P. (1987) 'Romantic love conceptualized as an attachment process', *Journal of Personality and Social Psychology*, vol. 52, no. 3, pp. 511–24.

Hess, J.A. (2000) 'Maintaining non-voluntary relationships with disliked partners: an investigation into the use of distancing behaviors', *Human Communication Research*, vol. 6, no. 3, pp. 458–88.

Hess, J.A. (2002) 'Distance regulation in personal relationships: the development of a conceptual model and a test of representational validity', *Journal of Social and Personal Relationships*, vol. 19, no. 5, pp. 663–83.

Hess, J.A. (2003) 'Measuring distance in personal relationships: the Relational Distance Index', *Personal Relationships*, vol. 10, no. 2, pp. 197–215.

Hester, M., Pearce, J. and Harwin, N. (2007) *Making an Impact: Children and Domestic Violence: A Reader,* Philadelphia, Jessica Kingsley Publishers.

Hinde, R.A. (1997) *Relationships: A Dialectical Perspective*, Hove, Psychology Press.

Hoffman, K.L., Demo, D.H. and Edwards, J.N. (1994) 'Physical wife abuse in a non-Western society: an integrated theoretical approach', *Journal of Marriage and the Family*, vol. 56, no. 1, pp. 131–46.

Homans, G. (1974) *Social Behaviour: Its Elementary Forms*, New York, Harcourt Brace Jovanovich.

Howard, J.A., Blumstein, P. and Schwartz, P. (1987) 'Social evolutionary theories? Some observations on preferences in human mate selection', *Journal of Personality and Social Psychology,* vol. 53, no. 1, pp. 194–200.

Jewkes, R. (2002) 'Intimate partner violence: causes and prevention', *The Lancet*, vol. 359, no. 9315, pp. 1423–9.

Jewkes, R., Levin, J. and Penn-Kekana, L. (2002) 'Risk factors for domestic violence: findings from a South African cross-sectional study', *Social Science and Medicine*, vol. 55, no. 9, pp. 1603–17.

Jones, A.S., Gielen, A.C., Campbell, J.C., Schollenberger, J., Dienemann, J.A., Kub, J., O'Campo, J. and Wynne, E.C. (1999) 'Annual and lifetime prevalence of partner abuse in a sample of female HMO enrollees', *Women's Health Issues*, vol. 9, no. 6, pp. 295–305.

Jones, B.C., DeBruine, L.M., Little, A.C., Conway, C. and Feinberg, D.R. (2006) 'Integrating gaze direction and expression in preferences for attractive faces', *Psychological Science*, vol. 17, no. 7, pp. 588–91.

Kirkpatrick, L.A. and Davis, K.E. (1994) 'Attachment style, gender, and relationship stability: a longitudinal analysis', *Journal of Personality and Social Psychology*, vol. 66, no. 3, pp. 506–12.

Koenig, B.L., Kirkpatrick, L.A. and Ketelaar, T. (2007) 'Misperception of sexual interests in opposite-sex friendships: four hypotheses', *Personal Relationships*, vol. 14, no. 3, pp. 411–29.

Langlois, J.H. (1986) 'From the eye of the beholder to behavioural reality: the development of social behaviours and social relations as a function of physical attractiveness', in Herman, C.P., Zanna, M.P., and Higgins, E.T. (eds) *Physical Appearance, Stigma, and Social Behaviour: The Ontario Symposium*, pp. 23–41, Hillsdale, NJ, Erlbaum.

Le Bon, G. (1895) *The Crowd: A Study of the Popular Mind*, London, Ernest Benn.

Lee, J.A. (1977) 'A typology of styles of loving', *Personality and Social Psychology Bulletin*, vol. 3, no. 2, pp. 173–82.

Lee, J.A. (1988) 'Love-styles' in Sternberg, R. and Barnes, M. (eds) *The Psychology of Love*, New Haven, Yale University Press, pp. 38–67.

Little, A.C. and Jones, B.C. (2003) 'Evidence against perceptual bias views for symmetry preferences in human faces', *Proceedings of the Royal Society of London* B, vol. 270, pp. 1759–63.

Madey, S.F. and Rodgers, L. (2009) 'The effect of attachment and Sternberg's Triangular Theory of Love on relationship satisfaction', *Individual Differences Research*, vol. 7, no. 2, pp. 76–84.

Markman, H.J. (1981) 'Prediction of marital distress: a 5-year follow-up', *Journal of Consulting and Clinical Psychology*, vol. 49, no. 5, pp. 760–2.

Maslow, A.H. (1962) *Towards a Psychology of Being*, New York, Van Nostrand Company.

McCarry, M. (2009) 'Justifications and contradictions: young people's views of domestic abuse', *Men and Masculinities*, vol. 11, no. 3, pp. 325–45.

Meyers, S.A. and Berscheid, E. (1997) 'The language of love: the difference a preposition makes', *Personality and Social Psychology Bulletin*, vol. 23, no. 4, pp. 347–62.

Milgram, S. (1963) 'Behavioral study of obedience', *Journal of Abnormal and Social Psychology*, vol. 67, no. 4, pp. 371–8.

Miner, E.J., and Shackleford, T.K. (2010) 'Mate attraction, retention, and expulsion', *Psichothema*, vol. 22, no. 1, pp. 9–14.

Monsour, M., Betty, S. and Kurzwell, N. (1993) 'Levels of perspectives and the perception of intimacy in cross-sex friendships: a balance theory explanation of shared perceptual reality', *Journal of Social and Personal Relationships*, vol. 10, no. 4, pp. 529–50.

Moreland, R.L. and Beach, S.R. (1992) 'Exposure effects in the classroom: the development of affinity among students', *Journal of Experimental and Social Psychology*, vol. 28, no. 3, pp. 255–76.

Morry, M.M. (2005) 'The attraction-similarity hypothesis among cross-sex friends: relationship satisfaction, perceived similarities, and self-serving perceptions', *Journal of Social and Personal Relationships*, vol. 24, no. 1, pp. 117–38.

Murstein, B.I. (1972) 'Physical attractiveness and marital choice', *Journal of Personality and Social Psychology*, vol. 22, no. 1, pp. 8–12.

Penton-Voak, I.S., Perrett, D.I., Castles, D.L., Kobayashi, T., Burt, D.M., Murray, L.K. and Minamisawa, R. (1999) 'Menstrual cycle alters face preference', *Nature*, vol. 399, pp. 741–2.

Perlman, D. and Oskamp, S. (1971) 'The effect of picture content and exposure frequency on evaluation of negroes and whites', *Journal of Experimental and Social Psychology*, vol. 7, no. 5, pp. 503–14.

Perrett, D.I., May, K.A. and Yoshikawa, S. (1994) 'Facial shape and judgments of female attractiveness', *Nature*, vol. 368, pp. 239–42.

Perrett, D.I., Lee, K.J., Penton-Voak, I., Rowland, D., Yoshikawa, S., Burt, D. M., Henzi, S.P., Castles, D.L., and Akamatsu, S. (1998) 'Effects of sexual dimorphism on facial attractiveness', *Nature*, vol. 394, pp. 884–7.

Povey, D. (ed.) (2005) 'Crime in England and Wales 2003/2004: Supplementary Volume 1: Homicide and Gun Crime', *Home Office Statistical Bulletin* No. 02/05, London, Home Office.

Rawlins, W.K. (1981) *Friendship as a Communicative Achievement: A Theory and an Interpretive Analysis of Verbal Reports*, Philadelphia, Temple University.

Reeder, H.M. (2000) '"I like you…as a friend": the role of attraction in cross-sex friendships', *Journal of Social and Personal Relationships*, vol. 17, no. 3, pp. 329–48.

Regan, P.C., Kocan, E.R. and Whitlock, T. (1998) 'Ain't love grand! A prototype analysis of the concept of romantic love', *Journal of Social and Personal Relationships*, vol. 25, no. 3, pp. 411–20.

Reis, H., Nezlek, J. and Wheeler, L. (1980) 'Physical attractiveness in social interaction', *Journal of Personality and Social Psychology*, vol. 38, no. 4, pp. 604–17.

Reis, H., Maniaci, M.R., Caprariello, P.A., Eastwick, P. and Finkel, E.J. (2011) 'Familiarity does indeed promote attraction in live interaction', *Journal of Personality and Social Psychology*, vol. 101, no. 3, pp. 557–70.

Rosch, E. (1973) 'Natural categories', *Cognitive Psychology*, vol. 4, no. 3, pp. 328–50.

Rosch, E. (1978) 'Principles of categorization', in Rosch, E. and Lloyd, B.B. (eds) *Cognition and Categorization*, Hillsdale, NJ, Lawrence Erlbaum Associates, pp. 27–48.

Rubin, Z. (1970) 'Measurement of romantic love', *Journal of Personality and Social Psychology*, vol. 16, no. 2, pp. 265–73.

Rubin, Z. (1973) *Liking and Loving: An Invitation to Social Psychology*, New York, Holt, Rinehart & Winston.

Rubin, Z. (1988) 'Preface', in Sternberg, R.J. and Barnes, M.L. (eds) *The Psychology of Love: vii-xii.* New Haven, CT, Yale University Press.

Sampson, E.D. (1989) 'The challenge of social change for psychology: globalization and psychology's theory of the person', *American Psychologist*, vol. 44, no. 6, pp. 914–21.

Sinclair, H. and Frieze, I. (2000) 'Initial courtship behaviour and stalking: how should we draw the line?', *Violence and Victims*, vol. 15, no. 1, pp. 23–40.

Smith, K., Coleman, K., Eder, S. and Hall, P. (2011) 'Homicides, firearm offences and intimate violence 2009/10: Supplementary volume 2 to Crime in England and Wales 2009/10 2nd Edition', *Home Office Statistical Bulletin* 01/11, London, Home Office.

Sprecher, S. and Duck, S. (1993) 'Sweet talk: the role of communication in consolidating relationships', *Personality and Social Psychology Bulletin*, vol. 20, pp. 391–400.

Sprecher, S. and Hendrick, S. (2004) 'Self-disclosure in intimate relationships: associations with individual and relationship characteristics over time', *Journal of Social and Clinical Psychology*, vol. 23, no. 6, pp. 857–77.

Stainton Rogers, R., Stenner, P., Gleeson, K. and Stainton Rogers, W. (1995) *Social Psychology: A Critical Agenda*, Cambridge, Polity Press.

Sternberg, R.J. (1986) 'A triangular theory of love', *Psychological Review*, vol. 93, no. 2, pp. 119–35.

Sternberg, R.J. (1995) 'Love as a story', *Journal of Social and Personal Relationships*, vol. 12, no. 4, pp. 541–6.

Sternberg, R.J. (1996) 'Love stories', *Personal Relationships*, vol. 3, no. 1, pp. 59–79.

Sternberg, R.J. (1998) *Love is a Story,* New York, Oxford University Press.

Sternberg, R. J. (2006) 'A duplex theory of love', in Sternberg, R.J. and Veis, K. (eds) *The New Psychology of Love*, New York, Yale University Press.

Sternberg, R.J. and Barnes, M.L. (eds) (1988) *The Psychology of Love*, New Haven, CT, Yale University Press.

Stets, J.E. (1990) 'Verbal and physical aggression in marriage', *Journal of Marriage and the Family*, vol. 52, no. 2, pp. 501–14.

Stith, S.M. and McMonigle, C.L. (2009) 'Risk factors associated with intimate partner violence', in Whittaker, D. J. and Lutzer, J.R. (eds) *Preventing Partner Violence: Research and Evidence-based Intervention Strategies*, Washington, DC, American Psychological Association, pp. 7–92.

Tang, L. (2010) 'Development of online friendship in different social spaces: a case study', *Information, Communication and Society*, vol. 13, no. 4, pp. 615–33.

Thibaut, J.W. and Kelley, H.H. (1959) *The Social Psychology of Groups*, New York, Wiley.

Turner, P.J., Gervai, J. and Hinde, R.A. (1993) 'Gender-typing in young children: preferences, behaviour and cultural differences', *British Journal of Developmental Psychology*, vol. 11, no. 4, pp. 323–42.

Watts, S. and Stenner, P. (2005) 'The subjective experience of partnership love: a Q methodological study', *British Journal of Social Psychology*, vol. 44, no. 1, pp. 1–26.

Watts, S. and Stenner, P. (2013) 'Definitions of love in a sample of British women: an empirical study using Q methodology', *British Journal of Social Psychology*, pp. 1–16.

White, G.L., and Mullen, P.E. (1989) *Jealousy: Theory, Research, and Clinical Strategies*, New York, Guilford.

Winch, R.F., Ktsanes, T. and Ktsanes, V. (1954) 'The theory of complementary needs in mate-selection: an analytic and descriptive study', *American Sociological Review*, vol. 19, no. 3, pp. 241–9.

Zajonc, R.B. (1968) 'Attitudinal effects of mere exposure', *Journal of Personality and Social Psychology*, vol. 9, no. 2, Monograph supplement, Part 2.

Chapter 7

How do you feel about that? The psychology of attitudes

Karen Hagan

Contents

1 Introduction

Have you ever told someone or been told by someone that you have a good attitude or a bad one? What is a good or bad attitude? We all understand this concept in everyday contexts; for example, a bad attitude is commonly understood as being surly and uncompliant – and in some cases, rebellious and sexy. Yet even this common understanding of attitudes is more complex than it may first appear; a teenager might be relatively proud of being told they have a bad attitude by a teacher, while to the teacher the accusation may have very negative connotations. To social psychologists, the concept of attitude means something slightly different from this everyday understanding. However, they too are interested in how one attitude is understood as good and another as bad. This is because psychologists understand attitudes as an evaluative position taken towards something and this something can even be an attitude itself.

Attitudes are important in society because they can have a strong influence on behaviour. For example, attitudes about disability can influence how able-bodied people behave towards people with disabilities and can also influence how people with disabilities themselves behave. So psychologists are interested in finding out about attitudes and how they influence behaviour, and they are particularly interested in how attitudes can be changed. Figure 7.1 reflects how sport has helped change attitudes toward disability. The Paralympic Movement (2014) claims that a third of people in the UK actually 'changed their attitudes toward people with an impairment' by the end of the highly acclaimed 2012 Paralympics Games in London. Visually associating impairment with more positive images, such as those of strength, drive and success, may improve self-esteem (Shapiro and Martin, 2010), encourage more positive attitudes towards disability, and change behaviour (Hernandez et al., 2004). However, understanding and manipulating attitudes has proved to be a particularly challenging area for social psychologists.

Figure 7.1 Anniversary Games, Olympic Stadium, August 2013: Rio Woolf meets his idol, Brazil's Alan Oliveira, who shattered his own T43 100 m world record at the games

This chapter will first set the psychology of attitudes into its historical context. It will outline some of the key features of attitudes, and discuss the range of purposes attitudes might serve. The cognitive, affective and behavioural components of attitudes will be explained, and then the two main social cognition models of the relationship between attitudes and behaviour will be discussed. The second half of the chapter introduces the topic of attitude and behaviour change. You will see that the focus on changing behaviour has had a profound influence on the development of attitude theory and research, preoccupying many psychologists and generating an extensive body of research. The chapter will then summarise the main criticisms of the traditional approaches in attitude research and conclude by introducing an alternative approach to attitudes from the perspective of discursive psychology.

Learning outcomes

On completing this chapter you should:

- have an understanding of the concept of attitudes
- be familiar with some key studies and explanations of attitudes
- have knowledge of selected research methods and types of evidence, and how they are used to develop theories of attitudes
- be able to evaluate the contributions of different kinds of approaches to our understanding of attitudes.

2 Historical perspectives on attitudes

From the 1930s through to the 1950s, the study of attitudes was a dominant theme in psychology. This research was shaped by the social context of the time, and psychologists were particularly exercised by local and global post-war problems. As noted in Chapter 2, Theodor Adorno and colleagues (1950), for example, carried out extensive work on the relationship between authoritarianism and prejudiced attitudes in the 1950s, following the revelations of the Holocaust and horror at the consequences of anti-Semitic attitudes. Carl Hovland and Irving Janis of the 'Yale School' studied persuasion, spurred on by Hovland's previous research with the US War Department into methods of improving and maintaining the morale of US citizens during conflict. Their studies of persuasion took the form of assessing, measuring and manipulating attitudes (Hovland and Janis, 1959). Louis Thurstone and Rensis Likert (cited in Ajzen, 2005) pioneered the quantitative measurement of attitudes. You will most likely be familiar with the **Likert scale**, even if unfamiliar with the name, as you would be hard pressed to find any person in the Western world who has not completed a questionnaire that employed a Likert rating (Figure 7.2). These methods were later adopted by marketing organisations, political activists and health promotion agencies, among countless others.

Likert scale
The sum of responses to several Likert items. Responses are usually provided on a questionnaire where items may be displayed with a choice of options on a continuum.

	Strongly disagree	Disagree	No opinion	Agree	Strongly agree
It is worthwhile taking extra time to save money.	☐	☐	☐	☐	☐
Own brands are as good as market-leading brands.	☐	☐	☐	☐	☐
I take advantage of special offers.	☐	☐	☐	☐	☐
I like to compare prices and get value for money.	☐	☐	☐	☐	☐
I make a shopping list before I go shopping and only buy items on the list.	☐	☐	☐	☐	☐
I like to try new products.	☐	☐	☐	☐	☐

Figure 7.2 An example of a survey question using the Likert scale

Nowadays, psychologists use attitudes to interpret behaviour, infer personality characteristics and make predictions about individuals' behaviour or intentions. The link between our attitudes and behaviours seems to be intuitive and obvious. However, as far back as 1934,

Richard LaPiere raised concerns that were subsequently to preoccupy attitudes researchers until the present day. In his research in the USA, LaPiere discovered dramatic inconsistencies between white Americans' attitudes toward the Chinese, as measured using a questionnaire, and their actual behaviour, based on his observations of how a Chinese couple with whom he was travelling were treated (LaPiere, 1934). This led LaPiere to comment sardonically that from a questionnaire response 'the diligent investigator will jump briskly from his factual evidence to the unwarranted conclusion that he has measured the anticipatory behaviour patterns' (p. 230). His study provided early evidence that there was 'no necessary correlation' between questionnaire responses and responses to the actual situation, a theme that was to haunt attitude research for decades.

Activity 7.1: Attitudes v. actions

Read the following extract and then answer the question below.

Extract from 'Attitudes v. actions' (LaPiere, 1934)

> Beginning in 1930 and continuing for two years thereafter, I had the good fortune to travel rather extensively with a young Chinese student and his wife. Both were personable, charming, and quick to win the admiration and respect of those they had the opportunity to become intimate with. But they were foreign-born Chinese, a fact that could not be disguised. Knowing the general 'attitude' of Americans towards the Chinese as indicated by the 'social distance' studies which have been made, it was with considerable trepidation that I first approached a hotel clerk in their company. Perhaps that clerk's eyebrows lifted slightly, but he accommodated us without a show of hesitation. And this in the 'best' hotel in a small town noted for its narrow and bigoted 'attitude' towards Orientals. Two months later I passed that way again, phoned the hotel and asked if they would accommodate 'an important Chinese gentleman'. The reply was an unequivocal 'No'. That aroused my curiosity and led to this study.
>
> In something like ten thousand miles of motor travel, twice across the United States, up and down the Pacific Coast, we met definite rejection from those asked to serve us just once. We were received at 66 hotels, auto camps, and 'Tourist

> Homes', refused at one. We were served in 184 restaurants and cafes scattered throughout the country and treated with what I judged to be more than ordinary consideration in 72 of them.
>
> [...]
>
> To provide a comparison of symbolic reaction to symbolic social situations with actual reaction to real social situations, I 'questionnaired' the establishments which we patronised during the two year period. ... The questionnaires all asked the same question, 'Will you accept members of the Chinese race as guests in your establishment?'... With persistence, completed replies were obtained from 128 of the establishments we had visited: 81 restaurants and cafes and 47 hotels, auto-camps, and 'Tourist Homes'. In response to the relevant question, 92 per cent of the former and 91 per cent of the latter replied 'No'. The remainder replied 'Uncertain; depends upon circumstances'. From the woman proprietor of a small auto-camp I received the only 'Yes', accompanied by a chatty letter describing the nice visit she had had with a Chinese gentleman and his sweet wife during the previous summer.
>
> (LaPiere, 1934, pp. 231–4)

Why do you think there was a disparity between the behaviour and the questionnaire responses in the extract above?

Discussion

The business people may have just been too embarrassed to cause a scene by turning customers away (though LaPiere seems to suggest they didn't show any signs of embarrassment or hesitation), or the couple may not have matched stereotypical ideas about Chinese people (though in the full published paper LaPiere noted that their appearance varied – on some occasions the Chinese couple had looked neat and tidy and on others they were travel-weary and dusty). In fact, there may be lots of reasons. The main point here is that there is often a disparity between what people say and what they do. As the chapter develops you will see that this remains a major challenge for attitude researchers and as yet there is limited understanding of such discrepancies.

2.1 Summary

Attitude research has been a preoccupation of social psychologists for many years as an area with great potential for application to real-world issues. However, it was apparent early on that the relationship between explicit reports of attitudes and their power to predict actual behaviour is complex.

3 The concept of attitude

3.1 Defining 'attitude'

So, if the common-sense understanding of 'attitude' is slightly different from the concept drawn on by social psychologists, let's look at psychologists' efforts to define the concept. Two popular and well-established definitions of attitude are:

> A psychological tendency that is expressed by evaluating a particular entity with some degree of favour or disfavour.
>
> (Eagly and Chaiken, 1993, p. 1)

> A disposition to respond favourably or unfavourably to an object, person, institution or event.
>
> (Ajzen, 2005, p. 3)

These definitions make three essential points. First, they state that an attitude is a 'tendency' or 'disposition'. In other words, an attitude is not simply an expression; rather, it is an *underlying* tendency or disposition that is expressed in our thoughts, feelings and actions. As a disposition is not directly accessible, it is regarded by social psychologists as a hypothetical *state* that is inferred from a raft of responses as opposed to being the response itself (Fishbein and Azjen, 2010). Second, regardless of whether we talk about entities or objects, we can have an attitude about anything that it is possible to evaluate. Third, an attitude locates the object in an **evaluative dimension**, or dimensions, of judgement. For example, my attitude toward psychology is that it is very interesting, and this has been an important aspect of my own career choices. Here the attitude object is psychology, the evaluative dimension is 'interesting–boring', and I have located psychology on the 'interesting' pole of the dimension. I have personally followed through this attitude with my behaviour, as I studied and taught psychology, and this clearly is reflective of my disposition. However, others may express similar views without following through with a related behaviour such as studying psychology. This is one of the dilemmas exposed by attitude research. I

Evaluative dimension
A measurement of a particular feature of an object, event or activity that shows direction and range.

am sure you can think of other examples where you have expressed an attitude and then not acted on it.

> Pause for thought
>
> 'Numerous attitudes have been assessed over the years and, as new social issues emerge, additional attitudinal domains are explored. Examples are attitudes toward the church, hospitals and doctors, smoking and drinking, open education, politicians and political parties, ethnic groups and nationalities, and social issues such as nuclear power, energy conservation, protection of the environment, and the like.'
>
> (Ajzen, 2005, p.1)
>
> 
>
> What attitudes interest you?

3.2 Significant features of attitudes

The definitions of attitude provide a basic idea of how we might understand the concept. In the following sections you will look at some of the significant features of attitudes in more depth. These sections begin to explore how and why attitudes are used to evaluate our social worlds.

3.2.1 Evaluative dimensions of attitudes

By any definition, attitudes are fundamentally evaluative and social psychologists are interested in identifying and measuring a wide range of evaluative dimensions. This is most often accomplished via the use of questionnaires. Items for responses must be along a *continuum* such as exciting–boring or pleasant–unpleasant. Generally, attitudes are formed from many bits of information and researchers typically collapse evaluations on a number of dimensions into a single overarching attitude. For example, we might collapse positive responses towards questions related to personal responsibility, individual initiative and economic freedom into an overarching positive attitude towards right-wing politics. Correspondingly, positive responses to questions about social responsibility, social initiative and economic equity might be collapsed into a positive attitude towards left-wing politics.

Our attitudes may, of course, be more complex and context dependent than this example implies. We may feel ambivalence towards an attitude object; for instance, we may favour economic freedom in principle, but also be concerned about resulting economic inequity in the local economy. You may have experienced difficulty because of these subtleties and tensions when completing an attitude questionnaire at some time. Exploring the specific dimensions of evaluation, as opposed to collapsing them into an encompassing attitude, may thus also be deemed important. For example, we may want to explore specific emotional reactions to issues of personal responsibility in order to get a better understanding of how the public may react to particular political–economic policies.

3.2.2 Strength of attitudes

If you watch the news, live political debates and chat shows on television, then the views and behaviours shown will leave you in no doubt that some attitudes are held with fierce conviction and help to shape our society.

Why are some issues, such as immigration, the welfare state, the environment and abortion, associated with such strong attitudes? Social psychologists have identified a number of dimensions that relate to the strength of our attitudes. These can help to explain the passionate responses evoked by particular issues or situations. You might want to think about the strength of the attitudes both for and against abortion or immigration as you read the dimensions below. Or you might consider some of your own, most strongly held, attitudes.

1 *Certainty*: conviction about an attitude can be affected by the amount, origin or nature of the information we have about the attitude object, including its perceived clarity and correctness. The more certain an individual is about their attitude, the more likely they will act in accordance with the attitude. Medical and scientific information, through claims of objectivity and scientific rigour, carry particularly powerful status and certainty. In addition, having social consensus from a group to which you feel aligned adds to the sense of certainty about an attitude (Prislin et al., 2012). For example, some people have strong attitudes to abortion because they have very 'certain' moral messages from their religious group, alongside some powerful biological/medical information and images (Figure 7.3).

Figure 7.3 A campaign against abortion

2 *Centrality/relevance*: the relevance of an attitude object for an individual is positively related to the strength of his or her attitude towards it. Take, for example, immigration as an attitude object. Immigration may be of great importance to workers or job seekers who feel that immigrants threaten them with the loss of job opportunities. Hence, members of those sectors of society may hold particularly strong attitudes to immigration.

3 *Relatability to other attitudes*: linked to centrality of attitudes, core attitudes seem to affect a range of other attitudes, while peripheral attitudes will have less influence. For example, for some people a negative attitude towards abortion may be related to a core, overarching set of beliefs and feelings about religious morality.

4 *Accessibility*: strong attitudes tend to be more readily accessible than others, that is, they tend to 'spring to mind' and be easier to recall. Fazio et al. (1989) found, for example, that accessibility ranges from having no readily available attitude to having a well-developed, tried and tested evaluation of the attitude object. They used the *time taken (latency)* to respond to a question about the attitude object as a measure of accessibility and found that quickly activated, highly accessible attitudes had a consistently strong influence on behaviour (Fazio and Williams, 1986; Fazio et al., 1989). At the extreme end of the range, having no readily available attitude means that an

individual must spontaneously construct one when required. Such inaccessible attitudes have not been tested over time and situation so may be based on inconsistent features and, consequently, will be less developed and weak.

5 *Stability*: there is a positive relationship between the strength of attitudes, their stability and associated behaviour. Strong attitudes are more stable over time and can have a greater influence over our behaviour. For example, when there are conflicting issues more stable attitudes will have a greater impact on the decisions we make. Stronger attitudes are also more resistant to change, so that when evidence is contrary to the belief held then it may be necessary to reinterpret or reject the contrary evidence (Fazio et al., 1989).

In general, the stronger the attitude, the more persistent it will be over time and situation and the more resistant it will be to change. Houston and Fazio (1989) argued that stronger attitudes are more likely to influence information processing. They found that people are most likely to devote more time and effort to thinking about attitudes that are stronger and about which they feel more certain. However, even strong attitudes can contain inconsistencies.

3.2.3 Cognitive consistency, cognitive dissonance

Attitudes are generally conceived as stable and enduring dispositions. In addition, some degree of consistency is assumed within and across attitudes, and between attitudes and behaviour. These assumptions are based on the common-sense understanding that most people, most of the time, act in ways that are consistent with how they have thought and acted before. People like to view the world around them as coherent and predictable. They like to believe they can anticipate how others will act so they might achieve a sense of control (Azjen, 2005). Social psychologists have explored this apparent affinity we have with consistency:

> Many theorists go beyond preferences to propose that consistency fulfils important needs in a person's life. Common to the different views is the assumption that maintenance of consistency in beliefs, feelings and actions is essential for a person's effective functioning in the world.
>
> (Azjen, 2005, p. 26)

Festinger (1957) introduced the theory of cognitive dissonance, arguing that people are psychologically uncomfortable with dissonance, i.e. with inconsistency. Cognitive dissonance occurs when two beliefs are incongruous with each other, and it is such an aversive state that individuals work hard to moderate either belief to move out of such a state (Haddock and Maio, 2012). Behaviour may even be disrupted when incongruous attitudes indicate actions that are mutually exclusive (Gawronski, 2012). Festinger argued that when faced with dissonance, people will both try to reduce the dissonance, and avoid information that may increase dissonance. To illustrate the point, think about the smoker who can talk about the dangers to health while lighting up another cigarette – they might tell themselves and others that they will stop when they are less stressed or they would 'rather die with lung cancer than grow old in a nursing home'. Alternatively, they might bring their behaviours in line with their attitudes and try to quit. In either case, their responses display the motivation to reduce what Festinger called cognitive dissonance.

3.2.4 Explicit and implicit attitudes

You have already come across the concepts of implicit and explicit prejudice in Chapter 4, Section 3.3, so you may be aware that implicit attitudes refer to spontaneous, non-verbal unconscious responses to an attitude object, while explicit attitudes can be seen in conscious verbal or written claims as direct attitude indicators. Attitude researchers explore both kinds of attitudes using different research methods and, as indicated by LaPiere as far back as the 1930s, explicit measures particularly have some limitations.

Explicit measures are the most commonly used in attitude research and are better at predicting deliberate, consciously controlled behaviour. The Likert scale in Figure 7.2 illustrates how questionnaires may be used to measure or rate explicit attitudes. Such questionnaires use a rating scale (e.g. from strongly disagree to strongly agree) that then allows researchers to convert responses into numerical values (e.g. strongly disagree = 1 and strongly agree = 5). It is essential that the items on the scale are actually testing what they are supposed to be testing and that they are all testing the same thing so that an overall score can be calculated (usually an average). The main problem with such explicit measures is that respondents may be unaware of, or unable to access, their own evaluation of an attitude object. They may

Explicit measures
These are direct measures of what people think or say, such as the responses collected in survey questionnaires.

also wish to disguise their true attitudes to give a more socially desirable impression (e.g. to not appear prejudiced towards others).

Implicit measures These are measures that attempt to access people's spontaneous associations with an object, event or activity, such as their behavioural responses.

Evaluative priming Where exposure to one stimulus (the prime) facilitates a response to another stimulus (the target). Primes facilitate categorisation (and speed of response) of target words when they possess similar characteristics to the target words.

Implicit measures use indirect methods, such as looking at spontaneous behaviours or associations related to the attitude object. These are better at predicting spontaneous, unconscious or impulsive evaluations (Strack and Deutsch, 2004). In experimental research, psychologists often rely on two approaches to implicit measures of attitudes: **evaluative priming** and the Implicit Association Test (IAT)). You will have the chance to read how evaluative priming and, similar to the IAT, the Implicit Relational Association Procedure (IRAP) have been used in specific pieces of research in Activities 7.2 and 7.3.

Box 7.1 Individual differences: self-monitoring

As if the picture of the relationship between attitudes and behaviour wasn't complex enough, there are individual differences in how people change their behaviours across different contexts. One example of individual differences is in self-monitoring. High self-monitors adjust their behaviour in accordance with the perceived situational cues while low self-monitors maintain behaviour true to their values and explicit attitudes. For example, Czellar (2007) found that consumers generally had positive *implicit* attitudes towards high-status brands but only low self-monitors were found to rely on these to guide positive *explicit* attitudes towards prestige brands. It was suggested that the judgements of high self-monitors were based more on situational cues, reading the attitudes of others and matching their own in order to fit in with the group.

3.3 What purposes do attitudes serve?

Attitudes help form our understanding of the world and our place in it by selecting and shaping the information we take in and how it is evaluated. They provide a basis for navigating our way in the world, guiding decisions and behaviour and communicating with others. For example, we typically develop relationships with like-minded people and share our attitudes to express our own and our group identity. Attitudes seem to meet certain social psychological needs, and it has been argued that the function of an attitude influences its strength and stability and vice versa (Haddock and Maio, 2012).

Some more specific purposes of attitudes include:

- *Object appraisal*: attitudes allow us to organise and simplify information about objects. For example, complex moral issues can become more manageable when they are condensed into a positive attitude towards religion. Smith et al. (1956) claimed that this purpose of attitudes allows processing to be more efficient, making it easier and quicker to make decisions about how we should act.
- *Utilitarian or instrumental function*: this function of attitudes is to maximise rewards and minimise costs, so it has an impact on the direction of the attitude. We are likely to have more positive attitudes about things that benefit us and more negative attitudes about things that cost us. For example, political party campaigns are all about convincing us they can offer us maximum rewards so we will have a positive attitude towards them, and cast our votes accordingly. At the same time, we tend to avoid supporting the parties that we believe may cost us, e.g. in taxes or health care.
- *Social identity/adjustment*: shared attitudes allow people to identify with each other. For example, we may support a charity campaign because we have a friend who works for the organisation or support a policy because it favours a group to which we belong.
- *Ego-defence*: attitudes can either enhance or damage our self-esteem. For example, autistic people who embrace ideas of neurodiversity do not hold such negative attitudes about autism as the general public and media so can be more positive about themselves (Bumiller, 2008). The esteem function can work on an individual level and a group level.
- *Value expression*: attitudes allow us to express our values about the world and communicate them to others. As we can see on television shows hosted by people such as Jeremy Kyle and Jerry Springer, these can be expressed in quite extreme ways, but attitudes also express our values more subtly or indirectly.

3.4 Summary

This section introduced the psychological concept of attitude. It explored how attitudes are essentially a way of evaluating and making sense of the world around us. Attitudes are complex, however, so this section demonstrated the source of some of that complexity in terms of how attitudes can differ in strength and consistency. The apparent discrepancies between what we say and what we do, and between our explicit and implicit attitudes, are among the most challenging issues in the field.

4 Models of attitudes

Attitudes are constituted from different forms of information and sources. The development of attitudes clearly starts early in life; we are socialised into particular attitudes through family, friends, media, marketing, education, politics and religion, and generally develop some coherence between our attitudes to a range of objects. This section will explore the main models of attitude formation, from models that describe the basic components of attitudes (Section 4.1) to models that attempt to explain the relationship between the components, attitudes and behaviour (Section 4.2).

4.1 How are attitudes formed?

The multi-component model of attitude, CAB (Cognitive, Affective, Behavioural), separates out the different constituents of attitudes. Each constituent will be explained here in turn before integrating them, in Section 4.2, into the most commonly used models of attitudes and behaviour:

- *Cognitive component*: cognitions consist of thoughts, memories, opinions and beliefs, and these all inform the understanding we have about an attitude object. We use our understanding of an object to build a judgement about it: an attitude. For example, I think of food as a necessity; I know it provides me with vitamins and other nutrients that I need and gives me energy. I also know that too much of it is a bad thing. My attitude toward food is complex. I know sugary foods are unhealthy but I still allow myself to eat some (quite a lot, actually). Fishbein and Azjen (1975) argued that attitudes can be calculated by taking into account knowledge about the object and the value we hold for it or its attributes:

  Attitude = expectancy (beliefs about the objects attributes) × value (ratings of the attributes)

  So to apply this to the food example, my attitude is in part the sum of my beliefs about the nutrients it provides multiplied by how important I rate these nutrients. I think fruit and vegetables have wonderfully healthy nutrients and I rate healthy nutrients very highly, but I am still overweight, so what about the other components?

- *Affective component*: the affective components are feelings and reactions you might have to the attitude object. Taking the example of food, I have to confess that I love a wide range of foods and particularly the ones that are bad for my health. French beans make me feel sick and slightly anxious as I was 'encouraged' as a child to eat my greens. This raises another interesting issue about the affective component: there is evidence that pairing affective information with an object can influence the affective component of the attitude towards the object. In the case of the French beans, my bad experience – and accompanying negative feelings – has resulted in a negative attitude towards French beans despite knowing of their health benefits.
- *Behavioural component*: the behavioural component of attitudes relates to past and future behaviours towards the attitude object. Although we generally think of the relationship between attitudes and behaviour as in the direction of attitudes shaping behaviour, research suggests that people also infer their attitudes from knowledge of their own previous behaviour. This does leave us with the quandary of deciding which came first, the attitude or the behaviour. Bem's (1972) self-perception theory claimed that people sometimes do not know their personal attitudes towards an object so they have to infer it from their own previous behaviour. Chaiken and Baldwin (1981) provided some support for this theory when they found that people's attitude to the environment was more positive after they completed a questionnaire that led them to believe they were environmentally friendly in past behaviours. People can also change the direction and strength of their attitude or add caveats when it is not supported or is contradicted by their subsequent behaviour – in other words, when there is cognitive dissonance.

Activity 7.2: Evaluative conditioning

Read about Hollands et al.'s (2011) study below and consider how it might be received by the following groups:

- consumers
- food producers and retailers
- government policy makers
- health care professionals.

Hollands et al.'s (2011) study assessed the impact of an **evaluative conditioning** intervention on attitudes. They wanted to see if 'pairing images of energy-dense snack foods with images of potential health consequences, such as of cardiovascular disease and obesity' would change food choices. Given current concern about the risks of poor diets and obesity, this is an important area of research for health promotion and government policy.

Evaluative conditioning
Enhancing or changing the feeling toward a stimulus by repeatedly pairing it with another stimulus that carries a stronger or opposite response.

Why did they take this approach? Building on early attitude research, many psychologists argue that our preferences originate from two sources: genetic predispositions and learned responses. Evaluative conditioning assumes that evaluations are primarily learned responses, so repeatedly pairing an object that has an existing positive or negative association (e.g. a large stomach) with an attitude object (e.g. a bar of chocolate) will produce a preference or dislike for the attitude object (Figure 7.4). Evaluative conditioning has been shown to have a disproportionately greater impact on implicit attitudes than on explicit attitudes, and implicit attitudes have a strong relationship with food choice behaviour (Conner et al., 2007).

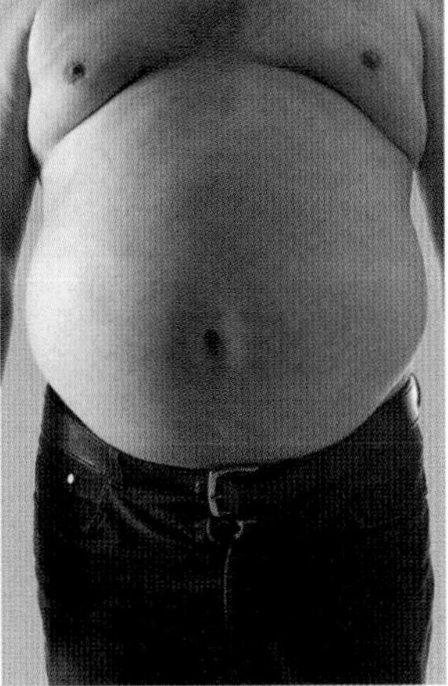

Figure 7.4 Example conditioning procedure images

In Hollands et al.'s (2011) study two groups watched a slideshow of five images of snacks shown randomly 20 times. The snack images were followed by a blank screen for the control group or an 'aversive body image' for the intervention group.

Afterwards, attitudes or outcomes were measured in three main ways:

- Behaviour – participants were required to choose between a fruit or a snack reward.

- The implicit attitude test (IAT) – participants sorted randomly presented items into two categories (fruit and snacks) and two attributes (pleasant and unpleasant). The speed of allocation was assumed to reflect mental associations so that, for example, a negative association with cake would be reflected by faster times on the category–attribute pair of snacks–unpleasant and slower on snacks–pleasant.
- A questionnaire using a seven-point semantic differential scale (e.g. seven options from 'not at all healthy' to 'healthy') was used to assess explicit attitudes towards different foods.

The results of their study showed:

- participants in the intervention group selected fruit significantly more than the control group in the behavioural measure
- the IAT scores for the intervention group showed a stronger preference for fruit over snacks than the control group
- there was an interaction between the effect of the intervention and the baseline preferences, such that the intervention had a stronger effect for participants with a higher baseline preference for snacks
- measures of explicit attitudes on the questionnaire were also in line with the behavioural and IAT measures.

So, in summary, evaluative conditioning did have an effect on attitudes towards food, and the stronger the initial preference for unhealthy food then the stronger the effect of the evaluative conditioning intervention. The implication here is that implicit attitudes may be treated as a mechanism for changing behaviour in evaluative conditioning through cognitive associations.

The importance of such a study is both theoretical and applied: first, it suggests there is a strong relationship between implicit attitudes and behaviour; second, it suggests that implicit attitudes can be manipulated.

4.2 Modelling the relationship between the components, attitudes and behaviour

For a long time social psychologists have struggled to understand why our attitudes are not very good predictors of our behaviour. A number of theoretical models have attempted to explain the conditions under which attitudes become effective predictors of behaviours but social cognition models have dominated the field. These models are based on the cognitive processing of attitudes with inputs, generalised processes and outputs. The two models discussed below, the theory of reasoned action (Fishbein and Azjen, 1975) and the theory of planned behaviour (Azjen, 1991), are regarded as core theories in the field of attitude research.

4.2.1 Theory of reasoned action

The theory of reasoned action (TRA) was designed to provide a model explaining how rational individuals decide to evaluate, and behave towards, an object (see Figure 7.5).

Figure 7.5 Diagram of theory of reasoned action working through the example of smoking

(Source: Stainton-Rogers, 2011, p. 239)

In the TRA, a person's expectations about a behaviour and evaluations (value of expected outcome) of that behaviour are summed to form an *attitude* towards the behaviour. At the same time, their perception of the opinions of others (normative beliefs) and how motivated they feel to comply with those opinions also are summed to form a *subjective norm*. The term 'subjective norm' essentially refers to the social pressure to conform perceived by the person. Fishbein and Azjen theorised that *intention* to perform a behaviour is a function of these two components: attitudes to the behaviour and subjective norms. This behavioural intention thus drives the *behaviour* itself.

Figure 7.5 uses the example of smoking to illustrate this model. Imagine the model is attempting to predict the behaviour of an individual; let's call her Michaela. Michaela's belief that smoking is bad and her expectation that giving up cigarettes will be better for her health are summed to form a positive attitude to stopping smoking. She perceives the opinion of her friends and family to be that giving up cigarettes is a good thing and she cares about what they think, so she is highly motivated to conform – these together form her subjective norm which creates social pressure on Michaela to give up. Michaela's positive attitude towards stopping smoking and the pressure she feels to do so drive her intention to stop. Finally, this intention results in Michaela giving up cigarettes (behaviour change). Well done, Michaela.

4.2.2 Theory of planned behaviour

The TRA was the dominant model of attitude research for a while, and it remains important. However, it soon became evident that attitudes and subjective norms did not always predict intention or behaviour very well. For one thing, TRA did not acknowledge the influence of people's beliefs about how much *control* (sometimes called *self-efficacy*) they had to perform the behaviour. If someone did not believe they had any control over the behaviour, they were unlikely to intend to do it or actually do it. To overcome this limitation, Azjen (1991) added the concepts of **control beliefs** and **perceived behavioural control** to TRA and created the theory of planned behaviour (TPB).

Control beliefs
A person's beliefs about the presence of factors that may impact on their performance of a behaviour, such as their skills or resources.

Perceived behavioural control
People's perceptions of their ability to perform a behaviour.

Perceived behavioural control – or an individual's belief that they can actually accomplish the behaviour – is a function of (a) their control beliefs about whether they have the abilities and resources, and (b) their perceptions about the power of those abilities to affect change. Although attitudes and subjective norms influence behaviour via behavioural intention, perceived behavioural control in the TRB influences behaviour directly as well as via shaping behavioural intention. So, in Figure 7.6 Michaela's brother, Icek, believes that it is possible to stop and that he has the willpower and self-control to do it. This influences not just his intention to stop smoking but, directly, his actual behaviour and he stops smoking. Well done too, Icek.

Figure 7.6 Diagram of theory of planned behaviour working through the example of smoking

(Source: Stainton-Rogers, 2011, p. 240)

4.3 Evaluating the models

The TRA and TPB have received empirical support from a large number of research studies. However, critics have pointed out a number of limitations. Manstead (2011) questioned the basic premise of perceived behavioural control within the TPB. He claimed that psychologists often try to apply the theory to behaviours that are questionably under our own volition, such as smoking or habitual behaviours that are repeated so often they are not completely under our control. More account could be taken of interaction effects in the theories too. For example, the relationship between perceived behavioural control and intentions can be negative when people have a negative/neutral attitude to the behaviour but can be positive when people have a positive attitude. If I had a negative attitude to dieting and felt I had strong behavioural control (was capable of dieting) then I would *not intend to diet*, but if I had a positive attitude to dieting and had a feeling of strong behavioural control then I *would intend to diet.* Manstead argued that the role of affect (because the models take a mainly cognitive stance) and of the 'social' (albeit included in the concepts of subjective norms and perceived behavioural control) were not sufficiently strong in the models. For example, we often like foods that are bad for us and busy modern lives result in a reliance on unhealthy fast or convenient food. In light of such criticism and limitations there have been numerous adaptations and additions to both models.

4.4 Summary

This section has introduced some of the psychological models used to understand attitudes over the past half century, particularly the relationship between attitudes and behaviours. Researchers have applied models such as the TRA and the TPB to an array of research topics. It has had some success in explaining the conditions under which attitudes often do predict behaviour. However, the section has also touched on some of the criticisms aimed at TPB. Although these have clearly opened up opportunities for further developments, they have not diminished the popularity with which the TPB continues to be applied. When you read on to explore how attitude research is used in behaviour change interventions, do remember your thoughts in Activity 7.2 on evaluative conditioning.

5 Attitude and behaviour change

We often want to understand why people behave as they do and we can probably all admit to putting some effort into changing our own and other people's behaviours: it is part of the everyday parenting role, for example. However, increasingly, psychological theory is used in more formal ways to inform interventions to change attitudes and behaviour. Furthermore, there are particular drivers or incentives in society – for example, economic, political, health and educational interests – which require more effective, evidence-based strategies. Health promotion agencies are particularly interested in changing behaviour to improve citizens' life chances and quality of life, while the retail industry focuses on changing consumer behaviour for profit. This section will identify a selection of theories of attitude and behaviour change and use some examples of research into interventions to illustrate and evaluate the approaches.

5.1 Theories of behaviour change

> By identifying the behavioural, normative, and control beliefs that serve as the underlying determinants of a behaviour we also gain important information about the kinds of beliefs that would have to be changed to effect and change intentions and behaviour. In fact, providing this kind of information is arguably the single most important contribution of our approach to the problem of effective behaviour change interventions.
>
> (Fishbein and Ajzen, 2010, p. 322)

There are many approaches to behaviour change grounded in learning and cognitive theories. These include methods that many of us use on an informal basis too, such as offering incentives, modelling behaviour, providing reinforcement and providing exposure or opportunities to perform a new behaviour. On a more formal level, you may have also come across cognitive behavioural therapy or associative learning techniques. However, the theory of planned behaviour provides a particularly popular starting point for behaviour change research and practice-based strategies. Interventions can aim to change any or all of the elements of the model in order to alter behaviour (Fishbein and Ajzen, 2010).

Sutton (2002) describes four steps to applying the theory of planned behaviour to developing interventions. These must be used to ensure that the target group and target behaviour are appropriately and sufficiently defined and measured:

1 The most frequently expressed and accessible (salient) behavioural, normative and control beliefs about the target behaviour must be identified.
2 A quantitative study must be completed, employing a TPB questionnaire, to access salient beliefs. These must be used to establish which components of the theory are the best predictors of behavioural intention.
3 From the analysis of the questionnaire results, the best predictors are deemed 'key beliefs'.
4 Key beliefs can then be used as targets in an intervention.

These steps relate to the theory of planned behaviour but they still leave the details of the intervention unspecified. However, it is relatively straightforward to derive strategies for behaviour change from TPB because it offers a simple causal and linear explanation. The predictors can be prioritised for the purposes of selecting which to use for the design of interventions. The relative weighting of the predictors, after statistical analysis, can offer guidance to prioritising. Generally, the more heavily weighted the key belief then the more influence it may have on changing the behaviour and the more usefully it may be addressed in an intervention. However, there also needs to be real opportunity to change the target in an intervention. For example, if a group of obese women hold positive attitudes toward healthy eating then this is not a likely target for intervention because there isn't much room for improving their attitude further – it may be more productive to design an intervention to increase their behavioural control beliefs. 'Stage-matched' interventions are a sophisticated form of intervention where the intervention includes different stages over a period of time. The adjustments to the intervention are designed to match the state of the individual because individuals' receptiveness and motivation both change as the intervention progresses (Ogden, 2012).

Most interventions are led by an information-giving approach, addressing the identified beliefs and attitudes, and attempting to change them to new beliefs that will in turn alter individuals' intentions and behaviours. For example, drivers often break speed limits with terrible consequences. A number of beliefs may motivate this behaviour. A typical target belief that driving at 30 mph within a 30 mph limit will result in being left behind the (illegally speedier) traffic can be addressed by delivering appropriate correctional information to the public. This may take the form of leaflets or television advertising, stating that where 30 mph limits operate there are obstacles, such as roundabouts and traffic lights, that mean trailing traffic has plenty of opportunity to catch up (Ogden, 2012). Interventions are usually developed to meet the most frequent and accessible beliefs of a large population, e.g. all drivers. Due to the diversity or individual differences within groups, addressing beliefs of a large population can mean that a significant percentage of individuals' salient beliefs are not addressed if they don't fit the norms. However, more tailored and creative interventions can be developed, albeit rarely, for specific groups and purposes.

5.2 Reviewing interventions using TRA and TPB

So how well do inventions using TRA and TPB work? Health promotion interventions provide some excellent examples of how they work in practice so we will look at one particular area, physical activity. Reviews of 72 studies that applied TRA and TPB to physical activity concluded that 'the majority of studies using the TRA/TPB in physical activity behavioural research have shown that attitudes have the most pervasive influence on intentions' (Hagger et al., 2002, p. 22). Attitudes overall were actually more than twice as strong predictors of behaviour as subjective norms and so attitudes were most often the targets for interventions. However, it is still important to complete the steps above for applying TPB to interventions as other elements of the model may be more important in specific situations.

French et al. (2013), for example, examined an intervention based on the TPB to get the general public to increase brisk walking. Their literature search yielded seven existing studies of walking behaviour that had already identified salient beliefs. These revealed that perceived behavioural control was the most salient belief on all reports with attitudes and subjective norms significant in only four out of the seven studies. Therefore, perceived behavioural control was adopted as a target for intervention, e.g. devising coping plans to overcome perceived barriers to walking. The result of the intervention was a significant increase in self-efficacy and intentions to walk more.

Happily, actual walking behaviour also increased and this increase was sustained even up to the follow-up point six weeks later.

5.3 Challenges of using social cognition models to develop interventions

You may already have begun to appreciate the challenges of behaviour change strategies after reading about the disjuncture between what people think and what they do. If we consider the numbers of people who continue to behave in unhealthy ways, for example, the success of health promotion interventions is clearly limited. Challenges are evident both in the short term, and in the long term to ensure the change is sustained. You may be familiar with the efforts of celebrity chef Jamie Oliver and his televised school meal project that demonstrated both these short- and long-term challenges. In his television series, he worked with schools to improve the nutritional value of school dinners and, through lobbying, achieved government engagement and action. The School Meal Review Panel and School Food Trust were set up to guide and promote the quality of school meals. He used information and persuasion to change beliefs and even provided opportunities to choose healthy food options. The medium of television was a strong aid but newspapers joined in and provided some mixed messages as they reported on the resistance to, as well as the support for, the project's aims (Figure 7.7). Although the School Food Trust has followed through with the campaign (Nelson, 2011), the long-term evidence on whether or not children's healthy eating behaviour actually changed has been mixed.

Figure 7.7 Jamie Oliver's healthy school lunch project; parents take orders for 'junk' food from children who rejected healthy lunch options

In many respects Jamie used interventions that were supported by psychological theory on producing behaviour change. He presented information to educate people into changing their beliefs and he addressed their fears with self-affirming interventions; for example, he worked with parents, school staff and the children to develop skills. The use of popular media, particularly television, should also have been a powerful way to deliver the message. However, this was perhaps part of the problem. As a television project, it incorporated an entertainment narrative. It engaged with individual stories at quite a shallow level and was unable to address the complexities of either the individual or group salient beliefs. It was also set in an unchanged wider social context of fast food and advertising which consistently circulates messages that are entirely contradictory to the project. Consumption behaviour is not just about information but about culture, economics, social groups, family and many other related issues. These could only be touched on in the lightest way in a television series. Sustained behaviour change takes time and multiple approaches (Ogden, 2012).

Box 7.2 Crossing boundaries

Research into attitudes covers a great range of topics but it also crosses the boundaries between approaches in psychology. Attitude research typically sits in the domain of social psychology, but some cognitive psychologists explore attitudes as networks of connections or schemas and use connectionist modelling to explore attitude structure, the relationships between different aspects of attitudes and the relationship between attitudes and behaviour (Monroe and Read, 2008). From a biological psychology perspective the development of MRI technology allows attitudes to be explored at the neuropsychological level. For example, the effects of persuasion can be mapped in neural networks (Klucharev et al., 2008).

5.4 Summary

This section has discussed how attitude research and social cognition models, the TRA and the TPB, have informed interventions to change behaviour. The models have been applied, for instance, to areas of health behaviour in an attempt to improve or prolong individuals' quality of life. It has dealt specifically with some of the achievements of attitude research and began to recognise some of the challenges that researchers face when they attempt to change our attitudes.

6 Discursive psychology and attitudes

In Chapter 2, Section 4, Stephen Gibson introduced the discursive psychological approach to social psychology and applied it to the topic of social influence. In this section, the discursive psychological approach will be developed further and applied to the topic of attitudes. The theoretical foundation of discourse analysis is drawn from social constructionism, which is concerned with how people construct their social worlds. Discourse analysis focuses specifically on the use of language in constructing meanings and practices. At the peak of this paradigm shift across the social sciences, often referred to as 'the turn to languages', Potter and Wetherell (1987) wrote an influential book entitled *Discourse and Social Psychology.* In it they argued there is no such thing as a stable, enduring mental state that psychologists label 'attitude'. Instead, they proposed an alternative way to understand thoughts, feelings and beliefs. Discursive psychology reframed the concept of attitudes as *evaluative positions* accomplished in and through everyday language. It is something that we do deliberately on occasion but which we mostly accomplish without much awareness. Through our talk about the world, we actively constitute the meaning of everything around us. We negotiate meaning in our talk with others and it changes depending on the context in which we use the language. For example, below is an extract from an interview I carried out with a mother following her child's assessment by two clinical psychologists:

Rosemary: 'Well we sat … well, they talked to us, the two girls talked to us about our concerns … and John wasn't in the room. I don't like talking about him when he is there and I don't think it is really fair. And then we sat in with him when he did the tests … so he did various written tests and imaginary play and I just, I could see he was just really uncomfortable with the whole thing. I felt a wee bit … I mean they were really nice girls but I felt John was a wee bit older than what … I don't think they targeted it, the assessment, necessarily for his age.'

This was part of an exchange with a researcher and was apparently not something said to the clinical psychologists, so already we can see that the context (with the researcher) may have facilitated a more critical evaluation. The evaluation is broached in a balanced way with moderate terms as more extreme criticism can be disregarded as unreasonable; some of the language, e.g. 'nice', is even complimentary to the professionals. However, although the professionals are 'nice', their competence is clearly questioned: 'I don't think they targeted it, the assessment, necessarily for his age'. The most powerful put-down, however, is the use of the word 'girls' to describe the professionals. This has the effect of reducing their status, stripping them, linguistically, of expertise, knowledge, experience and even maturity. Anything the 'girls' are reported as saying or doing is now set in such a framework and so can be treated with much less gravity, pertinence and even accuracy. Furthermore, Rosemary's comment on the 'girls' talking to the parents without John present, 'I don't think that is really fair', places the parent on the moral high ground. Rosemary connects the 'girls' to evaluations such as unfair and implies they were incompetent and even lacked respect for John. There are lots of evaluative statements here and they are doing something very active.

Note that in this approach an account like this is more than just an expression of an internal attitude towards a pre-given object. Rather, it plays a part in constituting the meaning of what attitude researchers would call an 'attitude object' and positions/evaluates it in relation to other objects. Discursive psychology focuses on the flexibility and variability of evaluative talk. We change our evaluations in different situations, with different people and for different purposes.

6.1 Variability in discourse

According to discursive psychologists, different evaluations of the same attitude object (e.g. immigrants) may be constructed in different contexts or at different times and so it is inappropriate to talk of a stable 'attitude'. While variability is not the focus of many traditional social psychologists, discursive psychologists argue that variability is inevitable and that 'one must assume that attitudinal stances contain both explicit and implicit aspects that may be contrary' (Billig, 1988, p. 83). In fact, variability is evident even in the talk of individuals with very strong views. Consider how we may hold very strong attitudes about, for example, healthy eating, welfare benefits or the environment but our talk is far from homogeneous as we move between positions over time and specific situations or different aspects of the issue. Billig (1989) analysed a family discussion on the monarchy and found that some variability and flexibility was drawn upon to argue and negotiate in the ensuing debate. For example, he highlighted how the father's talk spontaneously changed over the course of the discussion:

> At one point he says 'I'd love to get rid of them' ... yet a little while later, this had been softened: 'Probably I mean we may regret it if we got rid of them I don't know'.
>
> (Billig, 1989, p. 217)

This suggests that attitudes are not the stable dispositions presupposed by traditional attitude research. Although the father expressed anti-royalist views at times, when his talk was put in context this pattern of evaluation showed variation and complexity. In fact, his position on the monarchy had softened as a reaction to his son accusing him of supporting communism – a metaphorical red rag to a bull! In essence the father was able to construct a softened view strategically to avoid being associated with such an extreme position.

6.2 Discursive psychology and attitude research

Attitude research has treated the concept of attitudes as fairly unproblematic, but Potter and Wetherell (1987) provided three basic criticisms of attitude research, illustrating them through a piece of UK research on attitudes conducted by Alan Marsh in 1979 on 'coloured immigrants'. First, the category of the **object of thought** is usually more complex than attitude researchers assume. Potter and Wetherell claimed that 'coloured immigrants' is a complex and doubly contested concept because both 'coloured' and 'immigrant' can be contested. 'Coloured immigrants' is not a neutral concept either as it carries variable connotations in society. Most attitude objects of interest to psychologists are contested concepts that are not neutral; consider some of the objects discussed already in this chapter such as 'obesity'. The second criticism relates to the '**transformations**' that attitude researchers make in the coding of responses. For example, Marsh transforms the term 'extremely unsympathetic' to 'very hostile', a much more active and aggressive feeling that really may not relate to the respondents' actual disposition towards 'coloured immigrants'. Finally, the third criticism questions the fact that there is an assumption that a stable theoretical concept exists on a specific dimension; for example, Marsh's study assumes that an attitude to 'coloured immigrants' exists on a sympathetic–unsympathetic dimension. The discomforting experience of completing an attitude questionnaire highlights, in fact, the difficulty respondents have forcing decisions on simple dimensions, but does this mean such questionnaires and dimensions are not valid

Object of thought
The object, event or activity that is being evaluated. This term would most commonly be used by discursive psychologists as an alternative to 'attitude object'.

Transformations
Changing how the data is organised or coded, e.g. changing raw qualitative data into numerical data and/or subsuming data sets into overarching categories.

or useful? To offer a counter-argument, the multidimensional approach now taken by most attitude researchers allows them to measure attitudes on multiple dimensions and reflects greater complexity in the profile of an attitude. The social cognition models do allow for relationships between attitudes and behaviour that have some degree of complexity and have potential for embracing individual differences and variability. Although it may never be possible or desirable for cognitive social psychologists to reflect the variability that is accessible through discourse analysis, we must weigh up the benefits of being able to produce general rules, patterns and predictive power against the complex appreciation of the active construction of meaning through language.

Activity 7.3: Comparing two approaches to attitude research

Below are outlines of two examples of research in the field of autism. The first uses implicit measures of attitudes while the second uses discourse analysis to explore the construction of meanings. As you read them:

- consider the way the two published papers deal with evaluative ideas either as attitudes or as constructions
- note down your own ideas about the similarities and differences between them and the relative strengths and weakness of each.

Study 1: Attitudes to autism

The aim of the study by Kelly and Barnes-Holmes (2013) was to assess implicit attitudes of applied behaviour analysis (ABA) tutors and mainstream school teachers towards children with autism and correlate them with self-reported levels of psychopathology and professional burnout. They focused on implicit attitudes because previous evidence suggested that practitioners may feel compelled to suppress explicitly negative views of their clients as these would not be appropriate to their role. They used an Implicit Relational Assessment Procedure (IRAP) which they claimed participants could not deceive and which used response time to equate to mental associations, i.e. faster responses indicated closer mental associations.

The study found that both ABA and mainstream teachers 'showed implicit positive biases towards normally developing children but weak negative biases towards children with autism … for ABA tutors, their implicit attitudes, particularly negative bias toward autism, predicted professional burnout' (Kelly and Barnes-Holmes, 2013, p. 25). In addition, ABA tutors had more positive attitudes to normally developing children than had the mainstream teachers. Kelly and Barnes-Holmes offered possible explanations of the findings:

- ABA tutors may have been more forthcoming with negative attitudes and less motivated to conform to the social concern with positive framing.
- Attitudes tend to be more negative if working with students with more severe autistic symptoms. Although details of participants' client groups had not been identified, it is possible that the client group for the ABA tutors had more severe symptoms.
- They are actually in line with the philosophy of ABA tutors who aim to change symptoms of autism, i.e. if they were positive about them they would not be therapeutically motivated.
- ABA tutors with negative attitudes toward autism who rated high on the measures of psychopathology may have feelings of 'guilt and inadequacy in their professional roles' (Kelly and Barnes-Holmes, 2013, p. 26).

Study 2: Discourses of autism

A discourse analysis of media reports of autism was published by O'Dell and Brownlow in 2005, in the wake of the public reaction to Andrew Wakefield's claims of a link between the MMR vaccination and autism (Wakefield et al., 1998). O'Dell and Brownlow's paper aimed to demonstrate how, despite most studies concluding that there was no evidence to suggest they were causally linked, media reports at the time (focusing on the BBC online news site in the period between February 2002 and February 2003) created a moral panic about acquiring autism from vaccination and compounded society's negative understanding of autism.

O'Dell and Brownlow identified 'safeness and dangerousness' as a thematic dichotomy within the MMR–autism discourse. The language of autism in the media over this period centred around autism as a 'dangerous risk', concerning 'safety' over the vaccine and 'dangerousness' of the 'risk' of autism (O'Dell and Brownlow, 2005, p. 196). Autism was something to be avoided even at significant cost, such as at the risk of contracting rubella or causing a rubella outbreak. 'Brain damage' and 'vaccine damaged' terminology suggest the autistic person is broken, not acceptable or right, but the authors noted that this was 'in contrast to the more positive views of autism held by people labelled' (O'Dell and Brownlow, 2005, p. 195).

From the analysis O'Dell and Brownlow found that through media focus on the *dangerousness* of the vaccine, autism was constructed as something to be feared and avoided. Its meaning ranged from 'damaged' and 'faulty' to just a plain 'problem' (p. 198). O'Dell and Brownlow also examined media reports of 'parents' voices' in the MMR–autism link debate as a theme. The reported language used by parents comparing their child before and after vaccination was uniformly negative, contrasting the 'normal child', 'normal happy boy' and 'normal development' with the 'damaged' child who had 'lost language', 'went downhill very rapidly' and 'was about to lose the ability to even identify himself in the mirror' (O'Dell and Brownlow, 2005, p. 197).

You may see some similarity between the concept of attitudes and the discursive themes in O'Dell and Brownlow's analysis. For example, the safeness–dangerousness dichotomy could be an evaluative dimension on which to locate an attitude to the autism link to MMR vaccinations. While traditional attitude researchers may develop attitude questionnaires or experiments to get a picture of where people's attitudes sit on the dimension, discursive psychologists are more interested in how people may 'do evaluation' through language.

6.3 Summary

A contrasting approach to attitudes was developed in this section: discursive psychology. Discursive psychology essentially rejects the concept of attitudes as a stable inner state or disposition. The main premise for this rejection is the variability evident in attitudes. Instead, discursive psychologists assert that attitudes are more helpfully understood as dynamic evaluative constructions accomplished by people, together, within their everyday discourse.

You have had an opportunity here to compare brief summaries of two different approaches to how people think and feel about autism: one exploring attitudes and the other exploring evaluative constructions in language. Each offers different types of understanding but also has its limitations. Which did you find most helpful and why?

7 Concluding thoughts

When do attitudes predict behaviour? Attitudes are said to predict behaviour when there is a strong correlation between an attitude measure and behaviour. This will depend on a number of factors but we have covered some of the main areas. **Specificity** of the attitude and the behaviour must be matched. For example, measures for a general attitude toward the environment will not predict a specific environmentally friendly behaviour such as planting trees in the garden. An attitude must have a certain strength and **salience** to predict behaviour. At any one time an individual's decisions are influenced by a number of different attitudes so the strength of an attitude is as important as its relevance to the situation. Of course, opportunity to perform the behaviour must be available and the individual must perceive themselves to have ability to control their behaviour. Finally, any efforts to predict behaviour must also take into account the effects of social desirability; whether the behaviour will make them look bad will influence whether the person will behave in line with their attitude (Stainton-Rogers, 2011).

Specificity
The precise nature or exact aspects to which a behaviour or thoughts relate.

Salience
Importance or significance to a specific situation.

The chapter, while focusing on traditional attitude research, also introduced the discursive psychological approach to attitudes to encourage you to consider how the concept is contested. Key to this debate is how attitude researchers focus more on the individual and their cognitions, while discursive psychologists are more interested in the extent to which an individual is immersed in a social world. In fact, Potter (1996) accused attitude research of *atomism*, as treating attitudes as disjointed and independent.

Ogden (2012) argues that the social cognition models sometimes do not work. One of the most important aspects of all theories of attitude is to predict both intention and behaviour. However, a number of researchers claim the methods employed are less than adequate at predicting intention, with most managing between 40–50 per cent at best, and poorer again on predicting actual behaviour at around 19–38 per cent (Sutton, 2002). Additionally, some researchers have adopted methods that include a think-aloud component while completing a questionnaire and have discovered that participants' interpretation of questions is variable and sometimes inconsistent with the researchers' intended meaning (e.g. Darker and French, 2009).

However, despite these limitations and complexities, attitude research continues to be one of the most important and prolific areas of research in social psychology. Understanding and changing attitudes and behaviour can be used for commercial interests or political gain but it can also be used to improve health and longevity, and even help protect our planet. Researchers and funders are attracted by the promise of direct application to the applied social world across a wide range of topics and this is likely to continue well into the future.

Further reading

Maio, G.R. and Haddock, G. (2009) *The Psychology of Attitudes and Attitude Change*, London, Sage.

Mielewczyk, F. and Willig, C. (2007) 'Old clothes and an older look: the case for a radical makeover in health behaviour research', *Theory and Psychology*, vol. 17, pp. 811–37.

Ogden, J. (2012) *Health Psychology: A Textbook*, 5th edn, Maidenhead, Open University Press.

Potter, J. and Wetherell, M. (1987) *Discourse and Social Psychology*, London, Sage.

References

Adorno, T.W., Frankel-Brunswik, E., Levinson, D. and Sanford, D. (1950) *The Authoritarian Personality*, New York, Harper.

Azjen, I. (1991) 'The theory of planned behaviour', *Organisational Behaviour and Decision Processes*, vol. 50, pp. 179–211.

Azjen, I. (2005) *Attitudes, Personality and Behaviour*, Maidenhead, Open University Press.

Bem, D.J. (1972) 'Self-perception theory', *Advanced Experimental Social Psychology*, vol. 6, pp. 1–62.

Billig, M. (1988) 'Rhetorical and historical aspects of attitudes: the case of the British monarchy', *Philosophical Psychology*, vol. 1, pp. 83–103.

Billig, M. (1989) 'The argumentative nature of holding strong views: a case study', *European Journal of Social Psychology*, vol. 19, pp. 203–23.

Bumiller, C. (2008) 'Quirky citizens: autism, gender and reimagining disability', *Journal of Women in Culture and Society*, vol. 33, pp. 967–91.

Chaiken, S. and Baldwin, M.W. (1981) 'Affective-cognitive consistency and the effect of salient behavioural information on the self-perception of attitudes', *Journal of Personality and Social Psychology*, vol. 41, pp. 1–12.

Conner, M.T., Perugini, M., O'Gorman, R., Ayres, K. and Prestwich, A. (2007) 'Relations between implicit and explicit measures of attitudes and measures of behaviour: evidence of moderation by individual difference variables', *Personality and Social Psychology Bulletin*, vol. 33, pp. 1727–40.

Czellar, S. (2007) 'Self-monitoring and status motivation: an implicit cognition perspective', *Advances in Consumer Research*, vol. 34, pp. 332–4.

Darker, C.D. and French, D.P. (2009) 'What sense do people make of a theory of planned behaviour questionnaire? A think-aloud study', *Journal of Health Psychology*, vol. 14, pp. 861–71.

Eagly, A. and Chaiken, S. (1993) *The Psychology of Attitudes*, Fort Worth, TX, Harcourt Brace College Publishers.

Fazio, R.H. and Williams, C.J. (1986) 'Attitude accessibility as a moderator of the attitude–perception and attitude–behaviour relations: an investigation of the 1984 presidential election', *Journal of Personality and Social Psychology*, vol. 51, pp. 505–14.

Fazio, R.H., Powell, M.C. and Williams, C.J. (1989) 'The role of attitude accessibility in the attitude-to-behaviour process', *Journal of Consumer Research*, vol. 16, pp. 280–8.

Festinger, L. (1957) *A Theory of Cognitive Dissonance*, Oxford, Row, Peterson and Company.

Fishbein, M. and Azjen, I. (1975) *Belief, Attitude, Intention and Behaviour: An Introduction to Theory and Research*, Reading, Addison-Wesley.

Fishbein, M. and Azjen, I. (2010) *Predicting and Changing Behaviour: The Reasoned Action Approach*, New York, Psychology Press.

French, D.P., Darker, C.D., Eves, F.F. and Sniehotta, F.F. (2013) 'The systematic development of a brief intervention to increase walking in the general public using an "extended" theory of planned behavior', *Journal of Physical Activity and Health*, vol. 10, pp. 940–8.

Gawronski, B. (2012) 'Back to the future of dissonance theory: cognitive consistency as a core motive', *Social Cognition*, vol. 30, pp. 652–68.

Haddock, G.R. and Maio, G.G. (2012) 'Attitudes', in Hewstone, M., Stroebe, W. and Jonas, K. (eds) *An Introduction to Social Psychology*, 5th edn, Chichester, John Wiley and Sons.

Hagger, M.S., Chatzisarantis, N.D. and Biddle, S.H. (2002) 'A meta-analytic review of the theories of reasoned action and planned behavior in physical activity: predictive validity and the contribution of additional variables', *Journal of Sport and Exercise Psychology*, vol. 24, pp. 3–32.

Hernandez, B., Keys, C.B. and Balcazar, F.E. (2004) 'Disability rights: attitudes of private and public sector representatives', *Journal of Rehabilitation*, vol. 70, pp. 28–37.

Hollands, G.J., Marteau, T.M and Prestwich, A. (2011) 'Using aversive images to enhance healthier food choices and implicit attitudes: an experimental test of evaluative conditioning', *Health Psychology*, vol. 30, pp. 195–203.

Houston, D.A. and Fazio, R.H. (1989) 'Biased processing and a function of attitude accessibility: making objective judgements subjectively', *Social Cognition*, vol. 7, pp. 51–66.

Hovland, C.I. and Janis, I.L. (1959) *Personality and Persuasibility*, Oxford, Yale University Press.

Kelly, A. and Barnes-Holmes, D. (2013) 'Implicit attitudes towards children with autism versus normally developing children as predictors of professional burnout and psychopathy', *Research in Developmental Disabilities*, vol. 34, pp. 17–28.

Klucharev, V., Smidts, A. and Fernández, G. (2008) 'Brain mechanisms of persuasion: how "expert power" modulates memory and attitudes', *Social Cognitive and Affective Neuroscience*, vol. 3, pp. 353–66.

LaPiere, R.T. (1934) 'Attitudes versus action', *Social Forces*, vol. 13, pp. 230–7.

Manstead, A.S.R. (2011) 'The benefits of a critical stance: a reflection on past papers on the theories of reasoned action and planned behaviour', *British Journal of Social Psychology*, vol. 50, pp. 366–73.

Monroe, B.M. and Read, S.J. (2008) 'A general connectionist model of attitude structure and change: the ACS (Attitudes as Constraint Satisfaction) model', *Psychological Review*, vol. 115, pp. 733–59.

Nelson, M.M. (2011) 'The School Food Trust: transforming school lunches in England', *Nutrition Bulletin*, vol. 36, pp. 381–9.

O'Dell, L. and Brownlow, C. (2005) 'Media reports of links between MMR and autism: a discourse analysis', *British Journal of Learning Disabilities*, vol. 33, pp. 194–9.

Ogden, J. (2012) *Health Psychology: A Textbook*, 5th edn, Maidenhead, Open University Press.

Paralympic Movement (2014) *Official Website of the Paralympic Movement* [Online]. Available at www.paralympic.org/london-2012-overview (Accessed 02 August 2014).

Prislin, R., Shaffer, E. and Crowder, M. (2012) 'Populism versus elitism: social consensus and social status as bases of attitude certainty', *Journal of Social Psychology*, vol. 152, pp. 327–39.

Potter, J. (1996) 'Attitudes, social representations and discursive psychology', in Wetherell, M. (ed.) *Identities, Groups and Social Issues*, London, Sage.

Potter, J. and Wetherell, M. (1987) *Discourse and Social Psychology*, London, Sage.

Shapiro, D.R. and Martin, J.J. (2010) 'Multidimensional physical self-concept of athletes with physical disabilities', *Adapted Physical Activity Quarterly*, vol. 27, pp. 294–307.

Smith, M.B., Bruner, J.S. and White, R.W. (1956) *Opinions and Personality*, New York, Wiley and Sons.

Stainton-Rogers, W. (2011) *Social Psychology*, 2nd edn, Maidenhead, Open University Press.

Strack, F. and Deutsch, R. (2004) 'Reflective and impulsive determinants of social behavior', *Personality and Social Psychology Review*, vol. 8, pp. 220–47.

Sutton, S. (2002) 'Using social cognition models to develop health behaviour interventions: problems and assumptions', in Rutter, D. and Quine, L. (eds) *Changing Health Behaviour: Intervention and Research with Social Cognition Models*, Maidenhead, Open University Press.

Wakefield, A.J., Murch, S.H., Anthony, A., Linnell, J., Casson, D.M., Malik, M., Berelowitz, M., Dhillon, A.P., Thomson, M.A., Harvey, P., Valentine, A., Davies, S.E.J. and Walker-Smith, A. (1998) 'Ileal-lymphoid-nodular hyperplasia, non-specific colitis and pervasive developmental disorder in children', *Lancet*, vol. 351, pp. 637–42.

Chapter 8

How do we make sense of the world? Categorisation and attribution

Lisa Lazard

Contents

1 Introduction

Why did you decide to study psychology?

There are lots of different reasons why people study psychology, but most typically it stems from an interest in understanding why people do the things that they do. Trying to figure out why certain things happen and why people behave in particular ways is a routine part of everyday life. It is the main focus on daytime chat shows and debate programmes as well as being the source of conversations with the people around us. In other words, we spend a considerable amount of time thinking and talking about why, when and how things happen, and we do so in order to make sense of the world around us. Psychologists also ask questions like these to make sense of social-psychological events. As we have seen in the preceding chapters, such questions have included: *Why did the atrocities in the Second World War happen? When will people comply with requests? Why do individuals hold prejudicial attitudes? How do attitudes help us make sense of the world around us?*

The broad question of how we make sense of the world has been the focus of an approach called **social cognition**. This approach is concerned with how people select, interpret and remember social information. This may sound straightforward, but think for a moment about the sheer amount of information we come across in a single day. Simple, taken-for-granted activities such as walking past strangers in the street, meeting new acquaintances or judging the mood of a friend all require us to make sense of information so we can make judgements about what they are like and how they are likely to react. How do we process all this information? How do we make sense of it?

Social cognition
The cognitive processing of social information, including perceiving, considering and explaining people, events, relationships and social issues.

In this chapter, we will examine what psychologists have had to say about the processes of sense-making. This will include consideration of making sense of the vast amount of information we encounter as well as how we decipher the causes of events and people's behaviours. While this chapter focuses largely on what the social cognition approach has had to say about sense-making, it will also look at how other areas of psychology have explored how people make sense of the world.

Learning outcomes

On completing this chapter you should:

- have an understanding of the processes of sense-making
- be familiar with some key psychological studies and explanations of sense-making
- have considered similarities and differences in sense-making processes used in psychological research and those used in everyday life.

2 Social categorisation

M or F
Age.
hair color
bund.

> **Pause for thought**
>
> A friend has just asked you to describe the sales assistant who gave you a good deal on a mobile phone. How would you go about describing the assistant so your friend can identify them?

In the scenario above, you probably picked out information that makes the sale assistant distinctive – you might have described characteristics such as gender, approximate age, height and hair colour. This process involves categorising people by what we see as their key attributes. This process is called **social categorisation.** The importance of categories to our everyday lives should not be underestimated. Quite literally from the moment we are born we are assigned to a category – boy or girl?

Social categorisation
The process of categorising people, events and objects into groups based on common attributes.

Figure 8.1 Gender is a good example of a typical social category we use to make sense of people

The concept of social categorisation might feel familiar to you. This is because you have touched upon it in your reading about group processes and stereotyping in Chapters 3 and 4. The formation of in-groups and out-groups requires that the social world can be first categorised into separate groups. Social categorisation can be thought of as the mechanism that underpins those social–cognitive processes that require or use categorised information.

By assigning people to categories (such as gender, ethnicity, class, profession and so on) we are managing what information we need to process. Rather than processing all the information that we are initially confronted with when we meet someone, we match them to categories within which they seem to fit. That is, we categorise people on the basis of what we perceive to be similarities or common attributes between the person and the category of people to which we are allocating them (Schneider, 2004). Once we have matched a person to a category, we assume that they share all the characteristics that typify that group of people. We come to see them as having these characteristics even though we might not have seen concrete evidence of the person possessing them (Macrae and Hewstone, 1990). It is this process that makes us feel we know someone even if we've only met them for a brief amount of time.

Categories are thought to be made up of a vast amount of related concepts, so it is perhaps not surprising that concepts link across categories. Messick and Mackie (1989) suggest that categories are linked horizontally and vertically. For example, the descriptors Asian, Indian, British and Vietnamese could be linked together horizontally by the broader concept of ethnicity. Vertical links represent a hierarchical progression from broader conceptual links down to more specific ones that characterise a category of people. To see what these links might look like, let's take the example of British **stereotypes**. At a general level, Britishness may horizontally link to other racial identities, but becomes distinguished as separate because of category-specific attributes (tea-drinking, reserved, sarcastic). This may link across and down to other categories such as 'British man', which might be linked to more specific categories such as 'gentleman', 'football hooligan', and so on. The links between categories allow us to classify people into a number of social categories. The activation of one or more of these social categories shapes how incoming information is processed, how it becomes represented and how it is subsequently remembered.

Stereotype
An over-generalised belief about the characteristics of individuals that is based on their group membership.

2.1 Summary

Social categorisation is a concept that is popularly seen as underpinning many social psychological phenomena. The categories themselves are thought by some psychologists to be semantically linked both horizontally and vertically, which is thought to go some way in explaining how people and events can straddle some categories.

3 Schemas

Social categorisation allows us to organise information and, in doing so, simplify our social world. Social categories allow us to anticipate what certain groups of people are like and what we can expect from them in particular situations. This makes our social world more predictable because we have a reasonable idea of what to expect. The importance of predictability is best demonstrated when things do not turn out as expected. This can be seen in the widespread public shock during the 2011 London riots when footage of what looked like good Samaritans helping injured student Ashraf Hazig to his feet turned out to be a mugging (Figure 8.2).

Figure 8.2 The incident involving Ashraf Hazig during the 2011 London riots

The case of Ashraf Hazig illustrates how our interpretations of events are shaped by what we expect to happen in these circumstances. We expect most people would try to help an injured person, so we would draw on categories about helping behaviour to interpret the situation. What we would not expect is a re-victimisation of the injured person, which is what made this case so shocking.

Schema
A cognitive structure that contains information relating to specific subjects, people, events or issues.

The concept of the **schema** has been used to understand how expectations guide our interpretations. The development of the idea of schemas has been attributed to the classic work of Bartlett (1932) on how people remember stories and images. He used the concept to explain why English participants transformed the content of a Native American folktale to resemble English ideas when asked to retell the story. For example, words like "'boat' invariably, sooner or later replaced 'canoes', and 'rowing' replaced 'paddling'" (Bartlett, 1920,

p. 36). This suggested that when we process information, we organise it in a way that is meaningful to us, which helps us to remember it. The idea that information is organised into meaningful patterns formed the basis of schema theory.

In social cognition research, the term schema describes a cognitive structure that contains general knowledge and expectations about social objects (e.g. people, events and social issues) that we have garnered from experience. It can also include abstract attributes and ideals of social objects of which you might not have had direct experience. For example, think back to Chapter 3 for a moment to the example of how groups are divided up in secondary school. Groups may include 'the geeks', 'the jocks', 'the fashionistas', and so on. You may have an image about what a typical 'geek' or 'jock' might be like and you can still summon this image even if you haven't actually met anyone from these categories or groups. Psychologists have identified different kinds of schema. These include:

- **Event schemas.** These can be thought of as a script for what will happen and when in specific settings or circumstances (Shank and Abelson, 1977). For example, witnesses of the mugging of Ashraf Hazig seem to have used a script about helping behaviour to initially interpret this situation. We use event schemas to anticipate what will happen in a range of situations from extreme events, such as witnessing an attack, to more run-of-the-mill activities, such as visiting a restaurant.

Event schemas
Cognitive structures that contain information about social activities and situations.

- **Person schemas.** Grant and Holmes (1981) describe person schemas as implicit personality theories, which refer to a set of assumptions about which personality traits go together. For example, if someone is friendly, we might also assume they are outgoing, sociable and good natured even if we have not seen any evidence of these other traits. This allows us to flesh out our impression of someone, which can be useful when we need to make sense of new people quickly.

Person schemas
Cognitive structures that contain information about people's personality traits.

- **Role schemas.** These are packages of general knowledge about social roles. Roles include those based on markers such as gender, age and race as well as roles we have secured for ourselves such as occupational roles. These different roles are not always easily separated out. For example, imagine a typical nurse and a typical firefighter. What may well have come to mind is a woman in the nursing role and a man in the firefighter role. This highlights how

Role schemas
Cognitive structures that contain information about social roles including both acquired and ascribed roles.

different roles such as occupational ones can intersect with other kinds of roles.

It is important to remember that the knowledge contained in schemas is socially shared; this knowledge is recognised and understood by the people around us. This is why, in the case of Ashraf Hazig, a number of witnesses shared the same interpretation.

The use of schemas in storing knowledge means we only need to perceive or recognise a few pieces of information for the whole structure to be activated and used. For example, in the case of Ashraf Hazig, seeing people rush over and guide him from a slumped position on the floor to a standing position initially activated the social category of 'help', which guided the initial interpretation of the situation. However, we abandoned this interpretation because the act of a stranger standing behind someone and opening their bag is not consistent with the social category of help. It is important to remember that the mugging of Ashraf Hazig happened very quickly. The idea of schemas has provided psychologists with a way of understanding how it is that we can process complicated information that is presented to us briefly and, for the most part, effectively to arrive at a conclusion.

3.1 Evaluation of schemas

The construct of the schema makes sense of how people understand and process the vast array of information encountered on a daily basis. It also explains the efficiency with which we deal with information and how it is that we are able to draw relevant interpretations and conclusions that quite often serve us well.

Schematic processing
The processing of social information that is based in pre-existing schemas.

There are, however, some costs to the efficiency of **schematic processing**. This is aptly demonstrated in the study by Taifel and Wilkes (1963) that you came across in Chapter 4. You may recall that, in this study, participants were asked to estimate the length of grouped and ungrouped lines. You saw that this produced a category accentuation effect where participants tended to exaggerate the similarities between objects grouped in a category. Participants also tended to exaggerate the differences between categories. The act of categorising central to schematic processing invites us to pay attention to the similarities and emphasise the differences between categories or groups. As the Tajfel and Wilkes study shows, we begin to see what we expect to see; that is, schematic processing can be self-confirming. The problem with self-confirmation is illustrated in a classic study by Darley and Gross (1983) (Box 8.1).

Box 8.1 Schemas as self-confirming

In their experiment, Darley and Gross (1983) asked two groups of participants to watch a video of a young girl called Hannah. In one version of the video Hannah was portrayed as of high socio-economic status where she lived with professional parents in a wealthy area. In the second version, she had working-class parents and lived in a poorer area. In both cases, Hannah was rated by participants as having average academic ability – socio-economic status did not seem to influence how participants viewed her.

Some participants were also given a second video to watch that showed Hannah completing a test. However, it was not possible to tell how well she was doing. Despite this, those who had seen the high socio-economic status video and the exam video rated her as achieving more highly than those who had watched the exam video and believed she was of lower socio-economic status.

It seems participants interpreted the exam video according to their expectations – they expected individuals from high-status backgrounds would have higher academic ability. This also demonstrates that participants overgeneralised the extent to which Hannah was like a typical person of either higher or lower socio-economic class. In other words, participants used a class-based stereotype to make sense of Hannah.

As Darley and Gross's study suggests, problems can occur when characteristics (like those described in implicit personality theories) or roles become associated with important social markers such as race, gender or disability. This can lead to stereotyping which, as you saw in Chapter 4, can lead us to overgeneralise category information to apply to all members of the group. For example, it was mentioned earlier that gender can become associated with occupational role schemas (e.g. female nurse, male firefighter). A number of studies have shown that both children and adults tend to misremember gender-inconsistent roles (for example a male nurse and female doctor) as gender consistent (female nurse and male doctor) and this is particularly true of male-consistent roles (e.g. Kleider et al., 2008; Wilbourn and Kee, 2010). What this points to is that, while schemas can aid remembering, they can also produce biases and inaccuracies in what we remember.

3.2 Summary

Schema theory has been extremely influential in how we come to understand how we deal with incoming information and what we do with it. Schematic processing essentially is a means for simplifying the world. Social cognitive accounts represent our internal processing systems as limited yet based on rational procedures.

4 Attribution theories

So far we have looked at how people process information encountered in everyday life and draw inferences and conclusions from it. One thing we do when trying to make sense of a sequence of events or actions is try to ascertain the causes of them. During the course of your reading, you might have asked yourself: *What caused a person to give the wrong answer on a line estimation task when they knew the 'right' answer? What makes someone stay in a violent relationship? What caused them to voice a different opinion from the majority?* The processes we use to assign causes to events have been explored in theories of attribution.

Interest in everyday **attributions** can be traced back to the work of Fritz Heider (1958), who was interested in what he called **common-sense** or **naïve psychology**. This refers to how people develop their own theories about why people do what they do or why events occur. According to Heider, we develop causal explanations in much the same way as scientists. That is, we use the information we have at our disposal to build and test a plausible theory about what caused a particular chain of events or actions. Central to Heider's ideas was the question of how we perceive people's intentions.

Attributions
The processes by which we assign causes to social events, processes and people's behaviour.

Common-sense (or naïve) psychology
The everyday processes people use to make sense of social objects.

Activity 8.1: What do you see?

Look at Figure 8.3.

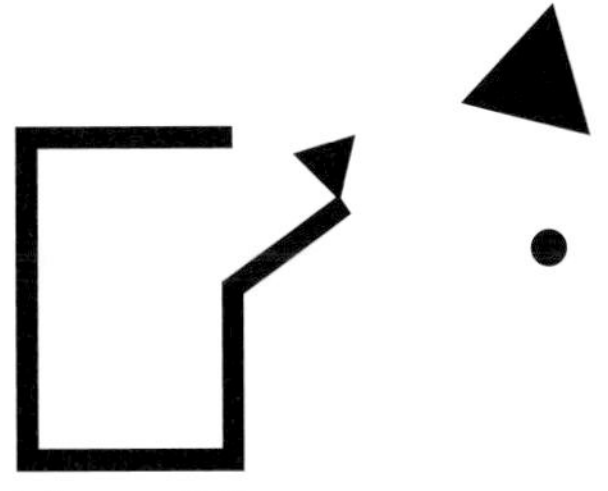

Figure 8.3

Write down what you see happening here. Don't just describe the shapes but note what you think is happening in the overall picture.

This image is taken from an early experiment conducted by Heider and Simmel (1944). They asked participants to watch movies of shapes in motion. For example, one movie contained a large triangle, a small triangle and a circle that each moved in different directions and at different speeds near a rectangle. One side of the rectangle included a section that opened and closed like a door. After watching the movies, participants were asked to write down what they saw. What was interesting is that participants often personified the shapes – they brought them to life by attributing personality traits and intentions to them. They wrote of shapes deliberately opening and closing the door, even suggesting that two of the shapes were in love! Like Barlett's study mentioned earlier, these participants were attempting to make their response meaningful by structuring it using familiar ideas. What sparked Heider's interest was how participants in this experiment used personal intention to connect a series of quite unconnected events (e.g. the movement of the shapes).

Phenomenal causality
The process of perceptual impression of causes of events and behaviour in the social world.

Using the concept of **phenomenal causality** (how we develop a perceptual impression that one thing causes another), Heider developed the notions of **personal causality** and **impersonal causality**. Personal causality describes actions with intent. For example, in the case of Kitty Genovese, which you came across in Chapter 5, we might draw the conclusion that the attacker deliberately set out to assault a woman that night. Impersonal causality refers to the unintended consequences of actions. So, for example, a neighbour who heard Kitty's screams but did not call the emergency services because they assumed help must be on the way did not intend her to suffer.

Personal causality
The idea that a person intended to cause an event or set of circumstances.

Impersonal causality
The idea that a person unintentionally caused an event or set of circumstances.

According to Heider, it is important to examine everyday explanations at a common-sense level. We build our explanations of the world not from an objective standpoint but from the standpoint of our own perceptions, which he called our 'subjective environment'. For Heider, it is crucial that psychologists examine common-sense-making because the explanations individuals use to understand and structure their world are important for understanding the strategies they use to understand and respond to social information.

Dispositional (or internal) causes
Causes of an event or behaviour located within the person (e.g. personality traits, ability, emotional state).

When building our theories about causes, Heider suggested we also tend to try to separate out the person from the situation to determine whether causes are dispositional or situational. **Dispositional causes** are internal to the person (Bob talked to people at the conference because he is an extrovert), whereas **situational causes** are external to the person (Bob talked to people because his boss wants him to

Situational (or external) causes
Causes of an event or behaviour located in the environment.

network). For Heider, the more we come to see a cause as dispositional, the less likely we are to perceive situational forces at play. This aspect of Heider's work influenced developments in later attribution theories such as the theory of **correspondent inference** (Jones and Davis, 1965).

Correspondent inference
How we attribute causes to internal or external factors.

4.1 Correspondent inference

Correspondent inference theory (Jones and Davis, 1965) is concerned with how we make internal attributions (a behaviour is indicative of a stable and enduring disposition or trait) or external attributions (a behaviour is caused by situational influences).

Pause for thought

Identify two causal accounts where an internal and an external attribution has been made. These accounts can be taken from your own experiences or from the media (e.g. recent television programmes you have watched or newspapers you have read). Try to identify how an internal or external attribution conclusion has been reached. What evidence has been presented to support these claims? Try to remember these as you read through the following explanation. Do they match Jones and Davis's theory?

According to this theory, we make attributions by making inferences about actions and the effects of that action. For example, imagine that John agrees to give Matthew his revision notes. Jones and Davis suggest that, to work out what this act means, we look at what the effects of John's actions are. One obvious effect is that the action helps Matthew, but other effects might include repaying a real or an imagined debt (for example, Matthew lent John his textbook some weeks ago or John will feel guilty if he doesn't help Matthew). To make the inference that John shared his revision notes as an act of kindness, we would need to be able to draw the inference that there was not much in it for him. So we would need to rule out that John wasn't going to receive a reward of some kind or that the act wasn't a payment of a debt between the two.

We would also have to be sure that the effects we were observing were freely chosen by John. If John was somehow coerced into giving away his notes then this wouldn't tell us much about his character. In other words, if we conclude that someone's behaviour is not freely chosen – that there were external circumstances that produced the behaviour (e.g. they were forced to in some way or there was some sort of reward for doing a particular behaviour) – we are likely to infer that the behaviour is shaped by external rather than internal influences.

Why is making internal or external attributions important? Jones and Davis suggest that internal attributions are actually more useful to us because we assume that if an action reflects the person's character then we can be surer that is how they will behave across situations. For example, if we conclude that John is generally a nice guy then he will probably be nice and helpful in other situations. So if your car breaks down, John might be the friend to call to give you a lift. External attributions have less predictive value because if a person acts because they are responding to the social context, this means their behaviour is likely to change across situations. So if John shared his lecture notes because Matthew was calling in a debt then we can't conclude that this is an act of kindness. In this case, we can't say with any certainty that John will be helpful in other circumstances.

Correspondent inference theory draws our attention to the number of different effects we process to draw conclusions about causality. It points to the need for certain information to be present before we make an internal or external attribution. Consideration of the kind of information we use when making attributions is further explored in Kelley's **covariation model**.

Covariation model
How people attribute causes by running a complex cognitive analysis of possible causal factors.

4.2 Kelley's covariation model

In his covariation model, Kelley (1967) embraced the notion of Heider's 'intuitive scientist' as an analogy of how laypeople assess relevant information to construct attributions. According to the covariation model, we attribute causes to actions by cognitively running a procedure that is similar to a complex statistical procedure called analysis of variance (or ANOVA), to which you will be introduced later in this module. This layperson version of doing an ANOVA involves identifying factors that appear to be associated or correlated with a particular behaviour. Based on the outcome of our analysis, we attribute cause to a factor that appears to be the most likely impetus for the behaviour we have observed. To see what this looks like in practice, let's take our earlier example of John's offer to lend Matthew his revision notes. How might Matthew make sense of John's offer? Kelley's model would suggest that Matthew would run a complex analysis of possible causes before arriving at a conclusion involving three important pieces of information:

1 *Consistency*: does the person behave in the same way in the same situation across time? Has John offered to help at other assessment points?
2 *Distinctiveness*: is the person's behaviour unique to this situation or do they often behave in this way? Has John offered to help other people or just Matthew?
3 *Consensus*: do other people behave in the same way in a particular situation? Has everyone offered to help or is this unique to John?

We judge the extent to which a person's behaviour is consistent, distinctive and similar to other people's behaviour (consensus) in order to work out whether the behaviour is internally or externally caused. The formula we use looks like this:

Internal attributions = high consistency + low distinctiveness + low consensus

External attributions = high consistency + high distinctiveness + high consensus

How might you use this formula in practice? To see how this works, let's slot in possible evaluations that Matthew could make about John's behaviour. To arrive at an internal attribution (John's a nice guy), Matthew would need to work out if John has offered to help Matthew before with assignments (highly consistent). Matthew would also need to decide if this is typical behaviour for John – he also helps other students with assignments (low distinctiveness). Matthew would look at what other students do. If no one else helps out other students with assignments, it would seem that helping is specific to John (low consensus). Taken together, the evidence might suggest that John is disposed to be kind and helpful.

To make an external attribution, Matthew would still need to consider if John has helped him before (highly consistent), but he would need to come to the conclusion that it is not typical behaviour for John as he doesn't offer to help students on the other modules he is taking (highly distinctive). So why is Matthew helping John? If Matthew looks at what other students do with their revision notes, John's behaviour might make more sense. If everyone shares their notes then it would seem that helping is part of the student culture on this particular module (high consensus). In this case, the act of sharing notes doesn't make John an intrinsically nice guy. Rather, John's behaviour is a reflection of what is considered normal in that particular situation.

4.2.1 Evaluation of classic attribution theories

The work of Heider, Jones and Davis, and Kelley provided the foundations of attribution theory. Rather than seeing them as competing theories of how everyday attribution processes work, it is important to see the ways in which they complement each other's contribution. Heider's writings inspired the subsequent theory and experimental work of Jones and Davis and Kelley. Jones and Davis's ideas attempt to explain attributions made in more contained situations, whereas Kelley's work attempts to explain attributions that are made when people have detailed knowledge across different times, situations and actors. Indeed, there is experimental support that suggests people do seem to make use of information described in these theories when making attributions. For example, McArthur (1972) found that people's attributions of cause changed when consistency, distinctiveness and consensus information were altered. This suggests that this information is important in forming particular attributions.

Both correspondent inference theory and the covariation model attempt, however, to describe the process of what people could *ideally* do when forming attributions. Neither theory claims to describe what people *actually* do.

Activity 8.2: Assigning a cause

Take a moment to recall some instances of when you assigned a cause to a person's actions or events. What information did you consider? On reflection, did your sense-making process resemble that described by Jones and Davis or by Kelley?

You might find that while some of the sense-making activity you engaged in when assigning a cause drew on some elements of the theories described above, it did not resemble the rational, logical calculus in quite the same way as proposed by either Jones and Davis or Kelley. In everyday life, most people do not systematically seek and test evidence in this way. For this reason, these theories could be accused of lacking mundane realism. Ahn et al. (1995), for example, when discussing the covariation model, raise the point that just because people are able to use these three pieces of information doesn't necessarily mean they will do so.

In a series of experiments, Ahn and colleagues asked participants what information they would want in order to put together an explanation of the causes of certain events. Their results suggested that participants wanted to delve into certain aspects of the event while neglecting others. For example, when assessing the causes of a car accident, they might focus more on the issue of whether John was drunk rather than, say, consistency information about how many accidents John has had. Participants focused on this information because it was seen to be more salient. They then dug deeper about this issue to collect evidence about their initial ideas for building and discounting aspects of their causal account.

You might be asking what the point is of describing ideal attribution processes when everyday sense-making is not ideal. Jones and McGillis (1976) suggest that, by providing the ideal of causal sense-making, we can then compare it with everyday sense-making to see the ways in which people's causal accounts deviate from logic by drawing on biased thinking. It is attribution bias that we will look at in the following sections.

4.3 Summary

Attribution theories attempt to explain how we come to conclusions about the causes of events and actions. Heider's ideas about common-sense psychology, correspondent inference theory and the covariation model have been influential in how we understand the way people make internal or dispositional attributions and external or situational attributions.

5 Rational decisions?

We have seen that early attribution theories used the 'naïve scientist' metaphor to understand how people develop causal explanations. A key assumption underpinning this work is that our cognitive processing of causal information is like the 'rational' processes used in scientific procedures. If you think about how we come to make causal inferences in the course of everyday life, it might strike you that they are not always clean-cut. Our accounts of events and the people that feature in them may contain biases because, as Heider (1958) noted, we develop our ideas from our subjective viewpoints. Psychologists have identified a number of common patterns in how we bias our causal accounts. Common kinds of bias include the fundamental attribution error, the ultimate attribution error, actor–observer effect and the false consensus effect. We will now look at these biases in more detail.

Figure 8.4 Cognitive processing: a key assumption of the social cognition approach is that our processing systems are rational and logical

5.1 Sources of attribution bias

In Chapter 5, you read about the abduction of James Bulger – the toddler taken and subsequently murdered by two 10-year-old boys. When the case was initially reported in the media, I remember wondering how people could stand by and let the child be led away. What was wrong with these people? Where was their sense of social responsibility? As we later found out, witnesses had chosen not to intervene because they assumed the boys were brothers. My initial response can be described as a **fundamental attribution error**. This is the tendency to attribute the causes of other people's behaviour to internal dispositions rather than consider what situational influences might have shaped people's actions.

Fundamental attribution error
The tendency to ascribe other people's behaviour to internal rather than external factors.

One of the most widely cited studies demonstrating this error or bias asked American participants to consider a speech written about the political figure Fidel Castro, who was hugely unpopular in the US at that time (Jones and Harris, 1967). The speeches were either pro-Castro, anti-Castro or neutral. Importantly, Jones and Harris told some participants that the speech-writer had a choice about what position to adopt in the speech, while others were told the writer had no choice. The participants were then tasked with working out the writer's true attitude towards Castro. What was interesting is that even in the no-choice condition, participants still made a fundamental attribution error. They saw the speech as reflecting the writer's true internal attitude even when they were told that the writer didn't have a choice in the matter.

So far we have talked about how we make errors as individuals but, as you saw in Chapter 4, we also make attributions as part of groups. Pettigrew (1979) suggested that in groups we can make the **ultimate attribution error**, which he describes as an intergroup misattribution that is rooted to some extent in prejudice towards an out-group. Our tendency to attribute dispositional attributions is heightened when we perceive the out-group as acting problematically. However, even when the out-group behaves positively, there is a tendency to attribute it to situational influences or dismiss it as an exceptional case and not representative of the behaviour of the out-group in general. For example, Hunter et al. (1991) demonstrated that both Catholics and Protestants in Northern Ireland were more likely to attribute internal causes to out-group violence than to expressions of violence by in-group members. A similar pattern of attributional bias was observed in

Ultimate attribution error
The tendency for people to attribute negative out-group behaviour to internal causes and positive out-group behaviour to external ones.

the attribution responses of Hindu and Muslim students for the causes of Hindu–Muslim intergroup rioting (Ruback and Singh, 2008).

What's interesting is that we don't tend to make the fundamental attribution error when we account for our own behaviour. It seems that we tend to overuse external attributions when we talk about the causes of our actions. This phenomenon is called the **actor–observer effect**. We can see the fundamental attribution error and the actor–observer effect in play in many of the major historical events that have been discussed in previous chapters. The overwhelming national and international response to those who committed acts of violence in the Second World War and in Abu Ghraib was that there must be something wrong with these people to be able to stomach the violence they inflicted. However, it is unlikely that those involved would attribute internal causes to their own behaviours. It is more likely they saw themselves as responding to the culture in which these behaviours had become normative and acceptable (see Chapter 2 for Zimbardo's causal account of Abu Ghraib). As Plumm and Terrance (2009) point out, the actor–observer effect can have profound real-world implications. Consider for a moment how jurors are positioned in relation to the actors (e.g. the victim and defendant). It is possible then that jurors, by virtue of their position as observer, may be more inclined to attribute the defendant's actions to internal causes such as personality traits or errors in judgement rather than the complexities of the social context in which they are located.

Actor–observer effect
The tendency for people to ascribe their own behaviour to external rather than internal factors.

The point should be made, though, that the very definition of error or bias means that attribution mistakes are the exception rather than the rule. Some psychologists have argued that the impact of the actor–observer effect in people's sense-making has been, on occasion, overstated (Quattrone, 1985). The business of attributing causes to others and our own behaviour is complex; the distinction made between being an actor and observer and the difference between internal and external attributions are far from clear cut in everyday practice. For example, as you saw in Chapter 3, in group decision-making tasks, individuals can easily be positioned as both actors and observers (Wallace and Hinsz, 2009).

It is important to remember that attribution bias might be expressed by individuals but that does not mean the expression of bias happens in a social vacuum. Some psychologists have argued that when we make attributions, we consider what inferences and conclusions other people might make in the same instance. If we think that other people would come to a similar conclusion then we can be surer that our attribution judgement is a sensible one. The problem is that sometimes we overestimate how likely it is that people would think and act in the same way. This is known as the **false consensus effect**. For example, in one of four studies conducted by Ross et al. (1977), university students were asked if they would be prepared to wear a sandwich-board to advertise a restaurant. Those who agreed to wear the advertisement reported that a large percentage of other students would also agree to wear it. Likewise, those who refused to wear it thought the majority of other students would also decline. This study demonstrates that we tend to assume that, by and large, our perspectives on the social world are shared ones. Why would this be important to us? Some psychologists have suggested that to feel as though our perspectives are shared by others validates the positions we take and the responses we give in our social world.

False consensus effect
A form of attributional bias where we overestimate the extent to which other people will do as we do.

5.2 Summary

Psychologists have identified a number of sources of bias that may impact the everyday formulation of causal accounts. These include the tendency to attribute other people's actions to internal causes (the fundamental attribution error), to attribute our own behaviour to situational influences (the actor–observer effect) and to think that most people think the way we do (the false consensus effect). This section also explored the tendency of attributing out-group negative behaviour to internal causes and positive out-group actions to situational influences (the ultimate attribution error).

6 It's not my fault: excuses and blame

You might have noticed that the sources of bias described above can be tied to the notion of responsibility. We seem to place responsibility squarely on other people when it all goes wrong rather than pay attention to the circumstances they might well have found themselves in. We, on the other hand, seem to be quite happy to accept responsibility for good things but not for the bad; hence the cry – it's not my fault (Figure 8.5).

Figure 8.5 Just an excuse? We are often critical of excuse-making in everyday life but at some point, most of us will have made an excuse

Weiner et al. (1987) explored excuses by considering what particular dimensions of attribution are involved in excuse-making. We have already described some key attribution dimensions including internal/external causes. Other dimensions include: stable/unstable (degree of permanency of action or event); controllable/uncontrollable (degree to which someone is in control of an action or event) and intentional/unintentional (degree to which someone intends for something to happen). According to Weiner et al., excuse-making involves assigning an outcome to an external cause that was uncontrollable and unintentional. In other words, when we made an excuse, we say we were caught in circumstances beyond our control and that we certainly didn't intend for our actions to have the effect they did.

We are often quite critical and dismissive of excuse-making, but at some point or another most people will make an excuse (Schlenker et al., 2001). This is because, despite its negative connotations, excuse-making can produce positive outcomes for both our sense of self and our relationships. For example, removing one's self from sources of negativity and moving the entire burden of responsibility from ourselves to other situational factors allows us to maintain a positive self-image and relieves feelings of stress. It also allows us to moderate our relationships by providing a means through which we can negotiate more palatable accounts of our actions and by implication more palatable resolutions (Higgins and Gallagher, 2009). For example, if you forget to keep a promise, you are unlikely to say that you forgot because it wasn't very important to you. This is not likely to result in a calm discussion or a smooth resolution. You are more likely to cite uncontrollable external circumstances that got in the way of you upholding your promise as you intended. This is because this explanation is likely to reduce any negative feelings and provide a path to a calmer resolution of conflict.

Importantly, excuses acknowledge what is considered acceptable and unacceptable. If you thought it was acceptable, you wouldn't feel the need to excuse it! The process of making an excuse is a way of aligning oneself with social norms about 'good' behaviour. In addition, although we have a tendency to dismiss excuses, in practice it seems that we prefer to hear a justification of problematic behaviour rather than other accounts such as 'I did it because I wanted to' or 'I just didn't think' (Greenberg, 1993). As Miller (2001) suggests, offering a justification or excuse communicates a level of respect to those negatively impacted by an incident – it acknowledges the negative experience and treats them as deserving of some kind of explanation.

For Maruna and Mann (2006), what is particularly interesting is how some psychologists have treated offender excuse-making. They suggest that offender excuse-making has been treated as a different phenomenon from everyday excuses. More specifically, offender excuses that assign outcomes to external causes (e.g. I started shoplifting when I was made redundant) or internal but unstable or uncontrollable factors (e.g. I shoplifted in a moment of madness) have been treated as evidence of cognitive deficit that produce errors in thinking. As Maruna and Mann point out, this understanding of offender excuse-making puts offenders in a no-win situation. If they use excuses, even those that align them with social norms of acceptability, then this is taken as evidence of erroneous thinking associated with criminality. If they accept responsibility, then this is still evidence of criminal thinking. Either way they become seen as criminal 'types'. Maruna and Mann argue that a focus on the internal erroneous thinking processes of offenders can distract psychologists' attention away from how the expression of criminal behaviour arises from complex situations, often involving both internal and external factors. For this reason, Maruna and Mann suggest that some psychologists seem to be making something akin to the fundamental attribution error when it comes to thinking about what role excuses play in criminal behaviour.

6.1 Psychology and the naïve scientist

Maruna and Mann's argument around the possibility that psychological work can contain attribution bias raises questions about the difference between the attribution of causes made by psychologists and those made by the person on the street. Of course, there are differences. Heider referred to everyday attributions as naïve psychology for a reason. Psychologists have training in using research methods that are designed to identify systematic patterns. However, just because there are differences between the causal accounts generated by psychologists and those generated by non-psychologists, we must be careful not to ignore the similarities. Psychologists, like everyone else, approach the topics they are interested in and the questions they have from their particular perspectives, and those perspectives are not formed in a social vacuum. Those perspectives too are shaped by the current social context in which they are located. These issues are raised in a review of attribution research described in Box 8.2 (Anderson and Doherty, 2008).

Box 8.2 Attributions in sexual violence research

The importance of reflecting critically on assumptions is highlighted in Anderson and Doherty's (2008) review of attribution research on the issue of sexual violence. Attribution research on this topic has largely been born out of observations that victims of sexual violence might experience negative reactions from others. Such negative reactions are often based on myths and stereotypes that victims may be in some way accountable or responsible for their experience (for example, dressing 'provocatively' or taking unnecessary risks such as walking home alone). Myths and stereotypes about sexual violence have been a source of concern because of the negative impact they have on victims.

Anderson and Doherty describe how attribution research on sexual violence typically focuses on the factors that are brought to bear on causal attributions as well as judgements of responsibility and blame. Much of this research uses **vignettes** to study sexual violence attributions – these are short hypothetical stories that describe an assault. The content of the vignettes is manipulated to make the victim and perpetrator look, for example, more or less to blame for the ensuing violence. This is achieved by incorporating features in the story that could trigger participant use of myths and stereotypes to make sense of the incident.

Vignette
A short story or description of events, people or actions that is used in research to elicit participant attitudes, perspectives and beliefs.

Anderson and Doherty point to a number of problems with using traditional attribution theories to explore people's sense-making on this extremely sensitive issue. As you have seen early in the chapter, attribution research is underpinned by the image of individuals as rational and logical information processors. However, judgements based on myths and stereotypes have been widely described as biased and irrational. Anderson and Doherty point to how using theories that emphasise logic to study irrational cognitive processes is an odd choice and one that can potentially make negative myth- or stereotype-based judgements look as if they are logical conclusions to make. They suggest that this message is often built into the structure of the experiments – much research sets up the victim and perpetrator as having an equal chance of being selected as the cause of the assault. The question of who is responsible for violence then becomes a matter of debate. Anderson and Doherty argue that the logic underpinning these studies actually reflects the sort of myth- and stereotype-based judgements used in everyday life. The danger with this research is that it runs the risk of reinforcing such myths rather than challenging them as biased and irrational ways of thinking.

As Anderson and Doherty's review suggests, bias can shape how we design, run and interpret psychological studies. This means that what is of particular importance to psychological work is to reflect carefully on our own assumptions to understand the impact they can have on our work. This can be seen in Maruna and Mann's account as they try to unpack the reasons why offender excuse-making has been treated as an altogether different category from everyday behaviour. They argue that:

> This misattribution is fully understandable. Those individuals who have never committed a certain offence themselves must find the idea of someone making excuses for crimes … abhorrent. It can be comforting to believe that offences are the product of bad people not circumstances. After all, if criminal acts can be committed by fundamentally good and decent people in bad circumstances, even the best of us have the potential to commit such atrocities.
>
> (Maruna and Mann, 2006, p. 166)

This sentiment resonates with some of the research you have read about in previous chapters, such as Milgram's and Zimbardo's classic work on social influence. The point is that psychologists are not resistant to assumption and it is always good practice to reflect on how it may impact the research process.

6.2 Summary

This section has shown how some researchers have attempted to apply classic attribution theory to psychological theorising. You have seen that, in some contexts, psychologists may have overemphasised the importance of internal attributions, which serves to downplay the importance of social context. The section has also discussed the importance of viewing theoretical claims in social context by examining the potentially damaging impact to victims of crime when victim-blaming is positioned as an inevitable result of rational information processing.

7 Rationality revisited: making sense of the sense-making person

Threaded through psychological research on both schema and attribution theory is the portrayal of individuals as rational beings, to a greater or lesser extent. Recall that earlier in this chapter I said that schema theory explains how we make sense of a vast amount of information. Underpinning this idea is that our cognitive system has a limited capacity – we cannot possibly attend to all the information thrown at us day to day, so we become selective about what we attend to. We cut corners to save time, energy and capacity, which is why we rely on processes such as stereotypes and schemas to make sense of our social world. The point is that this may be rational and sensible given our cognitive limits.

The image of human beings as limited information processors has led to an understanding of individuals as '**cognitive misers**'. We have to be miserly with our information-processing capacities to avoid overload and to do this we use shortcuts or heuristics to compensate for the limitations of our cognitive system. This could be read as suggesting we are at the mercy of our cognitive capacities – we view the social world in terms of our pre-existing assumptions and expectations and have very little choice in the matter. This portrayal of humans gives the impression that we are rather passive in how we select and process information.

Cognitive misers
A view of people as having a limited capacity cognitive system and as constrained, to some extent, by assumptions and expectations when perceiving and processing social information.

This doesn't account for how we actively choose what information to attend to and what we discard, however. For this reason, Fiske and Taylor (1991) suggest that rather than simply being miserly, we process information with respect to our needs. Rather than being 'cognitive misers', they describe people as '**motivated tacticians**', which they define as 'a fully engaged thinker who has multiple cognitive strategies available and chooses among them based on goals, motives and needs' (Fiske and Taylor, 1991, p. 13). This model of the social perceiver stresses that although we may have a limited capacity for information, we also make choices. The motivated tactician, then, would seem to move us away from conceptualisations of the individual as passive and mechanistic. It would also seem to provide a way of explaining the process of excuse-making mentioned earlier. The process of excuse-making involves selecting information-processing strategies that move us towards the goal of getting off the hook!

Motivated tacticians
A view of people as active participants in social information processing. Cognitive strategies are chosen on the basis of goals or need.

The motivated tactician metaphor draws our focus to the individual who rationally uses the strategies at their disposal to meet their goals. As has been noted in previous chapters, we must exercise some caution with individualistic accounts of psychological phenomena because what we end up missing is how we are never isolated from the social context but become located and shaped by it. For example, the formulation of excuses can be seen as a source of attribution bias or as a strategic goal-orientated activity that is responsive to a local context. What this version of excuse-making does not quite capture is how it is a process that is undertaken with another person. When we give an excuse, we are not simply describing what we think actually caused our actions; we are also engaged in the process of negotiating a tricky issue with another person. This does not have to take the form of a battle of one person's causal account over another's but can be a process of negotiating an agreement on the cause of the issue. This issue has been taken up in **discursive psychology**, which emphasises that one of the issues with schema and attribution theories is that they view language or **discourse** as a medium through which we can tap into people's cognitive internal worlds.

Discursive psychology
This focuses on how social actions and practices are performed and produced in and through discourse.

Discourse
A term that broadly emphasises the meaning-making qualities of language and text.

Pause for thought

Recall your experiences of writing essays or assignments. You may well have written an essay plan but did your thoughts evolve as you wrote? Can you think of examples of an idea that came to you through the process of writing?

A key insight from discursive psychology, as you saw in Chapters 2 and 7, is that when we produce an account of an event or describe a person we do so using language. However, language is not simply used to represent social objects; that is, words are not just labels we attach to things out there in the world. We use language to do things – forming an explanation, making an excuse and/or attributing blame or responsibility are all social actions. This places attribution work in the broader social context where the cause of an event is worked up in the process of social interaction. This is a similar process to how new ideas and insights evolve through the process of writing things down. You might have found when writing assignments that you articulate ideas in ways that you had not conceived of fully prior to writing your assignment. The idea of language or discourse as social action is further illustrated in the work of Edwards and Potter (1992): see Box 8.3.

Box 8.3 Crossing boundaries: talking about consensus – from social cognition to discursive psychology

As we saw in Kelley's covariation model, when individuals make causal attributions they draw attribution conclusions using three kinds of information: consistency, distinctiveness and consensus. While all three pieces of information are important, some researchers have suggested the consensus information seems to be particularly important to us when trying to work out the cause of something. For example, we can say there is consensus if everyone laughs at a joke. So if we are trying to work out what caused the laughter, we can be more confident that it was the joke that caused the laughter if we have this sort of consensus information. However, we do not have consensus if Claire is the only person who laughs. In this case, the laughter tells us more about Claire's personal humour preferences.

Edwards and Potter (1992) point out that in our exchanges in real-life settings, consensus is not only used to assess the causes of events but is used as a way of achieving a strong position when communicating our version of events. Consensus can be used to make our point seem credible. This is demonstrated in their classic study of a political incident that happened in 1988 between Nigel Lawson (who was the Chancellor of the Exchequer at the time) and ten journalists. While this incident happened some time ago now, Edward and Potter's study is a nice illustration of how ideas from attribution theory can be theorised quite differently from a discursive psychological perspective.

The political incident centred on newspaper reports that Nigel Lawson had told journalists at a briefing that the government was planning to undertake a controversial move to alter benefits available to those of pensionable age. This move was met with widespread condemnation by the press and other politicians. Nigel Lawson responded by saying that he had never said this to journalists in the briefing. In the exchanges that followed, the notion of consensus was used to create two different versions of reality.

Consensus was used by the press to make the journalists look like they were telling the truth about what Lawson had said in the briefing. This can be seen in the extract below taken from a broadsheet newspaper:

> The reporters, it seemed, had unanimously got it wrong. Could so many messengers really be so much in error? It seems doubtful.
>
> (*Guardian*, 8 November 1988, cited in Edwards and Potter, 1992, p. 109)

Edwards and Potter suggest that the idea of 'unanimous' consensus is used in this extract to make the journalists' version of events seem more credible. It works by appealing to the idea that it's unlikely that so many people could have got it wrong.

Consensus information was also used in Nigel Lawson's version of events. This can be seen in the following extract taken from a discussion in the House of Commons. In this discussion, Lawson denied he had said anything about benefits in the briefing, but another MP pointed out that the journalists would have taken notes in the briefing to remind them what had been said.

> Mr Lawson: Oh yes they will have their shorthand notes and they will know it, and they will know they went behind afterwards and they thought there was not a good enough story and so they produced that.
>
> (Edwards and Potter, 1992, p. 116)

The unanimous consensus of the journalists is being recast as a conspiracy. Lawson disputed the idea that the fact all the journalists said the same thing meant they were telling the truth. Instead, he suggested that consensus across the journalists' stories indicated they got together to produce a good newspaper story. Consensus information is being used to portray the journalists as deceitful and Lawson as a victim of collusion.

From this perspective, excuse-making can be understood as a negotiated outcome. What actually 'caused' the chain of events isn't strictly the issue. Who is 'right' and who is 'wrong' is played out as attributional versions of events are built up, contested and defended. Excuse-making can therefore be conceptualised as a negotiated reality (e.g. Maruna and Mann, 2006). This description of attribution is very different from those described earlier that centre on the logic of attribution processes undertaken by rational individuals. From a discursive psychological perspective, the rationality or irrationality of the attributing individual is not at issue. This is because discursive psychology focuses on attribution as a social action. What is of interest here is how these social actions are performed in our accounts of the causes of events and for what purpose. As Edwards and Potter (1992, p. 94) argue: 'a discursive psychology of attribution proposes an active rhetorical process which requires at least two participants. Rather than viewing the entire process from the perspective of an inference making perceiver … we have to examine how versions are constructed and undermined within a discursive manipulation of fact and implication.' What this suggests is that attribution is a process that is grounded in social interaction, which means it is thoroughly located in social processes.

8 Concluding thoughts

This chapter has looked at the question *How do we make sense of the world?* primarily through examining ideas emerging from the social cognitive tradition. You have seen that this approach effectively strips things back to basics to consider how we make sense of incoming information and how we then take the information we have distilled to form explanations of our social worlds.

It is important to remember that psychologists may well be experts but they are also people who use the same processes that they study. That is, psychologists are also selective about the information they attend to when forming research questions and designing studies and they also make attributions based on what they see. As discussed in this chapter, assumptions and expectations may inform the research process.

To embrace this aspect of psychology rather than glossing over it brings with it a critical dimension to the work that psychologists do; that is, to recognise that current social and historical contexts in which they produce studies contain assumptions and expectations that may allow them to see things they may not think to question. It may allow them to question those assumptions that they take for granted as just 'common-sense'. Critically reflecting on psychological work as 'ordinary' people may well provide insights that they might fail to see as 'psychologists'.

Further reading

- This book is a solid introductory textbook on social cognition including schema and attribution theory. It provides a detailed review of research evidence and links these topics to other issues covered on the module so far.

Augoustinos, M., Walker, I. and Donaghue, N. (2014) *Social Cognition: An Integrated Introduction*, 3rd edn, London, Sage.

- This classic text offers some insights on attribution theories and links to common-sense understandings of the social world.

Hewstone, M. (ed.) (1983) *Attribution Theory: Social and Functional Extensions*, Oxford, Basil Blackwell.

- This classic text describes some of the challenges that discursive psychology has made to the field of social cognition.

Edwards, D. (1997) *Discourse and Cognition*, London, Sage.

References

Ahn, W.K., Kalish, C.W., Medin, D.L. and Gelman, S.A. (1995) 'The role of covariation versus mechanism information in causal attribution', *Cognition*, vol. 54, pp. 299–352.

Anderson, I. and Doherty, K. (2008) *Accounting for Rape: Psychology, Feminism and Discourse Analysis in the Study of Sexual Violence*, London, Routledge.

Bartlett, F.C. (1920) 'Experiments on the reproduction of folk-stories', *Folklore*, vol. 31, no. 1, pp. 30–47.

Bartlett. F.C. (1932) *Remembering: A Study of Experimental and Social Psychology*, Cambridge, Cambridge University Press.

Darley, J.M. and Gross, P.H. (1983) 'A hypothesis-confirming bias in labeling effects', *Journal of Personality and Social Psychology*, vol. 44. no. 1, pp. 20–33.

Edwards, D. and Potter, J. (1992) *Discursive Psychology* London, Sage.

Fiske, S.T. and Taylor, S.E. (1991) *Social Cognition*, 2nd edn, New York, McGraw Hill.

Grant, P.R. and Holmes, J.G. (1981) 'The integration of implicit personality theories, schemas and stereotypes images', *Social Psychology Quarterly*, vol. 44, no. 2, pp. 107–15.

Greenberg, J. (1993) 'The social side of fairness: interpersonal and informational organisation of justice', in Cropanzano, R. (ed.) *Justice in the Workplace*, Hilldale, NJ, Erlbaum.

Heider, F. (1958) *The Psychology of Interpersonal Relations*, New York, Wiley.

Heider, F. and Simmel, M. (1944) 'An experimental study of apparent behavior', *American Journal of Psychology*, vol. 57, pp. 243–59.

Higgins, R.L and Gallagher, M.W. (2009) 'Reality negotiation', in Synder, C.R. and Lopez, S.J. (eds) *The Oxford Handbook of Positive Psychology*, Oxford, Oxford University Press, pp. 475–82.

Hunter, J.A., Stringer, M. and Watson, R.P. (1991) 'Intergroup violence and intergroup attributions', *British Journal of Social Psychology*, vol. 30, no. 3, pp. 261–6.

Jones, E.E. and Davis, K.E. (1965) 'From acts to dispositions: the attribution process in person perception', in Berowitz, L. (ed.) *Advances in Experimental Social Psychology*, New York, Academic Press, pp. 219–66.

Jones, E.E and Harris, V.A. (1967) 'The attribution of attitudes', *Journal of Experimental Social Psychology*, vol. 3, pp. 1–24.

Jones, E.E. and McGillis, D. (1976) 'Correspondence inferences and the attribution cube: a comparative reappraisal', in Harvey, J.H., Ickes, W.J. and Kid, R.F. (eds) *New Directions in Attribution Research,* vol. 1, New York, Wiley, pp. 389–420.

Kelley, H.H. (1967) 'Attribution theory in social psychology', in Levine, D. (ed.) *Nebraska Symposium on Motivation*, Lincoln NE, University of Nebraska, pp.192–238.

Kleider, H.M., Pezdek, K., Goldinger, S.D. and Kirk, A. (2008) 'Schema-driven source misattribution errors: remembering the expected from a witnessed event', *Applied Cognitive Psychology*, vol. 22, no. 1, pp. 1–20.

Macrae, C.N. and Hewstone, M.R.C. (1990) 'Cognitive biases in social categorisation: process and consequences', *Advances in Psychology*, vol. 68, pp. 325–48.

Maruna, S. and Mann, R.E. (2006) 'A fundamental attribution error? Rethinking cognitive distortions', *Legal and Criminological Psychology*, vol. 11, pp. 155–77.

McArthur, L.A. (1972) 'The how and what of why: some determinants and consequences of causal attribution', *Journal of Personality and Social Psychology*, vol. 2, pp. 171–93.

Messick, D.M. and Mackie, D. (1989) 'Intergroup relations', *Annual Review of Psychology*, vol. 40, pp. 45–81.

Miller, D.T. (2001) 'Disrespect and the experience of injustice', *Annual Review of Psychology*, vol. 52, pp. 527–53.

Pettigrew, T.F. (1979) 'The ultimate attribution error: extending Allport's cognitive analysis of prejudice', *Personality and Social Psychology Bulletin*, vol. 5, no. 4, pp. 461–76.

Plumm, K.M. and Terrance, C.A. (2009) 'Battered women who kill: the impact of expert testimony and empathy induction in the court room', *Violence Against Women*, vol.15, no. 2, pp. 186–205.

Quattrone, G.A. (1985) 'On the congruity between internal states and action', *Psychological Bulletin*, vol. 98, pp. 3–40.

Ross, L., Greene, D. and House, P. (1977) 'The false consensus phenomenon: an attributional bias in self-perception and social perception processes', *Journal of Experimental Social Psychology*, vol. 13, no. 3, pp. 279–301.

Ruback, R.B. and Singh, P. (2008) 'Inequity in Hindu–Muslim riots: a test of two biases', *Journal of Applied Social Psychology*, vol. 4, pp. 982–98.

Schneider, D.J. (2004) *The Psychology of Stereotyping*, New York, Guilford Press.

Schlenker, B.R., Pontari, B.A. and Christopher, A.N. (2001) 'Excuses and character: personal and social implications of excuses', *Personality and Social Psychological Review*, vol. 5, pp. 15–32.

Shank, R.C and Abelson, R.P. (1977) *Scripts, Plans, Goals and Understanding*, Hillsdale, NJ, Lawrence Erlbaum.

Tajfel, H. and Wilkes, A. (1963) 'Classification and quantitative judgement', *British Journal of Psychology*, vol. 54, pp. 101–14.

Wallace, D.M. and Hinsz, V.B. (2009) 'Group members as actors and observers in attributions of responsibility for group performance', *Small Group Research*, vol. 40, no. 1, pp. 52–71.

Weiner, B., Folkes, V.S., Amirkham, J. and Verette, J.A. (1987) 'An attributional analysis of excuse-giving: studies of naïve theories of emotion', *Journal of Personality and Social Psychology*, vol. 52, pp. 316–24.

Wilbourn, M.P. and Kee, D.W. (2010) 'Henry the nurse is a doctor too: implicitly examining children's gender stereotypes for male and female occupational roles', *Sex Roles*, vol. 62, no. 9–10, pp. 670–83.

Glossary

Actor–observer effect

The tendency for people to ascribe their own behaviour to external rather than internal factors.

Anonymity

According to LeBon (1960), anonymity refers to the loss of the sense of responsibility in the context of a crowd.

Attraction-similarity hypothesis

This hypothesis suggests that similarity can cause attraction but levels of attraction can also influence our perceptions of similarity.

Attributions

The processes by which we assign causes to social events, processes and people's behaviour.

Autobiographic memory

The system of memories that individuals hold about their personal experiences, including memories of places, events, episodes and people that have featured in their lives.

Autonomy-orientated help

The helper provides partial and temporary help to the person being helped. The underlying assumption of autonomy-oriented helping is that, given the right tools, a person can help themselves.

Aversive racism theory

Aversive racism theory seeks to explain a complex form of modern prejudice in which individuals express egalitarian attitudes towards other members of other ethnic and racial groups, but also, more subtly and indirectly, behave in ways that express negative feelings about such groups (e.g. avoidance of interaction).

Beauty–money trade off

The beauty–money trade off proposes that attractive men and women tend to marry people who have higher levels of wealth and resources than themselves. Reciprocally speaking, affluent people tend to marry partners who are more attractive.

Bystander effect

The finding that the more people there are present in an emergency situation, the less likely it is that any one of those people will help. This finding arose from a programme of research conducted by John Darley and Bibb Latané.

Cognitive misers

A view of people as having a limited capacity cognitive system and as constrained, to some extent, by assumptions and expectations when perceiving and processing social information.

Collective effort model

This model suggests that working as a group reduces motivation because participants realise that their individual contributions cannot be evaluated on an individual basis.

Common-sense (or naïve) psychology

The everyday processes people use to make sense of social objects.

Companionate love

Calm, stable feelings more overtly related to affection and friendship than to sex.

Compliance

Social influence arising as a response to a request.

Conformity

Social influence arising from adherence to group norms.

Contact hypothesis

The hypothesis that positive interaction between members of different groups tends to reduce intergroup prejudice.

Contagion

According to LeBon (1960), this refers to the idea that, in a crowd, every sentiment and act is contagious to the extent that an individual will readily sacrifice their personal interest to the collective interest.

Control beliefs

A person's beliefs about the presence of factors that may impact on their performance of a behaviour, such as their skills or resources.

Correspondent inference

How people attribute causes by running a complex cognitive analysis of possible causal factors.

Cost-benefit analysis

A cost-benefit analysis compares the costs and benefits of a particular course of action. So, Hamilton's cost-benefit analysis compares the costs (c) of altruism with the benefits (b). The benefits are weighted by the coefficient of relatedness (r). Altruism may evolve when $r \times b > c$.

Covariation model

How people attribute causes by running a complex cognitive analysis of possible causal factors.

Dependency-orientated help

This is where the helper assumes that the person being helped cannot help themselves. The helper provides a 'full solution'.

Diffusion of responsibility

When other people are present (or believed to be present) in a helping situation, responsibility for taking action is spread out among them.

Discourse

A term that broadly emphasises the meaning-making qualities of language and text.

Discursive psychology

The detailed study of how language is used to construct the world and perform social actions.

Dispositional (or internal) causes

Causes of an event or behaviour located within the person (e.g. personality traits, ability, emotional state).

Dogmatic personality

A personality characterised by simplistic thought processes and beliefs that are held inflexibly and with disregard to evidence.

Electronencephalography (EEG)

A technique used to explore brain activity by measuring electrical fluctuations along the scalp that arise as a result of neural processes.

Empathy

The ability to take another person's point of view and to imagine how they are thinking, feeling or perceiving.

Entitativity

The degree to which a group is a unified and coherent whole.

Evaluative conditioning

Enhancing or changing the feeling toward a stimulus by repeatedly pairing it with another stimulus that carries a stronger or opposite response.

Evaluative dimension

A measurement of a particular feature of an object, event or activity that shows direction and range.

Evaluative priming

Where exposure to one stimulus (the prime) facilitates a response to another stimulus (the target). Primes facilitate categorisation (and speed of response) of target words when they possess similar characteristics to the target words.

Event schemas

Cognitive structures that contain information about social activities and situations.

Explicit measures

These are direct measures of what people think or say, such as the responses collected in survey questionnaires.

Explicit prejudice

An overt, consciously held, negative response towards members of other groups.

False consensus effect

A form of attributional bias where we over-estimate the extent to which other people will do as we do.

Familiarity

A subjective feeling of recognition provoked by a situation, event, place, person or object we recognise from memory.

Friendship

A voluntary interdependence between two people over time which facilitates the socio-emotional goals of the participants.

Functional magnetic resonance imaging (fMRI)

A neuroimaging technique that measures brain activity by detecting changes in blood oxygen levels.

Fundamental attribution error

The tendency to ascribe other people's behaviour to internal rather than external factors.

Good communication model

In this model, love and admiration are freely expressed. The ultimate relational goal is the personal growth of both partners through open and honest reflection and communication about problems and the inner workings and progress of the relationship.

Good management model

With this model, problems and conflicts are avoided and the relationship itself is rarely a central topic of conversation.

Group cohesiveness

All those processes that function to hold the group together.

Group polarisation

The tendency of group members to shift their position to a more extreme one after group discussion than the one they expressed initially.

Groupthink

A mode of thinking in which the desire to reach unanimous agreement overrides the motivation to adopt proper, rational, decision-making procedures.

Halo effect

Attributing positive traits and characteristics to a person we like, even when we have little or no evidence to support these attributions.

Inclusive fitness theory

A concept drawn from the area of evolutionary biology, which attempts to account for the existence of altruism (behaviour that was troubling for evolutionary theory). Helping others (particularly those with a higher degree of genetic relatedness to themselves) is suggested to enhance the survival or propagation of an organism's genes, and therefore becomes understandable from an evolutionary perspective. According to inclusive fitness theory, then, fitness could be enhanced by means other than reproduction.

Individualism

The ways that people identify themselves and focus their goals, with an emphasis on personal freedom and achievement.

Individualistic bias

The tendency to either explain social phenomena in terms of individual psychological processes (explanatory individualism), or to see the individual as the locus of rationality and morality (normative individualism).

Informational influence

Social influence based on the belief that others are better informed than we are.

Impersonal causality

The idea that a person unintentionally caused an event or set of circumstances.

Implicit measures

These are measures that attempt to access people's spontaneous associations with an object, event or activity, such as their behavioural responses.

Implicit prejudices

Negative responses towards members of other groups that operate outside of the individual's conscious awareness or intention.

Intergroup processes

The relationships between groups.

Intragroup processes

The internal workings of a group.

Just-world hypothesis

Coined by Lerner, this term describes the belief that people deserve what they get and get what they deserve.

Likert scale

The sum of responses to several Likert items. Responses are usually provided on a questionnaire where items may be displayed with a choice of options on a continuum.

Longitudinal study

Studies that monitor and chart the development of psychological variables over long periods of time.

Love as a social construction

Definitions of love differ across and between societies, cultures and social groups. These different definitions act as a behavioural resource for people interacting within a particular collective.

Matching hypothesis

The idea that we are attracted to people with similar physical attractiveness to our own.

Meta-analysis

A technique for combining data from different studies on the same topic, and analysing them together, to derive an overall conclusion.

Minimal group studies

A set of studies that demonstrated how even trivial or arbitrary group divisions (e.g. based on art preferences) can be sufficient to create in-group favouritism and discrimination.

Motivated tacticians

A view of people as active participants in social information processing. Cognitive strategies are chosen on the basis of goals or need.

Normative influence

Social influence that occurs because of pressures to 'fit in' with a group, or more broadly with what we perceive to be expectations about what we should do.

Obedience

Social influence arising in response to a direct order.

Object of thought

The object, event or activity that is being evaluated. This term would most commonly be used by discursive psychologists as an alternative to 'attitude object'.

Passionate love

A powerful and changeable emotional state which is closely tied to feelings of sexual arousal.

Perceived behavioural control

People's perceptions of their ability to perform a behaviour.

Person schemas

Cognitive structures that contain information about people's personality traits.

Personal causality

The idea that a person intended to cause an event or set of circumstances.

Personal relationships

Voluntary interdependence between two people intended to facilitate the socio-emotional goals of the participants over time.

Persuasive arguments theory

An informational approach to social influences, it describes the process by which arguments are drawn into and used in decision making.

Phenomenal causality

The process of perceptual impression of causes of events and behaviour in the social world.

Prejudice

Prejudice is the negative evaluation of members of other social groups.

Prosocial value orientation

Proposed by Ervin Staub, prosocial value orientation (PVO) is a personality characteristic that includes a concern for the welfare of others, and is associated with a range of helping behaviours.

Proximity

Being near in space, time, order, occurrence or relation.

Reciprocal altruism

An alternative theory of altruistic behaviour from evolutionary biology that suggests people may help others (at an immediate cost to themselves) so that person will be able to help them in return in the future.

Rhetorical psychology

The study of how social life consists of rhetoric (argumentation), with people constantly engaged in rhetorical struggles to define the world in one way or another.

Role schemas

Cognitive structures that contain information about social roles including both acquired and ascribed roles.

Salience

Importance or significance to a specific situation.

Schema

A cognitive structure that contains information relating to specific subjects, people, events or issues.

Schematic processing

The processing of social information that is based in pre-existing schemas.

Self-categorisation

An awareness of one's membership in a social group.

Self-disclosure

The sharing of personal information and feelings.

Situational (or external) causes

Causes of an event or behaviour located in the environment.

Social categorisation

The process of categorising people, events and objects into groups based on common attributes.

Social cognition

An over-generalised belief about the characteristics of individuals that is based on their group membership.

Social comparison theory

A theory that suggests we compare our abilities and opinions to those of other people in order to make sense of how to behave in the world.

Social facilitation

How individual performance is impacted by the presence of others.

Social loafing

The tendency of individuals to make less of an effort when they are working collectively with others than when they are on their own.

Specificity

The precise nature or exact aspects to which a behaviour or thoughts relate.

Stereotype

An over-generalised belief about the characteristics of individuals that is based on their group membership.

Suggestibility

According to LeBon (1960), an individual in a crowd enters a special state not unlike hypnosis, in which they lose consciousness of their acts and are directed by the behaviour of the crowd as by a hypnotiser.

Transformations

Changing how the data is organised or coded, e.g. changing raw qualitative data into numerical data and/or subsuming data sets into overarching categories.

Ultimate attribution error

The tendency for people to attribute negative out-group behaviour to internal causes and positive out-group behaviour to external ones.

Vignette

A short story or description of events, people or actions that is used in research to elicit participant attitudes, perspectives and beliefs.

Violence

A phenomenon that can include physical, emotional and sexual abuse and a wide range of coercive, intimidating and controlling behaviours.

Volatile model

In this model, communication is emotion-laden and unpredictable. Partners say exactly what they think whenever they think it and express all things in an uninhibited and passionate way.

Acknowledgements

Grateful acknowledgement is made to the following sources:

Every effort has been made to contact copyright holders. If any have been inadvertently overlooked the publishers will be pleased to make the necessary arrangements at the first opportunity.

Cover
Copyright © iStockPhoto.com/Jamie Farrant

Figures
Figure 1.2: adapted from Zoll, C. and Enz, S. (2010) 'A questionnaire to assess affective and cognitive empathy in children', Opus Publikationsserver, Bamberg www.opus-bayern.de/uni-bamberg; Figure 1.3: Copyright © Eric Gay/AP/Press Association Images; Figure 1.5: Copyright © Jean Decety; Figure 1.6: Copyright © Arno Massee/Science Photo Library; Figure 1.7: adapted from Zahn-Waxler, C. M. et al (1992) 'Development of concern for others', Developmental Psychology, vol. 28, no. 1, American Psychological Association; Figure 1.8: Copyright © Jean Decety; Figure 1.9: Copyright © Jean Decety; Figure 2.1: adapted from Sherif, M. (1966) *The Psychology of Social Norms*, Harper & Row; Figure 2.2: Asch, S. E. (1956) 'Studies of independence and conformity: A minority of one against a unanimous majority', Psychological Monographs: General and Applied, vol. 70, no. 9, American Psychological Association; Figure 2.3: Courtesy of Professor Jerry Burger; Figure 2.4: Copyright © Philip G. Zimbardo; Figure 2.5: Copyright © AP/Press Association Images; Figure 2.6: Reicher, S. and Haslam, S. A. (2006) 'Rethinking the psychology of tyranny', British Journal of Social Psychology, vol. 45, no. 1, British Psychology Association; Figure 2.7: adapted from Reicher, S. and Haslam, S. A. (2006) 'Rethinking the psychology of tyranny', British Journal of Social Psychology, vol. 45, no. 1, British Psychology Association; Figure 3.1 left: Copyright © Marmaduke St John/Alamy; Figure 3.1 centre top: Copyright © David Ramos/Getty Images; Figure 3.1 centre bottom: Copyright © O. Louis Mazzatenta/Getty Images; Figure 3.1 right: Copyright © Caro/Alamy; Figure 3.2: Copyright © Jimmy Sime/Getty Images; Figure 3.4: adapted from Zajonc, R. B. et al (1969) 'Social enhancement and impairment of performance in the cockroach', Journal of Personality and Social Psychology, vol. 13, no. 2, American Psychological Association; Figure 3.6: Copyright © Universal History Archive/UIG via Getty

Images; Figure 3.7: Copyright © Ben Macfayden/Press Association images; Figure 3.8: Copyright © Barcroft Media/Getty Images; Figure 4.1: Rex Features; Figure 4.2: Copyright © Richard Harbus/ Getty Images; Figure 4.3: Courtesy of Joshua Correll; Figure 4.6: Hugenberg, K. and Bodenhausen, G. V. (2003) 'Facing prejudice; Implicit prejudice and the perception of facial threat', Psychological Science, vol. 14, no. 6, Copyright © 2003. Reprinted by permission of Sage Publications; Figure 4.7: Copyright © Julio Etchart/Alamy; Figure 4.8 left: Harris, L. T. and Fiske, S. T. (2009) 'Social neuroscience evidence for dehumanised perception', European Review of Social Psychology, vol. 20, no. 1, Copyright © European Association of Social Psychology. Reprinted by permission of Taylor & Francis Ltd, www. tandfonline.com on behalf of European Association of Social Psychology; Figure 4.8 right: Harris, L. T. and Fiske, S. T. (2006) 'Dehumanizing the lowest of the low', Psychological Science, vol. 17, no. 10, Copyright © 2006. Reprinted by permission of Sage Publications; Figure 4.11 left: Copyright © Greg Marinovich/AP/ Press Association Images; Figure 4.11 right: Copyright © AP/Press Association Images; Figure 4.16: Courtesy of John Dixon; Figure 5.1: Copyright © Steven May/Press Association Images; Figure 5.2: Copyright © Peter Singer/The Life You Could Save www. thelifeyoucouldsave.org; Figure 5.3: Copyright © Young People of the Year Ltd; Figure 5.4: Courtesy of Ervin Staub; Figure 5.5: Copyright © Alexander Chadwick/Press Association Images; Figure 6.2: Perrett, D. I., May, K. A. and Yoshikawa, S. (1994) 'Facial shape and judgements of female attractiveness', Nature, vol. 368, no. 6468, Macmillan Publishing; Figure 6.3: Dunn, M. J. (2010) 'Effects of manipulated prestige-car ownership on both sex attractiveness ratings', British Journal of Psychology, vol. 101, no. 1, The British Psychological Society; Figure 6.4: Dunn, M. J. (2010) 'Effects of manipulated prestige-car ownership on both sex attractiveness ratings', British Journal of Psychology, vol. 101, no. 1, The British Psychological Society; Figure 7,1: Copyright © Mark Davidson/Alamy; Figure 7.2: Copyright © Snap Surveys Ltd, Figure 7.3: Copyright © Peter Muhly/ AFP/Getty Images; Figure 7.4 left: Copyright © Bon Appetit/Alamy; Figure 7.4 right: Copyright © Frank Chmura/Alamy; Figure 7.5: Copyright © Wendy Stainton-Rogers; Figure 7.6: Copyright © Wendy Stainton-Rogers; Figure 7.7 left: Copyright © News UK & Ireland Ltd; Figure 7.7 right: Copyright © Adam Berry/Getty Images; Figure 8.1: Copyright © Angela Waye/Shutterstock; Figure 8.2: Rex Features Ltd; Figure 8.3: Heider, F. and Simmel, M. (1944) 'An experimental study of apparent behaviour', The American Journal of Psychology, vol. 57, no. 2, University of Illinois Press; Figure 8.4: Copyright © Photobank Gallery/Shutterstock; Figure 8.5: Copyright © Wavebreakmedia/Shutterstock.

Index